EXIT 48
THE ART OF NEVER GIVING UP

DALE ROGERS
NATHAN MILLER

Copyright by 2020 © Dale Rogers
All rights reserved. No part or this publication may be reproduced, distributed, or transmitted in any form by any means, or stored in a database or retrieval system, without the prior written permission orthe publisher.

Published by Dale Rogers Studio
Visit our website at dalerogersstudio.com
First published in 2020

Rogers, Dale.
Exit 48: The Art of Never Giving Up/ Dale Rogers ; with Nathan Miller.
p. cm.
ISBN 978-1-7362927-1-6
1. Memoir —Non-Fiction —I. Title.

Printed in China

*Dedicated to my mother and Father...
Without them, this book and the Big Dog
Show would never have been possible*

1

When I first heard the banging from the door, I did nothing. I was still half asleep, staring up at the ceiling in my shop clothes. It wasn't until I heard the second volley of bangs come from the front door that I jumped up and pulled myself out of bed. I stumbled down the staircase to the window beside the door and swiped the curtain. A man was standing in the rain, my walkway light outlining the silhouette of his campaign-cover hat and the .45 on his belt. I opened the door, peeking my head out into the downpour.

"My name is Officer Coughlin. I'm with the State Police Department."

He reached his hand out slowly and stared at me with a gruff, serious look on his face. I stepped out of the doorway and shook his hand.

"Dale Rogers."

He shifted his feet and sighed.

"Alright Mr. Rogers, listen—I think we caught a dog that belongs to you running down I-495. Go grab a coat and meet me at my cruiser if you want it back. I'd suggest you move quickly accounting the current position it's in."

I nodded and jogged up the stairs to my bathroom. There was a windbreaker strewn across the tiles when I switched on the lights. I stumbled to the sink with it half tangled around my head. The white

DALE ROGERS

fluorescents made me wince as I dug around for a bottle of mouthwash and ran the faucet. I splashed cold water up onto my face to wake myself up. For a moment, I looked in the mirror at the person staring back at me—disheveled and soaking wet, eyes bloodshot. I wondered if he could keep at it. There was a cop in my driveway waiting for me to go hunt a giant dog on the highway in the rain, I thought. I closed my eyes and threw my head back. The bathroom light floated like a shadow behind my eyelids. I opened them to the clock on the wall, reflecting into the mirror. It read a quarter past one. In a few hours, I'd have to start the day. Everybody I knew was asleep. They'd gone to bed early and are anticipating their morning commute. They'd wait in a drive-through for a bagel and coffee, jump on I-495 or I-93 to wherever they were going to make their payroll. After work, they'd hurry home and eat dinner or maybe watch the game. It was times like this, I could understand them better—understand them and the decisions they'd made for themselves and understand the way some of them looked at the path I chose for myself.

I ran from my front door to the cruiser and hopped in the passenger seat. I hesitated for a moment; I'd never been in the front seat of a police cruiser. It smelled like shoe grease and wintergreen and cleaning detergent. An industrial mounted laptop glowed in the direction of the officer. I could see a few things around the car I didn't recognize. Most of them were small modules with strange buttons mounted on the dash. At least one of them I imagined was to control the siren and lights.

We drove in silence most of the way, aside from the occasional sound of the officer spitting chew into a foam Dunkin Donuts cup he kept in the cupholder. Now and then the police radio would jabber. I was trying to think of something to talk about to make the whole ordeal a little more bearable.

"Does that control the siren?"

"Nope."

I nodded and he spat into the cup. Maybe it was best I didn't talk. All of the lights in the houses we passed were off; the streets were empty. We were getting close to the Exit 48 on-ramp when he threw the chew that was in his mouth out the window and wiped his hand on his pant leg.

"So, what is it?" the officer asked.

His voice startled me awake, and I jumped in my seat. I didn't notice I was dozing off.

"What is what?"

"You know—that thing you got on the highway. What is it?"

"Well, it's an eight-foot-tall dog."

The officer scoffed and smiled for the first time since I'd met him. He shook his head.

"I could've guessed that much. I mean, *what's the point*. Why'd you have it sitting there in the first place?"

I'd heard that question a million times. It was the primary topic I discussed when people found out the dog belonged to me. I never took offense to it. An eight-foot dog on the side of the highway certainly wasn't a practical thing to build. I'd let them give me a bewildered look and then give them one right back. I wanted to tell them it was strange to demand a reason or meaning. I never thought about this whole art thing as more than a matter of creating something to enjoy; like opening a new restaurant or planting trees in a park. I didn't think there was meaning more agreeable than that. That was never the answer they were looking for.

"I'm just hoping somebody will see it and want to adopt it."

The officer laughed.

"Well, it looks like you certainly got your wish tonight."

We pulled a big loop on the highway to get to the Exit 48 off-ramp. As the officer pulled the car into the grass, I saw the tail peeking out from the curve. He pulled forward until I saw the whole thing, the rain dousing it in the headlights. It looked massive in the road, stretching ten feet across and blocking nearly the entire stretch of pavement. Its head lay seeping into the grassy hill that came up as the asphalt met the median. Small currents of water flooded beneath it and trailed down the off-ramp.

"Yessir, there she is. We've got no idea yet who tried to drag it away. Teenagers maybe—anyways, whoever it was must've never bothered to walk up and check how big the damn thing was before they tried to drag it away."

I rubbed my face and looked at the dog in the open street. There was something about the whole thing perplexing me.

"What about the fence?" I asked.

"The what?"

"The fence. I set it up behind the big chain fence around the property. It has to be at least five feet tall. How did they lift it over? No way a couple of kids could have."

The officer laughed, and I felt confused.

"Sometimes," he said and flicked on the spotlight mounted to his side mirror. He swiveled it across the street.

"Sometimes all you gotta do is go straight through."

The metal piping of the fence lay tangled and warped in the spotlight, the chain-link scattered and strewn about the grass. It looked as if a tank had barreled through it, or maybe like an elephant had charged through the field and stomped right on over it.

EXIT 48

The land in front of it was torn up and I could see where the dog had been heaved through the mud like belted tire tracks. Parts of the ground were pitted and filled with water, which is where I assumed the perpetrators had discovered the dog was indeed quite heavy and dug themselves in.

We stepped out into the street. I threw on the hood of my windbreaker. The rain was biting and oppressive—the kind that pours over New England as autumn settles and the land begins to flush into colors of orange and magenta. It signals the first moments of the year when you hold your palms to your face and blow hot breath into them. It forces everything down into the earth and is the rain you find yourself working in, unlike that of the summer months which are meant for sitting and enjoying the hot air and smell of green and earth rising.

The officer asked me what I wanted to do about my dog laying in the street. I asked him if we could just drag it back over the pavement and remnants of the fence. I'd deal with the rest in the morning once I could get a hold of my brother Harold, I told him. He shrugged and said it was fine. We dragged the giant piece of steel across the road, stopping now and again to catch our breath and find our grip.

"You know, driving by I always thought this thing might be made of wood."

"Lots of people do."

I had built the dog from sheets of COR-TEN steel. US Steel developed COR-TEN developed COR-TEN in the earlier part of the last century as an alternative to other steels that needed to be painted to avoid corrosion. The steel has a property that causes it to create a thick, oxidized surface layer that acts as a protective shell to the rest of the material. I welded the dog in my garage and applied a solution to accelerate the weathering process and give it an even color. The result was a metal sculpture coated in a deep, uniform reddish-brown. It looks almost like mahogany or some other hardwood.

 I remember being young and watching the weathered boxcars pass over the Merrimack River. There was something I liked about the way they looked. The place I grew up was littered with farm equipment the same color—deep hues of orange and brown rough to the touch. I'm not sure if I was thinking about those memories when I began making sculptures; it just seemed like the material lent itself to the world I grew up in. It was the color of the railways, the trees in the autumn, and the mounds of leaves they left on the forest floor as winter approached. It was the color of the old remnants of the industry that built the Merrimack Valley and the rest of the Eastern coastline. It was something I knew well, and it was something I knew was tough and meant to last.

 The Dog was almost out of the road. Each time we stopped, I couldn't help but look over my shoulder at the cars flying down the interstate. I kept thinking about one of them flying onto the off-ramp and cutting a turn hard and hitting us while I tried to lug my sculpture out of the street. I wouldn't even be able to hear it over the steel grating against the asphalt as we dragged my sculpture. I wondered how they'd explain it in the newspaper. Would they call me an artist? A sculptor? A crazy man trying to move the giant steel dog he welded together out from the middle of an interstate in the rain? It didn't matter to me so much at the moment. I was cold and soaked through my shirt with rain and sweat and covered up to my knees in mud. I could tell the officer wasn't having a good time either, and I felt bad he would have to sit in his cruiser filthy and wet until his shift was over. He seemed like a good sport.

We managed to get the dog back to where it belonged and left it there laying on its side. I wiped the mud on my hands on my coat and shook his hand. I couldn't thank him enough. I didn't have the money for a tow by a longshot.

We walked back to the car and the officer scraped the mud from his boots along the pavement.

"You know, we didn't catch whoever did this yet."

I put my hands up and shrugged.

"Part of the trade I suppose."

"My point being—"

The officer put his hand on the driver's door of the cruiser.

"They could come back whenever with a truck or some other way to move it next time."

I was walking around the hood of the car and looked back at the officer.

"If someone wants a piece of my art that bad, they might as well just take it."

We pulled off the grass onto the Exit 48 off-ramp. The rain was still coming down hard. It pelted the roof of the cruiser with such intensity it sounded like a continuous static. The cold of the rain and wind on my face had made me forget how exhausted I was. I slouched in the passenger seat and began to feel my eyelids get heavy. The numbers on the dash read two-thirty in the morning now. As we began to drive towards my house, I twisted my head back and looked at my sculpture lopsided in the rain. I thought about how I'd have to come down once the sun came up and figure out a way to prop it back up. It wasn't easy the first time around, and it wouldn't be easy tomorrow I also wasn't quite sure what I was going to do about the five-foot fence that now looked like a pile of rubble in the dark. I was sure I'd end up having to pay somebody. I counted on my hand how many hours of sleep I could squeeze in. Three hours—four? I thought about Auguste Rodin rolling *The Thinker* across a street in the rain, or Michelangelo asking his brother if he could come to help him fix one of his sculptures at six in the morning. It was pretty hard to imagine, and it was pretty difficult to think of myself in the same light. There's no room for Rodin's or Michelangelo's anymore, and I knew I needed to figure out a way to make more money at this before my artwork crushed me like it crushed that chain link fence. It was pretty comical people were stealing my art before I could even tell them who I was. I could get a laugh out of it, but it seemed like another dull blow in a fight I'd already lost. I would have never guessed it would change my life forever.

2

The city I'm from is Haverhill, Massachusetts. It is one of the many cities along the Merrimack that once marked the region as the continent's industrial epicenter. If one were to start on a raft fifty or so miles North in Concord, New Hampshire, they'd chase an echo of those days. Many decrepit mills, factories, and receding storefronts lean against the shores of the river, painting the backdrop of the water in shades of rust and faded red brick. The river eventually turns eastward into the Greater Lowell area. Beyond Lowell sits Lawrence, and beyond that sits Haverhill—the city I grew up in and where I live to this day. Beyond Haverhill, the industry along the Merrimack begins to thin into small suburban and rural communities until the water pours into the ocean by the old fishing town of Newburyport, Massachusetts.

A little over a century ago, my great grandfather worked along the Merrimack at the Haverhill Paperboard Company. On his way home from the mills, he'd often cross the railroad tracks that cut through the arteries of the city. When the day came that he was struck by a train, the railroad company made quick work of ensuring he'd sign the paperwork that freed them from any liability. To keep things quiet, a representative left him a small stipend of money by his hospital bed. He later used that money to purchase the two and a half acres of land, the single horse, and the donkey that would one day become the dairy farm I grew up on. The earliest and best memories of my childhood were on the farm. As the generations trickled down, homes were built by each family member to raise their branch of the family. My neighborhood and family were interlocked, and most of the time we all had little reason to travel outside the piece of the world we'd carved out for ourselves. It felt safe and comfortable, and the fields stretched outward so far that I had trouble imagining a world outside the life we built.

It was 1978 and I was seven years old, just beginning to learn my way around. My house sat side by side with the houses of my cousins, uncles, and aunts. If I followed the road up the grassy clearing I'd pass the feed crop, and across from that the grazing fields, which sloped down to the brook and was where the cows would huddle in the sun. Further down the road were the cow barns, the manure house, various tool and equipment sheds, the milking parlor, and two massive silos that peaked out over the hills.

Across the street from the barns was the house of my grandparents. My great grandfather built the house when he bought the original two and a half acres of land. I loved to visit my grandparents in the early morning and sit while they ate breakfast. I'd watch from their window as the older boys of the family and the farmhands gathered around the bottling plant next to the house. I'd hear the belts moving glass milk bottles far into the afternoon.

It was around this age that the rest of the children on the farm and I began to set out on our adventures. Behind the fields was a group of large pine by a brook. It was for the most part untouched by any adult on the property. We began to make it our special place to go to be unbothered by the thoughts and trivial opinions of adults. We built fortresses and monuments from brush and stones and stolen pieces of scrap metal. We discussed matters important to us, settled fights—sometimes in the dirt and pine needles and between whole groups of us, rolling around and gnashing our teeth. On calmer afternoons we were more attentive to the world around us. One day we sat under the trees on a pile of stones, drinking warm bottles of coke and watching chipmunks scurry and chase each other. There were entire droves of them running back and forth. My brother Harold stood up and pointed towards them.

"It's like a whole chipmunk village!"

I looked out at the army of chipmunks, amazed. It looked as if we had stumbled upon a secret society of them. From that day we called that area under the pine trees 'Chipmunk Village.' I would go there for years after into my adult life, oftentimes walking down there to think or even to just watch the chipmunks run about.

There was a ladder by the barns that led up to a hayloft. We'd jump from bale to bale, kicking hay dust up into the blades of light that sunk through the weathered boards of the barn. I'd climb to the highest bales up in the corners of the ceilings and look out at the land from knotholes in the wall. I loved the colors—especially in the autumn time. The maples would darken through the months behind the grass fields, the wheat veering into a thickened gold. The machinery scattered around the fields was interesting to me; especially the old pieces. They were often painted maroon, crimson, or emerald green. After years the finish would corrode, and rust patches would bloom over the surface and tangle between blotches of sun stains.

Almost everything was touched by that deep russet color. The tool shed was littered with wrenches, hammers, bits, and bolts. Along the walls were hoses, sickles, and saws swallowed completely by swathes of auburn, crimson and bright veined orange rust. Even my uncle's old international harvesters had ripened to a patina. I would sometimes sit in them with my cousins or brother and we would pretend we were traveling the world.

One day, my father took me to fill the vending machines. In those times my family not only raised the cattle and bottled the milk but delivered it too. The perimeter of land around our farm was filled mostly by factories and industrial warehouses. I'd get bored going to work with my father and I'd ask him why he cared so much about the factory owners.

"Every workplace has a lunchroom, doesn't it?"

I didn't see why that mattered, and I didn't understand why he had to go every day and fill the vending machines or fix them when they broke. "So much of a farmer's life is based on things they cannot control, and an industrial park full of cafeterias was a stroke of grace" he said.

I was picking up a crate of milk cartons from the bed of the truck. My father was talking to a man in a white shirt and a red tie.

The man's sleeves were rolled, and a cigarette bobbed in his mouth when he talked.

"Want some help loading it in?"

My father smiled and shook his head.

"No, no. You look like you've got enough on your plate. Besides, that's what I brought him for."

My father pointed his chin towards me, and the man laughed. The milk crate I was carrying made me waddle like a penguin.

"Look at that, a regular working man. Wish I could get these freeloaders to work that hard."

There was a group of men by one of the factory entryways. They looked disheveled and a bit dirty. Most of them wore Dickies and tucked work shirts as they ate sandwiches outside and smoked. I didn't think it was very nice of the man to call them freeloaders. They looked like they were working harder than him, after all. My father looked much more like them to me than the man in the shirt and tie. I wondered why they both liked each other.

"Well Mr. Stewart, I believe it. That's why I do most of my business with cows."

Mr. Stewart laughed and hacked up smoke. His face turned red like a balloon and my father patted him on the back. I walked behind him to the back of the pickup and lugged another crate of milk off the bed. My father had a milk crate in one hand and the keys to the cash box jingling in the other.

"Say, Rogers, I forgot to tell you."

He'd yet to make it to the vending machine and was looking back at Mr. Stewart with the keys ringing around his finger.

"I think somebody picked the lock again the other night. I locked it back up when I found it open in the morning." "Well—"

My father walked over and picked up the empty cash box from the vending machine and shook it.

"That's no good."

He tossed the cash box back in the vending machine and tilted the brim of his hat. Mr. Stewart sighed and rubbed the back of his neck.

"Say, Rogers. Don't worry about my cut this week. The last thing I need is for you to close down and have people complaining about no milk."

Mr. Stewart smiled, and my father shook his hand and patted his back. He and my father exchanged words and Mr. Stewart laughed and coughed smoke again. We loaded the rest of the milk into the vending machine and headed off towards the next factory.

We drove to the next stop; a tool company down the road by the highway. My father whistled and hung his arm out the window. When he pulled the truck off into the Knight Tool Company parking lot he stepped out and shut the door with the window open.

"Now remember—"

I was still in the passenger seat waiting for him to speak. He walked around the back of the truck and I heard the metal of the milk crates scrape against the steel bed. He came back around to the window and peered in.

"No matter what you do in life, there won't ever be anything wrong with brightening someone's day."

I was looking up at him. Through the shadow cast by the sun, I saw him wink.

"It helps you save a little money too."

He had a natural way of moving a conversation in the direction he wanted simply by being agreeable and warmhearted. He only gave what was necessary when talking—what a person cared to hear. He never overstayed his welcome when speaking and always listened intently no matter how long somebody went on talking.

I followed him out to Knight Tool Company. Afterward, we went to the next stop, and then the next. We drove about the dirt roads that connected the factories, supply houses, and leased industrial space, filling their vending machines. I was tired by the end of it. My father said the day was only half over; he was headed back to the bottling plant.

When we weren't learning the trade, we children found ways to occupy ourselves. There was a bull on the farm. Sometimes we would climb the fence and inch towards him while he grazed in the field—sometimes six or seven of us all at once, tiptoeing around leaves and fallen brush towards the giant creature. We wouldn't make it very close before I'd see the muscles in the bull's neck tense up and hear him huff into the grass. Somebody would yelp and then we were running, faster and faster with the sound of the bull's hooves shaking the earth behind us. I was heavy and slower than most of the pack. The fastest of the bunch would see me wild-eyed with the bull closing in as they yelled by the fence. I don't remember ever thinking of the bull catching me while I was running. If I were to think about it, I would've stopped and choked up and god knows what would've happened afterward. I only thought about the fence. The faster I ran, the closer I would get to where I had to be.

At first, the world outside was a confusing place for me. Soon into beginning kindergarten, I began to hear my teacher speak strangely about me to my mother. She'd often tell my mother I was *special*, which I found strange as she often seemed displeased with the answers I gave in classes. My parents began taking me to a place they called *Boston* sometimes in the afternoon. My mother and father would change out of their work clothes in the middle of the afternoon and I would sit alone on the bench seat of the truck as we drove. It felt strange and empty not being packed in with my brother and a cousin or two. The longer we drove, the more the road was filled with cars. Some of them looked like my father's truck, some that looked very different and were all kinds of spectacular colors. Behind the cars, I'd watch the skyline creep up over the horizon. The immensity of the steel and glass of the skyline was almost frightening. The winding concrete bridges, and whirring tunnels were nothing like what I'd seen in the Merrimack Valley and its stout, red-brick mills and narrow townhouses.

We'd end up at a big hospital with huge glass windows and waxed floors. I'd look back at the children we passed. Some were so sick they were on stretchers. I didn't feel sick at all—not even sick enough to go to the normal doctor.

They'd take me into a room, and someone would sit with me and ask questions. It was different from any other type of doctor's appointment I'd been to. It felt more like a game or a riddle. The person asked me to count on my hand or to explain the way I think about something or to solve a puzzle with blocks.

When he'd walk me back out to the lobby my parents would be there smiling. Every time the doctor or nurse would walk me out, there would be a very long talk between them and my parents before we left. It was unbearably long and dreary and I understood almost nothing they ever said. There was only one thing I heard from every doctor we visited that I understood. It was the word *"Special,"* and I thought it was a strange coincidence my kindergarten teacher had thought the same about me. I didn't feel very special.

In the autumntime, my family was busier than at any other time of the year. It was the most exciting time for me. Everybody would be out in old thermal undershirts yelling and walking with quick feet. Even the youngest of children were busy at work, as this was the time of year we prepared cattle for the competitions at the Topsfield Fair. Topsfield was southeast of Haverhill, nestled in a rural stretch of land that pressed up against the famous coastal towns of the Northshore such as Gloucester and Salem. Because of that it always managed to remain a quiet, unbothered place since its settlement centuries ago. As simple as a little town it was, common people spanning hundreds of miles in any direction knew and loved the place as home to the fair. It was a relic from an older New England; one that was at its height long before I ever stepped foot on the fairgrounds and one that gripped to pastoral traditions and cultures that had slowly crumbled with the majority of family-owned farms as the years passed and the country changed.

My uncle would keep a record of most of the cattle through the year and our job was to prepare a select few in the last months leading up to the show. The older a child on the farm was, the more responsibility they were given to tend to their cow until eventually, they'd grown into a regular dairy farmer. It was my first time competing in the competition and I was very excited. I'd never even been to the fair before. My brother and I usually just spent the weekends with my grandmother when the older ones went.

My uncle Richard brought us to the barns. Inside were the cattle eating at their troughs.

"Alright kids, pick quick and pick smart. I ain't doing any tradin' stock like last year."

The other children rushed past me. My older cousins had long picked their cattle and had been keeping records and training them through the summer. I moseyed about, trying to look each animal in the face while they squirmed between each other and edged for food. I looked over at my brother. He was leading Uncle Richard to his pick: a well-mannered Holstein. Her long eyelashes dipped slowly, and she chewed grain like she was daydreaming. She had the look grown dairy cows get that makes them look like wise old women.

I heard a commotion in the barn adjacent to me. A smaller

one of the bunch was digging wildly through the crowd of dairy cows to get to the grain. The cows huffed and stomped around her while she jerked her head and bumped into their flanks. Eventually, she got to the food trough and I knelt to touch her nose.

"I want this one."

My uncle walked up to me and laughed like there was gravel in his throat. He sighed and put his hand on my head.

"Son, that is a Heifer. Haven't you been listenin' to anything I tell you?"

I looked at him and felt confused. I watched his face shift from a grimace to a smile ear to ear.

"You know—maybe she suits you."

My older cousin laughed in the background. I was still confused but when he laughed at me it made me feel hot on the back of my neck and embarrassed. He was always laughing at things as if he understood them so well. I wasn't going to budge on my pick no matter what he was laughing at.

In the next couple of months, I learned what a Heifer was and why my cousin was laughing. My uncle Richard would stand out with all of us and watch while we tried to halter our cattle. I'd walk towards the Heifer with the rope-loop shaking in my hands. At first, she wouldn't let me anywhere near her. As soon as she saw the rope in my hands, she knew she didn't want it around her face and would turn right around. We weren't allowed to sneak up on them since we might get kicked.

"They'll take your little noggin right off with one boot."

My uncle Richard would yell it sporadically at us. It made the cattle much scarier to me. I imagined my head bouncing down the field like a kickball—all the way to the factories.

I'd walk around so I was facing her again, but she'd just turn the other way. I spent most of the first few weeks just walking in a circle. Eventually, she let me walk up to her but that wasn't much better. She'd let me get close enough to pet her but would tilt her head and stare so the white of her eye showed and made her look crazy. I'd try to get her head through the loop and she'd just jerk around and huff and grunt.

The more I was around her, the less scared I felt. I noticed she became calmer the less I fretted. I began to pat her every day and talk to her. She still wouldn't let me put the halter on her but otherwise was very calm and it almost seemed like she began to like when I'd come to visit.

Every day, I made sure to visit until she finally let me put the halter on her head and walk her. I'd walk her just like Uncle Richard showed us and then I'd tie her to the gate outside the cow barn.

When the day came for us to set up for the fair it was sweltering. The news forecasted blistering heat all weekend. It felt strange to be dizzy from the heat in the middle of October. My uncle said he'd never seen anything like it. The cattle were anxious and stubborn. Their trailer cooked like wrapped tinfoil on a grill in the sun as we dragged them by their halters up the ramp. I looped the halter on my Heifer by myself and my grandfather helped me load her into the trailer. I ran to his truck while he talked to Uncle Richard and my father. They were going to take the trailer with the cattle, and my grandfather and mother were going to take us in his pickup.

I was reeling with excitement. I had spent the summer around bonfires hearing stories about the fair and now I was going to have my own to tell. The heat only made me more restless. There is something about a swing in the weather that turns the world on its head—like everybody can feel a fresh static charge under their feet at the same time. I crawled into the back of my grandfather's truck and smelt the exhaust pooling in the window. My brother looked at the ceiling, tapping his hands against his thighs and trying to be patient. My grandfather walked to the car with my mother and fussed around, making sure we had what we needed for the weekend. He put the truck in drive and headed down the hill by our house. My brother and I bounced around the bench seat as we hobbled over gravel and dirt. I looked back at my home. The morning sun turned the white siding gold. I'd never slept away from home unless it was just for a night at my grandparents.

We drove the winding backcountry streets of the towns between Haverhill and Topsfield. My grandfather pointed each town out to us: North Andover, West Boxford, Boxford. The towns all looked the same to me, but I liked to listen and hear about each of them. My grandfather seemed to know a lot of history for a dairy farmer. I asked him how he knew so much about each town.

"Well—from driving through them to the fair when I was little—just like you two are right now."

I looked out at the passing pine trees and townhouses. A woman was walking her dog on the sidewalk and it stared at me as we flew by.

"Look here—"

My grandfather was looking at my brother and me through the rearview. He had his hand pointed towards the passenger side of the windshield. I followed his finger and saw a giant, corroded cage on the side of the road. It was tucked into a nest of bushes and sitting outside a farmhouse littered with dilapidated equipment.

"There's a monkey in that cage sometimes."

My brother cocked his head up. He had been dozing off but was now raising his eyebrows in disbelief.

"You're pullin' my leg."

"Am not. Seen it with my own eyes. They have a pet monkey and sometimes they keep it in that cage. If you're lucky you can see it when you're passing by."

My brother looked at me with bewilderment while my grandfather went on and on. He'd jumped topics by now to talk about the way things used to be—how he'd seen even crazier things than a monkey in a cage and it's all hidden forever now in the old backyards, houses, restaurants, and bars of these cities. I'd wish later I could remember more of his stories but all I could think about was the monkey. It haunted me. The school we went to had a book with photos of monkeys and we both agreed to watch for it on the way back. If we saw it, we would be able to tell the whole school what monkeys *actually* looked like in real life and not just out of some old book.

The fairgrounds were empty when we arrived. There were only the other farm families and different vendors bustling to set up. The ground was dusty like the road up to our farm. Uncle Richard showed up with the cattle a little later. We walked them in a line, each child with their cow and me with my Heifer. My mother led the way and my father and uncle grabbed supplies and rucksacks of feed from the trucks. I looked at the people setting up. Some of them looked like my family, some looked different. There were many scraggly haired, tough-looking men with sullied shirts and fancy jewelry.

"Carni-folk."

"My cousin was walking behind us chewing bubble gum loud. He walked with slow lumber like he'd been to the fair a million times.

"I'd watch out. They'll snatch you up and sell you for carnival tickets."

My brother rolled his eyes. I still sped up my walking a little. My Heifer tugged back at the rope. She still seemed agitated from the trailer.

"Look!"

My brother was practically shaking. Across the dirt lot, I saw what we had been waiting for all this time. It was Midway; the carnival and amusement park that sat in the center of the fair. It was all we could think about. From where I stood, I could see a giant wheel with little seats dangling from it. It was enormous; almost as enormous as the buildings in Boston.

"Do people sit on that?" I asked.

"What—the Ferris wheel? You bet. You can see all the way back to our farm from it." my mother replied.

All around the Ferris wheel were tents colored in deep reds and golds. In the distance, I could see a clown standing in the archway drinking out of a cup. Music was beginning to radiate from the center of the park, warping from the span of distance. I heard my mother speak over it.

"Here we are!"

It was a big barn with a steel top. My mother showed us where each of our cattle belonged and we tied them to the fence posts. She came up to us while we were pouring feed.

"Remember, no rides tonight or tomorrow. You two can go Sunday while we load the cattle."

We knew it before we showed up. We came to the fair for the cattle. Eventually, people began to arrive. We'd have to stand by our cattle and talk to them about everything cattle-related; things like

EXIT 48

life on a dairy farm, caring for cattle, what cattle eat, how we get the milk—endless questions from people floating around and petting the cows. I didn't know half the answers to the questions they asked me, so I decided it would be fine to make things up if I needed to.

The next day was the competition. I put on my white uniform and hat with the other children and rehearsed the show with my Heifer. I was nervous. Thousands of people went to the fair and this would be a large event.

When the time came to line up, I looked out at the crowd of people. Judges stood along a fence waiting to come up close. Families showed their cattle off, each person walking the mopey cows to their place in line. My cousin and brother went before me. Both of their cows walked perfectly well across the field. I closed my eyes for a minute and took a step. My Heifer took a step with me. I began walking and she stayed calm and stood by my side, but when we got to our place in line and the judges began to walk forward something happened. I felt my Heifer tense up; I tensed up too and held my breath. I looked out at the crowd staring and eating their fair food and it made me break out in a sweat. I tried to remember what I learned about staying calm to keep her calm, but it was too late. She jerked her massive head and it pulled me down. The Heifer walked across the open field, dragging me. I couldn't let go and let my cousin or uncle win. My uncle Richard came jogging across the field and got a hold of her as the crowd broke out in laughter. He had to tug the rope out of my hands and pull me up.

I walked home with my white outfit covered in mud and grass stains listening to my uncle and cousin cackle behind me. It didn't bother me. At least I didn't let go. Regardless of who laughed, I didn't care because I knew we were spending the day at midway the next morning. When my brother and I woke up we dressed as quickly as we could and told our parents we were off.

"Stick together," my father said.

We nodded and scurried off. It didn't feel strange for us to be left away from our parents. We spent most days acres away from them, exploring some hidden corner on the outskirt of a grazing field or swimming down by one of the brooks that bleed out from the Merrimack. When the sky would begin to turn reddish and the air would cool, we would know to begin back towards the golden light pouring out from the house. It would be a long walk for children our age, but we'd make fun along the way and come up with games for the next day or maybe debate whether the game we played that day was worth playing again. Now and again we'd get lucky and my uncle or one of the farmhands would be driving one of the old pickups from the barn to wherever they were headed. We'd jump up and down and holler until the headlights caught us in the dark and they let us climb into the bed.

Once, we wandered out to the very edge of the property while following a brook. My cousin told us we should follow it and build a new swimming hole wherever it led. The water led us to a drainage pipe on the connector that binds the Bradford area of Haverhill to I-495. We piled rocks by the side of the road, one by one trying to flood the brook. Above my head, I could feel the wind of cars rushing, the whirring noise, and the growl of the tires on asphalt. It was frightening but in a new and exciting way.

Being at the park with my brother felt the same. The entire thing was captivating to us; we had never seen anything like it. I could smell popcorn and cotton candy and cigarettes. I walked with my brother by the lines of tents filled with toys and bags of candy, all colored in pastel pinks and greens and blues. Groups of boys crowded around one another, watching intently at whoever was trying to hit a balloon with a dart or get a ball to land in a cup. When they would win, there would be an upheaval of roars and they would shake the boy who won, the lucky winner looking full of pride and bewilderment. When they'd lose there would be a choir of groans and the boys would kick the tent and curse like they'd seen their fathers curse at slot machines.

My brother looked around with his brows bent into a serious look. We had a mission, and he meant business.

"I don't see it nowhere."

We spun in circles scanning between hotdog stands and bumper car tents. My brother held his hand over his eyes like a naval captain. It was hard for me to stay focused; I had some quarters in my pocket and wanted to try a candy apple or win a cowboy hat at the BB gun target tent. We had a pellet gun sitting around on the farm and I figured I might be a better shot than the average kid but I didn't want to wander off. My brother couldn't stop thinking about what our older cousin told us the night before.

"You're going into midway tomorrow?"

"Yes."

We answered at the same time. I crossed my arms and felt proud and smug. Even covered in mud and grass stains I couldn't help but feel great. We were outside the Presbyterian tent. They were open late and if you went in and talked to them about God, they'd give you free balloons. They were old folks and didn't seem ever to notice we were the same kids coming in over and over again. We'd go outside the tent and sit under the lantern light and inhale the helium and then roll over laughing at the way our voices changed. My cousin wiped his forehead and leaned on one hip while we sat on the asphalt. His hair was tucked back in his backward cap and his cheeks were burned red by the late-season sun. He looked behind himself, snorted his nose, and then spit.

"You boys gonna ride The Corkscrew or what?"

I looked at my brother. I didn't know what my cousin was talking about. My cousin ripped the knot of a balloon with his teeth and inhaled until his cheeks filled. He sounded like a cassette track scrubbing.

"Don't tell me you've never heard of The Corkscrew!"

My cousin perched his eyebrows up as high as he could so that his face looked like an old ventriloquist dummy. My brother was fidgeting a little and shuffling his feet. His face began to flush red into a pout and I could tell he didn't know either.

"No sissies or losers can ride the Corkscrew. It's the wildest ride at Midway. Look—"

He began to float his hand upward on a steep incline, shaking it a little and making a mechanical noise with his mouth.

"You get pulled up to the top in a long cart like a caterpillar climbing up a tree, and then—"

His hand rushed downward fast, leveled itself, and then began to twist and turn, his finger spinning like a top.

"Straight down and then spun upside down, around and around like a screw, or like a fighter pilot doing divebombs."

"Woah," my brother whispered.

My cousin let the rest of the balloon go and we all watched it barrel roll as it flew sideways through the air. He looked out and spat again.

"Yep. Heard people were passin' out when they first brought it up here. Not a ride for sissies like you two."

My brother told him that he was wrong and that he'd see when we came back. He stomped away and I followed him to our sleeping bags to wait for the next morning.

I was getting hot now as we explored midway. I kept picking at my shirt and could feel sweat pooling in my back. My brother would wave for me to follow him, then we'd stop, and he'd look around again with his hands cupped around his eyes. I was about to walk over to the sprinklers when we heard the sound of people cheering and a loud motor ticking. It sounded like a belt from the bottling plant but huge and echoing.

"There it is!"

I ran with my brother. Overhead I could see massive yellow and black piping with a cart of people being pulled to the highest peak of the structure. We dug through the crowd of people around it to the fence. My brother climbed up on the bottom rung and looked up at the cart with his nose tilted to the sun. For a moment, everything was quiet. The ticking had seized, and the cart was up in the sky against the baby blue backdrop of the afternoon. Somebody waved from up in the air, and just then the motor started and kicked the cart forward. A deep metallic roar spread over the ground as the cart plunged towards the earth. The wheels screamed; people screamed. They turned left hard and twisted upside down, their arms hanging loose like pinned clothing in the wind.

My brother looked back at me. I felt a little nervous; I could tell he was too.

"Well come on, let's go. We aren't sissies."

We went to wait in line under the canopy. The line between the metal dividers was claustrophobic and full of people, but it was still cooler than out in the open sun on the pavement. Many of the people in line were much older than me. Teenage boys sat on the railing of the divider and swore and laughed loudly, flicking their cigarettes onto the beamed floor. A teenage girl looked our way and smiled. Her hair was thick and curly and full of hairspray, glitter on her eyelids. They were all very tall compared to me and wore clothes like people I'd seen in movies that were on cable sometimes in the evening time.

We waited for a long time. I was beginning to get tired. I sat on the ground and rested my forehead on the lower steel bar of the divider. It was cool to the touch and felt good in the heat. When the line moved forward for what seemed like the hundredth time, I suddenly found myself in the front. A teenager in a red polo-shirt was standing in front of me with a blue "L" shaped bar. He waved for us to come forward. My brother went first. The teenager squinted at him for a moment and motioned for him to go up to the carts. He looked back at me and ran to find a seat.

"Alright kid, let's go."

The boy was motioning at me. He told me to stand under the bar. For a moment he didn't say anything and just sighed. I was trying to figure out why he was holding it above my head and what it was for. It was painted a very bright blue, after all, and must be for something special.

"Sorry kid, you can't ride this one today."

I choked up. I was too nervous to ask him why or what the bar was even for. A teenager laughed from on top of the railing. I backed away and headed for the stairway. The people in line stared as I passed, their faces a hot blur. I caught the face of the girl who smiled at me; it was tilted now, her lip jutting out and her eyes glossy. I turned my head and ran down the staircase.

On the bottom step, I tried to think of why the boy wouldn't let me on The Corkscrew. I wondered if it was because I was a sissy or loser like my cousin said. My brother, Harold, was only 18 months older so I didn't think I was too young either. I closed my eyes and tried to dig for anything that anybody said about me that they didn't say about him. I racked my brain over and over, and then it hit me. I remembered the drive alone with my parents; the wide bench seat with nobody on it but me. I remembered trying to tell everybody about Boston because I was the only one who'd gone—my teacher talking about me at the end of class; what was it? I remembered the strange, strong-smelling room at the hospital where they asked questions and I remembered the word they all said to my parents: *Special*. I sat on the steps thinking that must be it, and for the first time in my life I did not want to be *special*—whatever it meant.

3

The first time I heard somebody say, "short bus," was on my first day of elementary school. I wore my new Red Sox Cap and backpack and stood with my cousins and brother and all the neighborhood kids at the end of our street. My mother had already explained to me I'd be taking a different bus than everyone else—that'd I'd have to wait just a little longer after they all got on the first one. I was confused about why I was on a different bus, but I trusted my mother and didn't want to make her upset.

We all stood around waiting. The older kids looked despondent and the rest of us gripped the straps of our backpacks and tapped our feet. We took turns peering around the corner to check if we could see it coming down the road. I looked over at my brother. His face was stretched into a frown and he rolled his eyes.

"I don't see why you gotta take a different bus."

I shrugged. My older cousin looked up from wiping his sleeve on his watch. He started saying something and stopped. We were both staring at him waiting to hear what he wanted to say.

"It's cause his brains are all twisted up. He's gotta ride the short bus."

I looked at Harold and said, "Short bus?"

My cousin sighed. I couldn't tell if he was trying to be mean or not.

"Shortbus—like the bus for looneys and retards. School says he's gotta take it cause he's special."

I looked down at the ground. When the first bus arrived, my brother patted me on the head and walked up the stairs with everybody. The engine grumbled and kicked dust as I waved to him from the tiny window by his seat.

My cousin was right about calling it a short bus. When it arrived, it was about half the size of an ordinary school bus. I was disappointed. I was excited to sit on a real, full-size school bus as the older kids do. This bus just looked like a van.

The doors swung open. A man with gray hair and sunglasses held the lever for the door in the driver's seat. He grimaced at me and motioned for me to walk up the steps.

"Let's go kid, let's go."

I hurried on up the steps and looked around. The bus smelt strange—like urine maybe. Between the rows of green vinyl seats were children. Some of them looked very strange, like people I'd seen at the carnival at Topsfield. Many were yelling and squirming in their seats. There were a couple of strange medical machines clanking around too. I walked by them fast and sat in the back.

The bus drove from our road through the outskirts of Bradford until we got to the common. I wiped the fog from the window and looked out into the dewy morning. There was traffic everywhere, jamming up the old looping streets that bleed into South Main Street. I smiled at the sight of the river as we traversed the bridge. It looked like a river of gold in the morning sun. The gold-covered the brick buildings along the water and caught the dew. I watched as we passed downtown, the people bustling out of storefronts, sub shops, and banks.

We followed Main Street up farther than I'd ever been. There was a stern postured brick building the bus pulled in front of and soon we were loaded out in a straight line. I looked at the playground out front. It was made of red, yellow, and blue piping tangled up in itself. Teachers led us to a coiling staircase where we climbed up to the top floor; the attic of the school. I looked down before we went into the classroom at the spiral to the bottom.

    They brought us in and told everybody to sit. I could tell it was different from the other classrooms. There was a foggy brown varnish over everything, and I could feel the curves in the floorboards when I walked. The light came through a single window and I could see the dust drifting through the room. I looked down. The light poured down onto the floorboards and I could see where the finish had worn through.

    The first few months were fine. If anything, they were just very boring. Most of the day I was up in the attic with the other children that came in on the short bus, watching the trees move outside. The teacher was different than the one I'd had at the church. If I didn't sit still at the church, I would be yelled at or brought to the back of the classroom and told to listen. She'd watch over us outside like a hawk and yell from the picnic table when somebody pushed somebody else over. This teacher was much younger, but she seemed much older to me. She'd sigh and try to perk up her eyes and seem excited. When the children spoke out, she tried to calm them at first but eventually sunk into her seat and drawled on about the lesson. It was difficult to hear, and when I could hear her, it was usually about something I did not understand at all. I'd zone out on the other children. Some of them were very strange. One wore shiny steel braces on her legs; another looked normal but would yell like he was in pain for no reason at all.

Outside I kept to myself. I'd walk to the corner of the schoolyard where a large pine tree hung overhead and throw rocks at it. I used to think about being a famous baseball player and figured I should spend my free time learning to pitch. I'd back up from the tree with the rock in my hands and zero in, standing perpendicular to it with the rock up against my chest like I was praying. I'd spit, fix the brim of my hat, and then drag my foot back through the dirt like an angry bull—just like I'd seen when my father watched the game on television.

Sometimes I'd see someone else at the end of the schoolyard. It was a boy from my class. He'd flutter back and forth like a ghost, always alone. I hadn't ever said anything to him until one day we were in line to practice spelling at the board. He had just gone, and it had taken a very long time. He lingered upfront while I tried to spell the word *"better."* I kept feeling I was ready to write it but when the chalk would touch the chalkboard my mind would go blank. I could feel the eyes from the line behind me burning into my back.

"We're a bit short on time today—tomorrow, Dale. James, you get back to your seat too."

The teacher nudged me along with her hand on my back. James followed me in a hovering kind of way.

"Hey—were you jus' makin' fun of me?"

"What?"

He had his arms crossed and seemed like he was trying to look mean. His clothes were giant on his lanky frame and he smelt like a wet dog.

"Jus' because I can't spell quick don't mean anybody's better than me."

He stuck his nose up and turned his cheek. I hadn't even paid attention when he went up; I was too nervous about when I would have to.

"I wasn't making fun. I can't spell quick either."

"Oh."

He stepped back and inspected me for a moment. He was a tiny, wiry-haired kid with eyes that vibrated in his head. I noticed his fingers moved around whenever he wasn't talking and that he shuffled back and forth. Even when it seemed like he was standing still he was moving one pace forward and back.

"Why you think that girl's got metal legs?"

I shrugged. He leaned in close to me.

"Glad I'm not her."

James began to talk to me at recess and at lunch. He talked a lot—at a mile a minute like radio static. I'd stand back from him because he always got too close and got spit on my face. I could never keep up with what he was saying. He had a blank look whenever I spoke like the words were flying over his head. Nevertheless, he was entertaining to be around. His ideas were crazy and strange, and he knew about things I'd never heard of. When I told him I was thinking of being a baseball player, he said he was sure he was going to be a stunt devil. He'd climb the tree and jump off from high up in the air. When he'd hit the ground and roll through the pine needles, he'd look up at me and say,

"Did you think that was cool? Were you scared?"

I'd be laughing and tell him yes. One day we were watching a group of boys play wall ball. They all wore clean, pressed sports jerseys and wore colorful Nike sneakers. A few girls straggled around them while they played and giggled in groups. Now and then a boy would go up and say something to make them laugh.

"I wish I could be friends with them. I wanna play wall ball with them and talk to the girls." James said.

"What do you mean? Why don't you?" I asked.

I was watching James chew through a tootsie pop. He had a blue film around the corners of his mouth. I never really thought about it, but I guessed then after I spoke that maybe he wouldn't mold so well with those boys. It never occurred to me that you couldn't be friends with somebody—even if you wanted to. A piece of me wanted to be friends with them too, but it seemed like a lot of work. I didn't look like them at all and had never played wall ball, and that seemed like the only thing they ever did at recess besides huddle in circles and laugh. I didn't know any of their names since I was in the attic all day.

"I can't be because I take that stupid bus to school and sit next to the girl with the robot legs."

I'd never tested the theory on myself. I figured I probably had a better shot than James, but then again, I had never really thought too much about what people thought of me when they looked at me or listened to me speak. I hoped I didn't look or act like James.

At home, I'd begun to start working a paper route. Since my bus showed up so late, I had time in the morning to meet the mailman at the edge of the neighborhood. He'd get a bundle of newspapers out from his truck and I'd put them in the front pocket of my backpack. I'd run from house to house through the neighborhood dropping newspapers off. I'd try to catch people as they were leaving for work because they'd sometimes tip me. I'd collect the coins and keep them in the side pocket of my bag.

Sometimes at the end of my route, I'd look around and check if anybody nearby was outside. If nobody was looking, I'd run off away from the property. There was a pizza shop I'd seen on the bus ride to school every day and I'd use my paper route money to buy myself French fries and a soda. I'd explore around the neighborhoods near mine and keep an eye out for my father's truck. I'd memorized his route delivering milk and I knew for the most part where not to be and when.

Most of the money I saved. I could only get French fries so often and my mother gave me enough to eat at school. I liked to hear the money jingle while I walked up the stairs to the classroom in the attic. I'd count it from under my desk and make sure I hadn't lost any. James was always asking if we could go buy candy at the store across from the school but I figured he lived in a neighborhood and took the same bus I did and should probably start delivering papers too if he wanted.

Once I learned I could skip school it was hard to keep myself there. I began to fake being sick. It started legitimately; I'd thrown up in the stall one day and got sent home with my mother. They didn't see me throw up; I'd just told them. It didn't take long for me to figure out I could do that whenever I wanted. My mother knew what I was doing but she'd just give me a somber look and smile while she stood in the old oak lobby of the school. She'd drive me home and I'd sit up front with her and play with the radio dial until I found a song I liked the sound of. It'd be warm and quiet in my living room while everybody else was out in the world. I'd discovered all different types of cartoons running through the afternoon. I'd never really sat indoors by the television during the day before that. I loved the way the characters looked and never cared about what they were doing. It fascinated me that the same thing could be drawn in so many different ways and that every cartoon made me feel a little different.

EXIT 48

It was over when my father caught on. He said it was important I went to school; that sitting and watching cartoons would make me lazy. He also said I'd thank him one day but being back in that musty classroom made me wonder what for. One day I was out at the schoolyard with James. I hadn't been to the schoolyard with him for a while, so I bought us bags of M&Ms at the school store. We passed the boys playing wall ball and James stared. I looked over and a few of them were looking at us and talking amongst themselves.

"Let's go talk to them. We'll see if we can play."

James looked like I had two heads when I said it. Before he could say no I started walking towards them. I looked back at him and waved for him to follow me. His fingers were moving wildly around each other, and his eyes bulged out of his head. He caught up to me and I could hear him panting in my ear when we got close.

"Can we play?"

All the boys stopped what they were doing and turned towards me. James gasped and tried to resist pacing. He looked in pain from standing still, his face flushed. A larger boy out of the bunch emerged from the pack and stared at us. He was almost my cousin's height and chewed bubblegum like him too, loud and exaggerated with his jaw kicking out to the side.

"How'd you get those M&M's?"

I didn't say anything, but I wasn't confused. I wish I'd listened to James.

"Ron says he's seen you buying them with a big bag of coins. I can hear em' jingling when you walk."

He stepped towards me and I felt the crowd behind him pulse forward. He bent down to my level and looked me in the eye.

"What's a retard like you need that money for?"

Retard. I'd heard that word walking to my classroom from the bus with the rest of my class. I knew enough of what it meant: that I was different than him—that I belonged on a different bus or stowed away in an attic. I felt my neck get hot like I was embarrassed, but it kept getting hotter like red coals until I clenched my jaw and felt my nostrils flare. I began to yell and lunged forward. Out of the corner of my eye, I saw the blur of something cut the air.

I'd gotten in fights before and I'd been hit before. Down at Chipmunk Village, I'd fight my brother over things all the time; even my older cousin sometimes. We'd meet there or get in a scuffle while we were playing a game. We'd put each other in headlocks, throw sand in each others' faces, tackle each other, or even throw punches at each other while we circled like barn cats.

None of the times somebody hit me in Chipmunk Village felt this way. At first, I barely felt it at all. For a split second, there was a rush of air against my head and then I heard a loud cracking noise that sent a deep jolt across the right side of my face. My momentum was still sending me forward. I tripped over myself. I couldn't hear anything but ringing by the time I hit the ground. I rolled on my back and tried to sit up. I saw another shadow graze the corner of my eye and there was a second sledge against my face. It drove the fat of my cheek into my molars and I felt the warm rush and taste of iron pool in my mouth. I felt it now. My entire head began to swell with ripe pain. It felt like something was pushing out from behind my eyes. One of the boys leaned in and punched me in the stomach. I coughed and the air left my body. I couldn't breathe and curled over on the pavement.

Looking out from laying on my side, I saw a pair of feet shuffling on the outskirt of the pack. I followed them up to James's face staring at me. He was backing away.

"James! Help!"

He shook his head and put his hands up. I felt a kick lay into my back. It sent a shock through my body, but the momentum helped me roll onto all fours. I swatted at the boys with my hand. One of them slapped it away and punched me hard in the face again. I crumbled back to the ground and put my hands over my head. The hitting subsided and I listened with my nose on the pavement as the boys dumped each pocket of my backpack until they found my money and walked off talking amongst each other. When I finally looked up the schoolyard was empty, and I sat against the wall ball wall alone for a good while and then gathered my things.

I went to class the next day with my face swollen. It felt as if my entire head was a bruise. When I walked in, I didn't look at James and I didn't look at my teacher. I wasn't upset with James, but I'd decided I had enough of him and almost everything at Walnut Elementary. At some point, I decided to slip back into the far corner of the class. We didn't have assigned seats and children got up and moved as they pleased. There wasn't much one teacher could do to control it. On the shorter end of the "L" shaped room were a few empty desks nobody touched all year. I began sitting there every day through all of elementary school and nobody seemed to notice. I drew on all of the desks, spending whole school days shading different scenes in pencil. On one of them, I drew a map of my paper route; on another, I drew a pitcher striking someone out. I sketched out cartoon characters I'd seen on TV and scattered them through all the different things I pulled from my brain.

At the center of it all was my desk, on which I drew a monkey in a cage. It was from the perspective of someone passing by on their

way to somewhere else, the monkey snarling and showing its teeth—
half in the frame and half out.

4

"Look here."

The bottles of milk rattled as they treaded the belt. My mother stood at its end with her hands raised in front of her like a quarterback. She snagged each bottle of milk quick and gently so as not to break them, her hand moving in a single motion and placing them in crates by her side. The air was dense, its coolness breaking against the kinetic heat of men moving from room to room. The concrete walls mangled the machines' roar to a steady drone, and under it, I heard the hoarse voices of the older men yelling at each other. A boombox in the corner of the room next door was almost inaudible under the hum and clamor, straining itself and frying the underbelly of the air with static.

Everybody was expected to work, and my mother and father told me it was about time I learned how to help at the bottling plant. One of us was going to end up with it, they said. My brother had already begun working and was in the room next door with the older men bottling and capping the milk. My job was simple: catch the bottles at the end of the conveyor belt and stack them in milk crates.

"Don't be fooled. It's not taking a stroll and dropping off papers."

My mother looked down at me sternly. When one was full, she lugged it quick to her left and added it to the growing stack of crates. On her right were the empty crates, which she dragged in bunches within arm's reach. She motioned for me to jump in. I took her place and began to reach over the lip of the belt to grab the bottles. I felt clumsy compared to her swift movements and my hands shook a bit. She stood with her arms crossed, nodding or yelling, "Catch up!" if the bottles began to accumulate.

By the end of the day, I was covered in sweat, grease, and milk. I had dropped a bottle and the sound of the glass hitting the pavement sprang onto the concrete walls and bounced through the plant. The entire crew hollered, and the milk propelled upward and soaked my clothes. I knew I couldn't stop; the belt would get backed up. At the end of the day, I mopped the mess and let the breeze cool the wet spots on my clothes as I walked home.

I graduated from Walnut Elementary to attend J.G Whittier Middle School. Whittier was closer to the heart of the city and its doors poured out with children and teachers from all walks of life. The schoolyard was a massive, spanning field ravaged by months of drought and the cleats of the various soccer teams from neighboring cities. Adjacent to the school were two basketball courts dismantled from years of use and high schoolers coming after dark to goof off. The school was planted in the center of suburban neighborhoods and children often lined the court on their bicycles and sat hunched over their handlebars as they let the morning dwindle.

It was the first day of school and I sat in homeroom gripping my math book. I was allowed to take a normal math course this year, and I wanted everybody to see I had a textbook just like them. I'd spent the last few years of my life in an attic and I was ready to be something new. For years, I'd given up on being normal; it simply wasn't possible. Every day I felt like I was an outcast and a freak, and when I tried to break from that mold somebody always proved to me that I was nothing more. I'd learned to keep quiet and back off. Over the summers, I became more reclusive on the farm, wandering off on my own to sit in the dry dirt or sneak into my uncle's shop to mess with the tools. I didn't think people had much to offer me and couldn't think of anything I could offer them, so I let it be how it was. My brother had begun to climb his way up the pecking order and spent a lot of time now riding bikes with kids I didn't know. My cousin was in high school and had gone from being a tormentor to being disinterested in all of us. Sometimes I'd see him and his friends tearing up part of our fields in a truck or drinking out of beer bottles and smashing them along the brook. I didn't say anything to anyone. I knew better.

I wanted people to see my math book. It was the only book I carried. I saw how the other kids heaved their stacks of books or carried them lazily under their arms and I wanted to do the same. I made sure I carried it with the front cover out under my arm so everybody could see I was in a real math class. I wanted them to look at it and know I was like any of them; maybe even smarter in some ways.

I didn't want just to be liked, I wanted to be admired. Throughout elementary school I watched my old friend James wiggle his way into the social structure. Like me, he knew he had to distance himself from everything in that class and on that bus. He found his way into social groups by clinging to people; by becoming their hype man. I'd often see him hovering around groups of boys like the ones that attacked me. They'd make him their punching bag, and when everybody laughed at him, he laughed right along too.

The teacher was passing papers around. All around her, children shifted and shouted. In the back corner of the class, a group of boys was chucking crumpled paper and eraser heads at each other. I watched a group of girls whispering. They flung their hair back and forth and gasped and rolled their eyes. I couldn't remember when they began to start acting like that. The boys around me seemed like they hadn't changed much besides the fact they were much larger now and knew some different ways to curse.

My teacher looked a lot like my old teacher at Walnut Elementary. She was young, but it seemed like she was tired all the time. I just assumed it was something that happened to adults. I'd see the same look on my parent's faces. Sometimes I'd drop the mail off in our kitchen and walk to the living room to watch cartoons. My mother would pace behind me reading through whatever was in the envelopes and she'd look tired and upset. Other times I'd walk out to the cow barns and see my Uncle Richard with that face looking at the cows, or sometimes my father when he'd walk slow from his deliveries, now with jugs of milk still in the truck.

My teacher was talking in the high-pitched, happy way they do whenever they look tired. She'd told our homeroom we were going to try and draw our own hands. I liked to draw. Sometimes I spent my free time drawing. I had a pad of paper I carried in my backpack that I'd take out far into the fields and I'd draw the silos or maybe the bull while he huffed and ate alone in his pen. I tried to draw in the styles of the cartoons I watched. I liked how I could draw the bull how I wanted, whether I wanted to make him stand up with a top hat or be tiny like a barn cat.

I pulled my pencil out from my pack and began to focus on my other hand. When I tilted it left or right the shadow crawled over my skin. I balled my hand into a fist and held it so my fingers were facing me. The first thing I drew was the outline of my fist, then the dark, creasing shadow my fingers made as they dug into my palm. When I'd worked out the rough sketch, I tilted my seat back and tilted my head. The outline was beginning to look like a tree line to me. The crease of my palm and fingernails looked like underbrush, the flesh of my lower palm a hill in the foreground. My bent knuckles were a bit too pointed to look like knuckles, but they looked like pine trees. I filled them in with branches and needles, scribbling thick gray strokes downward and wisping out from their centers.

There was a boy next to me who kept peering over at my drawing. He was stockier than me with tight black curls and a boxy head. Whenever I'd look over at him, he'd look away. I wondered if he was trying to copy me. It wasn't a test or quiz; I didn't think the teacher would even look at what we were drawing, and I wondered why he would even try to copy someone trying to draw their hand when he had to draw his.

"Why'd you draw it like that?"

It made me angry he was asking. I knew It didn't matter to him, and I didn't want to start middle school with someone calling me a name and telling the class I was strange or slow or dumb. I hadn't figured out a formula to deal with something like this yet. I needed time to think. I thought about the boys at Walnut that would hurt me just for talking to them—how after they tried to make a game out of it and hunt me in the schoolyard when they were bored of wall ball. I didn't want to be nice to anyone.

"Mind your business."

The boy scoffed and rolled his eyes. He filled his cheeks with air and exhaled.

"You don't have to be an ass. My drawing just looks different, see—"

He fumbled with his piece of paper and held it up towards me. The hand was drawn with a blue crayon and the paper was crumbled for some reason. It looked crude and the lines were jagged and shaky.

"I just did it how they made me do it when we drew turkeys for thanksgiving. Did you do that?"

"Yes."

I lied. Well, I'd drawn the turkey—just not in class. Too many of the kids in the attic couldn't do it. Some couldn't understand what the teacher meant, some couldn't sit still and squirmed around too much. My teacher botched the assignment and took all the drawing supplies back when kids started putting the markers in their mouths. The next day I saw the turkey drawings hung up around the school on paper plates stapled to the wall. I fell out of line on the way up to the attic and looked close and hard at one of the turkeys, trying to remember and memorize how the other classes had done it.

At the end of the day, I waited for when they'd get us ready to go down to the buses. It was always hectic as soon as my teacher called for help to round everybody up; the kids knew they were going home. They'd get up and stand on desks and holler and my teacher would scramble to calm them down.

I waited for her to be occupied with a particularly excited child and slipped back to the supply crate. I looked behind me quickly. She wasn't looking, so I pocketed the markers I thought I'd need: red, brown, orange—maybe yellow for the beak. When I got to the farm, I went to the dairies break room and stole a paper plate from the stack. I ran with it up to the hayloft where nobody would see or bother me. I grabbed the end of a splintered twelve-inch board that had peeled from the wall and fell down the stack, then I nestled myself between a couple of bales that had fallen apart and soft.

When I'd finished outlining my hand and drawing the legs and beak and eyes, I filled it in with streaks of brown and orange. I stood up and blew the hay dust off the plate and held my turkey by a beam of light coming through the wall. I thought it looked great and smiled. It was just as good as the ones I'd seen on the wall at school.

"See, I'd done it just like the turkey, but I just didn't add a beak or legs or feathers."

I looked at the outline of his hand on the paper. He didn't even add fingernails. I thought it was a little goofy. He leaned over and looked at my drawing. He squinted his eyes and nodded.

"I like how you did yours. Is that how hands look to you?"

I leaned back a little. His chair was balancing on two legs and he was practically falling over onto my desk.

"I started drawing my hand and then thought it looked like trees."

The boy clapped and nodded his head. He fell back into his chair and looked at me.

"Hell—I think I see it now! I woulda never thought of that. The fingers are trees!"

I smiled. I realized that nobody had ever seen one of my drawings, besides my mom and the janitor who had washed them off the desks at Walnut Elementary every few weeks. I liked that he liked my drawing. It made me feel proud and like I did a good thing. I sat up sometimes at night imagining people seeing my drawings and being very impressed, but I didn't think I could stand for them to call me a name or make fun of me if they didn't like it.

"Are you some typa' artist?"

"I don't think so. I draw cartoons sometimes."

The boy slapped the top of his desk. He talked loudly and

moved with big clumsy sweeps.

"No shit—which ones you draw?"

I told him about which cartoons I drew and I told him I drew other things. I explained the farm; how I liked to draw different pieces of old farm equipment and how I already had the marker colors to draw them—the red finish of a truck bed, the rust of an old monkey wrench. He nodded and asked me questions about the cows. He told me what his favorite cartoons were and said he didn't know much about farms besides what he saw at the fair because he lived in an apartment downtown.

The bell rang. I pulled out my list of classrooms and searched for the room number. Before I could turn the paper away the boy was peering over my shoulder at my classes.

"Huh—didn't take you for being in a class like that."

I ripped the paper away and shoved it into my pocket. I should've known it would turn out like this. I looked at the boy's blank face and felt enraged. I could feel my cheeks get hot as I began to grab my bag and walk backward.

"Yeah—I'm in the class with the slow kids. Can't read well. Want to know anything else?"

The boy burst out laughing with his hands on his knees. His face was flushed red and his laugh hobbled out of his mouth with a cumbersome slowness.

"I don't know what you're talking about, but I was talking about that math class! To think I was just about to say you must be smarter than you look. Listen—"

He walked over and punched my shoulder. I flinched but he put his hand out.

"I can barely read a full sentence myself. Don't get worked up so easy. My name's Tommy. Yours?"

"My name is Dale."

I shook his hand and looked at the floor. I felt bad for lashing out at him. It had been a while since another student asked me what my name is, never mind sat with me and talked about cartoons. He didn't seem too beat up about it though. He didn't seem bothered by much of anything.

"Alright, Dale. I'll see you at lunch."

He waved and headed out the door.

At lunch, we met up and ate food while we told jokes. He didn't seem like he fit on a rung on the social ladder at all. I was so used to being boxed out against my will that it seemed strange to see a person unconcerned. He wasn't picked on by anyone and didn't seem to take any precautions. Maybe it was because he was a big kid and could put up a fight; maybe everybody liked him. Then again, I didn't see anyone take much notice of him besides to say hello. His clothes were normal; they weren't expensive and flashy, but they were clean and normal enough to blend in. He seemed to be unconcerned with almost everything happening around him.

We began to hang out every day and based a lot of our friendship on making fools of ourselves. It was different from my old friend James. It didn't seem like either of us was clinging to each other for dear life. Plus, I enjoyed Tommy's company as a friend. It made me realize I couldn't remember if I ever even had a friend.

Taking the bus home from Whittier was unbearably long. After some begging, my mother agreed to drive me to school in the mornings so I wouldn't have to take the short bus and step off in front of anybody. I still had to take it home and made sure to rush on as fast as I could every afternoon and avoid any eye contact.

Throughout the entire city, anybody in our age group that qualified as "special" took the same bus home. We stopped at several different schools and picked up children with ailments I'd never even heard of. Some of them had such bad problems they couldn't talk or had to be wheeled onto the bus. I'd run from the school lot and jump on as fast I could so nobody would see me, and I could get my spot in the farthest seat back.

When I first saw the kids get on from Smiley School, I didn't know whether to laugh or cry. It seemed like a joke when they walked up the bus steps with their long hair and leather jackets. I couldn't imagine they'd come from somewhere named Smiley School. Some of them even had full beards. They walked slowly when they stepped into the aisle, the ceiling of the bus almost touching their heads as their work boots clunked against the steel grating of the floor. They scowled at any kid that looked their way and sank into the bus seats when they sat.

I was sure they couldn't be younger than my cousin. They sat around me in the back, and I tried to slide as far against the window as I could. I listened to them say all kinds of horrible things about girls they knew and guys they didn't like while they spit on the bus floor. I kept my face towards the window, watching a boy on a bike that flew downhill next to our bus. I didn't want to look their way; I knew it'd be trouble and there was nowhere to go if they decided to notice me. I could smell cigarette smoke wrapping around the back of my neck into my nostrils. They flicked their Zippos and ashed on the floor of the bus.

I was one of the last stops. I walked past the crumpled cigarette butts and broken pencils and crayons and stepped onto my street. I turned around and the bus driver wasn't looking at me. The smoke from his cigarette reflected in the sunglasses he'd worn since he first started driving me in elementary school. He pulled the latch and the bus door shut. Its tires kicked up a cloud of dust in the dipping sun. I watched it disappear and then took off in a jog to get some hours in at the plant before the machines went quiet.

The only problem that I'd seen Tommy have with anyone that first year was because of me. One day a boy recognized me from Walnut at recess.

"Who let the retard out of his cage?"

He had a crew with him, and they gave out a choir of laughs.

"Shouldn't you have somebody following you around?"

I gripped my math book until my knuckles turned white. I didn't get scared of people like him anymore; just furious. Tommy lumbered a few steps ahead of me, his shoulders slightly lifted like a professional wrestler.

"There he is!"

The boy was pointing at Tommy and forcing his laughter. Tommy looked back at me grimacing. I put my math book on the ground. I couldn't bear for my new friend to see me get put down.

At some point, I had to decide enough was enough. The boy was still laughing when I hit him in the face, his top and bottom teeth clicking against each other as he stumbled sideways. I immediately felt my feet leave the ground. I soared through the air and hit the pavement hard. The person that landed on me bounced off my rib cage. I saw Tommy drag the person across the pavement and begin pummeling them. Two more kids jumped on him like coyotes and took him to the ground, laying punches into his head.

The fight was over quickly. Right as kids began to swarm a teacher broke it up and we were all sent to the principal's office.

"Man—what pricks." Tommy said.

There was blood in the corner of Tommy's nose, and he had a scratch mark across his forehead. We both looked at each other and said nothing for a moment, then broke out laughing. I didn't mind if my lip was split. It felt good to have a friend.

I began to get more and more proficient at my job at the plant. Picking the bottles from the belt and crating them became muscle memory, allowing me to think while working. I'd think over the fragments of a lesson I learned in English class, mouthing each letter to words that would be on our weekly spelling quiz. I'd recite them until I could say the letters quick and untethered—in the way I could list multiplication tables or fractions to percentages. The plant also helped me become more outspoken. It was merely part of the language to yell and be garish. It wasn't a matter of hard feelings; it was just how they spoke. If they weren't yelling at you that's when you had to worry.

It helped condition me to be a bit crude myself. I began to speak my mind to other children my age and discovered not only that it minimized the amount someone could exploit me as a target, but also that I could be funny. One year toiled into the next and my methods became more intense. I found a niche and rolled with it. Children in my math class began to favor me as a clownish type, making a spectacle of myself and teachers and whoever else crossed into my line of fire. Nonetheless, no matter how funny I was, I still felt like a great distance between everyone and myself. For the most part, they liked me, but they seemed to take no interest in me unless I was making a funny face at them.

One Saturday, I was working the long shift at the plant. It was lunch break and I sat in the small break room next to the main building with the other men. They cackled and smoked cigarettes, passing them back and forth over a coffee table littered with old magazines. One of the workers grabbed a magazine tucked under the rest of the bunch and nodded at me.

"Hey kid, you ever dug through one of these?"

He threw the magazine at me and winked. It read *Penthouse* across the cover. Below the white lettering sat a naked girl on a chair. I smiled and felt my face flush. I opened the first page and heard the men erupt into laughter. I didn't know magazines like this even existed, never mind that we had one at the plant. As I skimmed through the different pictures of women, I wished I owned the magazine. It felt embarrassing to hold it in front of the workers, but I supposed if they did it then it was fine.

I flipped through the pages fast, trying to absorb whatever I could. In the middle of the magazine was an advertisement for a men's workout tape. The photo had two naked women clinging to a shirtless man. The man's muscles were massive, and he smiled at the camera like he knew his life was better than anyone looking at him. I'd never seen anyone with muscles like that. Most of the men at the plant were thin or fat.

On the way out from the breakroom, I caught a glimpse of myself in a window reflection. I'd gotten even heavier than when I was younger. My body looked soft and child-like, my face still round and hairless like a baby's. On top of the whole mess was a greasy head of hair cut straight across the eyebrows by my mother. I realized the missing piece of the puzzle.

When day broke into the night and all the men wandered out of the plant, I rushed past them into the breakroom. I dug through the pile of magazines and found the one with the bodybuilder. I looked out the window to see if anyone was watching me and then flipped to the page with the advertisement. It had a mail-in attached to the bottom. I tore the page out of the magazine and ran home.

The tapes came in a few weeks. We had a VCR set in the living room, so I began unplugging it every night and carrying it up to my bedroom when I'd get out from the bottling plant. The man that was in the ad was the man in the tapes. He had a funny voice, or at least one I wouldn't expect from looking at him. It was high-pitched, a bit nasally. He'd point at the camera as if he was talking directly to me. On occasion, he had a pretty woman in spandex with him that demonstrated the exercises.

I followed his instructions each night, doing sets of pushups or sit-ups or crunches. Eventually, the workouts began to involve weights, so I saved money and bought some of those too. It was rough at first. I'd wake up aching all over my body and it'd hurt to work at the plant. It helped me sleep at night, though, and I often felt less restless at school. It made it a little easier to focus in class; I felt less like something was crawling in my bones that kept me from hearing anything or sitting still.

Eventually, my body stopped hurting so much from the workouts and I began to look forward to it working out in my room. It felt like I was moving towards something and I went to bed knowing I was closer to being something better. One night my father found the tapes on my dresser. He looked at it and squinted.

"Snake oil."

He tossed the tape back on the bureau and walked towards the door. He began to shut it on the way out and turned so I could see his face through the doorway.

"Get the same thing for free from tossin' a milk crate into a truck."

He smiled and shut the door. My father and the other men on the farm were strong, but they were the type of strong somebody got from working. My father looked like anyone else I'd ever seen but could heave crates of milk like they were pillows. He was tan, but in a way like he'd been running a plow in the sun; not like he'd been laying out on a beach or boat. I wanted to be magazine strong; the type of strong people could see when I walked into a room.

When seventh grade rolled around, Tommy and I were in the same art class together. It was the first class we had together, and I began to look forward to it every day. On the first day of class, we had to sketch an apple on the table. I got lost in my sketch for a bit. I decided to make the apple melting onto the table as I'd seen in a book of Dali paintings by the bookshelf. I tried to think of a color apples couldn't have in real life and decided on a sky-blue apple with a stem that curled upward like a tornado.

I leaned over and looked at Tommy's sketch. I was taken aback. It looked like I could reach into the page, pick it up, and take a bite out of it.

"Since when can you draw like that, Tommy?"

"Don't know—think I always could and just didn't look at anything long enough. Started drawing stuff a lot last summer."

I thought back about his drawing of the hand and how it almost made me laugh. I felt jealous now. The cross-hatching and shadows were smooth, and I couldn't see a single line in the drawing if I stood back.

"Why didn't you tell me you could draw like this?"

Tommy shrugged. He was strange in that way. It was almost as if he was taking himself for granted, but not quite. I couldn't put my finger on it, and I couldn't figure out if it was admirable or sad.

"You didn't ask."

He smiled and went back to cross hatching, intricate and slow. He looked up for a moment at the apple and then put his nose back to his paper.

"Damn. I wish I could draw like that."

Tommy put his pencil down and looked at me for a moment. He shook his head.

"Well, I wish I could draw like you. You always see somethin' different in whatever you're drawing—like it's a hill you're trying to peek over. And me—"

He began to sketch again, casting the first beginnings of a shadow against the apple's stem.

"I guess whoever made me just made me good at seein' things how they are in front of me."

He went on with his drawing.

The same kids from Smiley were still on my bus in seventh grade. I figured at this point we were in the same grade, and I wondered if they'd just keep being in the same grade forever. They began to not mind me so much at this point. Some of them would even nod my way as they tossed cigarettes to each other and banged the packs against their wrists. They could be very funny, but always at somebody else's expense. When one of the children on the bus would moan or shout out, they'd mimic them and chuckle. They'd cross their eyes and stare at the cigarette between their lips and say something in a goofy voice like they were slow. There was a girl on the bus who looked at the ceiling and let her head sway the whole ride. When it was her stop, she'd still be staring at the ceiling as she walked down the aisle, which made her often bump into things and trip over herself each afternoon.

The Smiley kids found it very amusing and when they got picked up, they'd all be staring at the ceiling, swaying their heads and purposely falling over kids on the bus. They'd pretend to trip over each other and shove people into bus windows. The bus driver would scowl in the rearview and wait for them to get on with it. I'd laugh in my seat. They were very convincing after a while and they were more outlandish each day to keep up with their senses of humor. I didn't feel too bad for the girl. I didn't even know if she noticed what they were doing. I was on the same bus as her, after all. If anybody should be allowed to laugh, I thought it was me.

At home, I'd kept at it with the tapes into the summer and the new school year. To accompany my workouts, I began going for jogs before school. I'd wake up extra early before the sun peeked over the tree line and when the air was still dull and blue. I'd start at my house and jog down the street to where the fields met the fence line. From there, I'd run along the fence line until I ended up back at my driveway.

I liked to see the world wake up as I ran. The birds would scuttle and chirp as I cruised by. The shepherd dogs would trot next to me until I got too far from their herd. Sometimes I'd see a litter of stray barn kittens hunting in the grass blades, pouncing on grasshoppers and mice drinking dew as they woke. My uncle would be out letting the cows hobble into the fields to stretch their legs and graze. I'd wave to him and he'd wave on back.

I'd shower when I got back to my house. One morning I looked in the mirror at my face. It was beginning to thin out. I had lost weight. I'd stand in the mirror and flex my muscles like the man on the tapes. I didn't look anything like him, but I also didn't look how

I looked months ago. I was proud of that. Still, something about the way I looked tormented me. I stared in the mirror at my face and the wet mop of blonde hair that hung over my eyes. It wrapped around over my ears and to the back of my head like a soup bowl.

It began to irk me the more I looked. I opened my bathroom cabinets and fished around the piles of things stuffed into them. I tossed old soap boxes and rolls of toilet paper back until I found the electric razor I'd seen my father shave his beard with. I pulled the wire from a tangled-up hairbrush and plugged it into the wall. The rusty teeth hummed in my hands. I looked once more at my hair and ran the razor straight over the top of my head. I gasped and then laughed a little. I ran the razor over my head over and over until my head was buzzed like a military man. I looked in the mirror when I was done and smiled. It felt like I'd left a weight in the sink under my blonde locks.

People had begun to get to know me at school. I had a few more friends now from my math class, and Tommy and I would sit at a table of guys at lunch and all talk about girls or who did what to get in trouble and when. I thought at this point there was only one storm cloud following me around that set me apart from everybody else.

Every-other day since the first day of middle school, the school administration forced me to go to a special physical education program at the high school. I'd leave in the middle of the day with all the other short bus kids at Whittier Elementary and get shipped over to take swimming classes and play games I thought were for little kids. Since day one, the gym teacher seemed not to like me for some reason and would often comment on my weight. I'd grown to loathe him. The way he talked, the way he dressed—it reminded me of the boys that played wallball at Walnut Elementary. Eventually, he could tell I hated him, and he'd make me do extra laps in the pool or pickup WIFFLE balls from the gymnasium floor.

I could bear him, but I couldn't bear that the bus arrived back at Whittier right at lunch. It was easy to slip away when the bell rang after homeroom and go to my special classes, but there was no way around arriving back at lunch soaking wet from the high school pool. We'd pull right in front of the cafeteria windows and the old brake pads of the short bus would squeal in front of everyone. I'd step off with the rest, soaked like all of them and holding my math book in my hands so the whole cafeteria could see.

That was sixth and seventh grade, though, and I'd come too far to step off the short bus in front of the cafeteria. From the first day of eighth grade and on, I just didn't go. Nobody seemed to notice.

Skipping gym every other day freed up some time for me, and I ran into the predicament of where to go so I wouldn't be questioned. I snuck around the halls looking for the right place until one afternoon I was sitting in on something happening in the auditorium to kill time. When the classes began to file out, I slipped away behind the stage. I wandered in the dark for a bit until I found a peculiar door tucked back into the corner of the room. I looked around to see if anybody else was backstage and snaked up to the door.

The knob was rickety and corroded. I gave it a pull and it budged a little. I wound up and pulled on the door with both hands. It swung open and sent me stumbling backward. A rush of air that smelt like old newspapers rushed over me from the dark of the room. It was a little spooky and I felt nervous as I inched forward and felt for a light switch against the wall.

I found the switch and turned the light on. The room flickered and crackled until the dark gave way and exposed a much larger room than it initially seemed to be. It must've been a large storage closet at one point. Ancient-looking shelves were lining each wall, stripped empty now aside from books and boxes strewn about. A map of the world was crumpled and torn on the floor with a few boxes of screws and lugs.

I was elated. When I heard the echo of the bell ringing, I shut the storage room up how I found it and ran towards the Cafeteria. I met Tommy there in line. He was farther up, and I jumped up and down and motioned for him to move back to my spot. He threw his hands up and shook his head but walked back to meet me. I was panting.

"What're you all worked up about?"

I told him about the storage room and how he had to see it. We planned it out over our food. He had a study at the same time of the day. The teacher assigned to the study, as he said, was "old as hell" and didn't keep marks of who showed up.

The next time I was supposed to be shipped off to the high school, I went straight for the storage room. Tommy was already there, looking around confused in the dark behind the stage curtains.

"Over here."

I jogged over to the door and pulled it open. I flicked the lights on, and it was just as I left it.

"No kidding," Tommy exclaimed.

"Pretty cool, huh?"

Tommy was walking around touching the shelves. He picked up a crumpled piece of paper.

"This playbill is older than me!"

I walked over and looked at the yellowed piece of paper. The room was completely forgotten about and we both immediately began devising plans for it. All of the junk in the room went to the corner. We pocketed supplies from our art class and stockpiled them. Tommy bought six-packs of coke and put them under the shelves. I even snuck in a couple of milk crates from the farm to sit on. We took the dismantled shelving units and made makeshift isles. By the time we were in the latter half of eighth grade, we had a full-fledged secret art studio going.

We spent a big chunk of the day there painting and drawing. We'd meet up at the block before lunch, then a little later when we heard the bell ring, we'd stop at the cafeteria to grab food and come back for the rest of lunch and recess. We'd talk about nothing and everything. Sometimes we talked about art and what we liked about making art, sometimes we talked about work. We talked about the girls we thought were good looking, we talked about whether they thought we were good looking or not. Sometimes it was about being younger, sometimes it was about when we'd get older—sometimes we didn't talk at all and just worked on our art in quiet.

I walked with Tommy one day to the cafeteria to grab a bite to eat. As we got to the door, I saw one of my pieces from art class hung outside the door. It was a drawing of a massive, ridiculous hamburger that stacked up two feet high. Pinned to my drawing was a ribbon. I was overjoyed but confused; I hadn't entered any contests. The next day I asked my art teacher about my drawing.

"I entered it for you. Thought you might be too busy stealing markers to do it yourself."

He was a serious old man, and I took it as a serious remark he entered the drawing for me. I thought he must really like it if he did. It was the first of anything I'd ever won, and I smiled ear to ear while I walked back to the cafeteria door to look at it again.

After years, I was starting to feel normal. Whenever I felt lousy, I could go to the storage room and get away from the world. The more I hung out there, the less I felt like I had to stay sane. I'd completely thinned out by now, too. I was as built as one could expect an average eighth-grader to be from years of watching workout tapes. In a way, I was happy I had to work for it because it gave me something to be proud of.

Everybody in my grade knew who I was; people saw my name and asked me about the hamburger. It felt good to have people be interested in something about me. I felt like I was more than a class clown. I stayed in the room with the popular kids on my class field trip, I had my first kiss with one of the prettiest girls in the school at our spring social, and it all happened more naturally than I ever thought it would.

The last time I went to the storage room Tommy and I rounded up whatever art supplies we hadn't spent and put them in a cardboard box. We hung out there a bit and then flicked the lights off for the last time. I stopped by our art teacher's class before catching my bus and looked through the window on the door. Nobody was in there. I let myself in and left the box of supplies on the counter.

As my last days of middle school came to an end, I felt miles apart from the girl who waved her head around on the bus ride home, which is why it felt worse and worse each day I laughed at her. I sat in the back of the short bus and watched the kids from Smiley torment her. It'd risen in intensity over the years and became hard to watch. She was crying and I didn't want to laugh anymore.

"Come on, man."

I didn't know if I was talking to them or myself, but the words blurted out of my mouth. It felt so strange to be on the bus with all of these people. One of the Smiley boys walked down the aisle towards me and loomed above my head. I didn't say anything, I just stared upwards. He punched me in the teeth; I immediately grabbed my mouth and curled up. The Smiley kids laughed and the boy moseyed back to his seat. I straightened myself out and got off at the next stop. I wasn't upset; I knew it was goodbye. I let the short bus get smaller in the distance as it carried its passengers deeper into the city. I sucked on the inside of my cheek. My mouth tasted like iron and I could already feel my lower lip swelling.

I spit the blood from my mouth as the bus shrank to a tiny yellow speck. I waved goodbye to whoever sat by the far back window. It was the window where I once sat, but never again. I hoped them the best as I worked up a jog and ran home into the afternoon.

5

There was an old dolly in the woodshop. I rolled it through the crowds of people pouring out from classrooms as the bell rang. People moved in a way that reminded me of schools of fish. I nudged my way through, pushing the dolly into the backs of people's calves to get them to make way. As I passed teachers monitoring the hallway, none of them seemed to take interest in why I was moving a dismantled cubicle across the school. Maybe they figured I was in the stage crew or I was a custodian.

I first saw the cubicle while skipping class. Tommy and I were on the run from a teacher and we cut into one of the rooms by the auditorium. It was in a junk pile by an old upright piano. After the teacher gave up looking for us Tommy wanted to draw on the piano. He always carried sharpies in his pocket and drew little caricatures he thought were funny on whatever he could. I dug through the junk to pass the time. It took me a while to figure out what it was, but once I did, I knew I wanted it.

I dropped the cubicle pieces off outside my classroom and wheeled the dolly back to the woodshop. It was my sophomore year at Haverhill Highschool and there wasn't much for me to bother worrying about. High School was intimidating for the first few months. The school was massive compared to the elementary and middle schools in the city, and many of the older kids looked more to me like full-grown men and women. None of them were very welcoming, and I learned quickly that they'd take little interest in me if I stayed out of their way. I rarely saw anybody I knew if I didn't make an effort to see them. On occasion, I'd see one or two people I remembered. Sometimes they were people I once envied; people who sat at the very top of middle school politics called the shots. Now, they were staring wide-eyed and as afraid as anybody else. We were all the youngest in the school again, and it felt like everybody's position in the pecking order had vanished. In the end, the intimidating aspect of high school subsided and I found it liberating. Life had restarted again, and this time I knew better than to care about anyone's business but my own.

I was in normal classes now and managed just fine. I quickly found my home in the Highschool's 'A-Wing.' The A-Wing was a wondrous place to me. I figured its moniker stood for "Art Wing," but I wasn't sure. It was a part of the school separated from everything else, and only had classrooms that catered to creative types or shop kids.

Consequently, it was always like a little bohemian village nestled inside Haverhill Highschool. The teachers were interesting and archetypal, many of them relics of past counter-culture movements. The kids who hung around there were just as diverse in life paths and interests. There were musicians and band geeks, sculptors, painters, carpenters, and photographers. The halls smelt like sawdust and different chemicals used to develop the film. There were theater kids and stagehands, accounting the auditorium sat on the floor below, and sometimes you could hear one singing while they walked down the halls. Some kids just hung out there to skip class or to goof off. Above all, the A-Wing was a place at Haverhill Highschool for people who didn't have anywhere else to go.

I took the required freshman art class and quickly decided to spend most of my time in art classrooms. I filled whichever periods I could with art classes and quickly became close with a teacher named Mrs. Paradis. She saw a glimmer of light in my artwork and made sure to nurture whatever talent I had. She looked at my work and offered equal praise and criticism. When she spoke to me about my art, it was with a seriousness that nobody had lent to me prior. It made me feel dignified about art and like it was my calling. I began to obsess over art and the process of creating. I'd listen for any morsel of information I could from an art teacher's lectures and conversations between each other. Each day I felt like I was still hungry for more and it drove me forward.

Still, my tendencies would often get the best of me. As time passed and I settled into high school, it became more and more challenging to isolate myself. I had trouble focusing for long periods, and I would eat up my own creative time by floating around the classroom and poking my nose into other peoples' work. There were always a hundred conversations happening at once and I wanted to be a part of all of them. It felt like aspects of my life I'd always kept separate were competing and it was impossible to pick a side.

That was why when I saw the cubicle, I knew immediately that it was the answer. I sat outside my classroom sliding the pieces of white particle board together until I was encompassed by three blank walls. I grabbed a desk from the classroom and sat it in the middle. Mrs. Paradis had followed me outside and was staring at my new hideout. She smiled.

"As long as it walks its way into my room after class. I don't want to explain to the principal why I'm harboring thieves."

She laughed and went back to her classroom. I heard the door creak to barely peeking open and smiled. For some reason what she said made me feel good; like she was in my corner. Teachers had always looked right through me. They may have been kind, or patient—but not in any way more personal than a clerk at the convenience store. There was something transactional about when they spoke to me, and consequently, I didn't care much for anything they had to say. I didn't even consider a teacher ever taking more notice in me than they were paid to, so when she broke the rules for me it made me feel the same as when a friend vouched for me. I wasn't sure how much it mattered whether the cubicle went in the classroom or not, but it made me feel like she was going out on a limb for me. She was willing to take a risk to help me create my art and it made me think she might think I had a shot.

At home, most of the cows were gone now. The world was changing, my father said. Nobody kept vending machines full of milk anymore. Many businesses that knew us on a first-name basis had liquidated or been bought out or moved away. People didn't get milk delivered to them anymore and dairy farms across America were swallowing each other and building partnerships with massive brands. The only cows we kept on the property were for the sake of novelty, as we still brought some to the fair to compete.

We were luckier than some farms. There was a spring that ran under the land that we used for cattle and other things around the farm. My father saw the signs when the world became obsessed with bottled spring water. We quickly rebranded and transitioned to selling bottled water rather than bottled milk.

My brother and I had worked our way up at the plant. Keeping the belts running every day brought us closer together again.

We'd joke or swap gossip while we worked to keep the day trotting on. Afterward, I'd hang out with his friends or he'd hang out with mine. There'd be days he'd say something that would make me take a step back and realize how different we'd become. Other times I'd watch him talk to another guy at the plant and I'd feel like I was looking at myself. I began to think the similarities were what made siblings difficult. Differences were easy and absolute. They were things I could either love or hate—admire or look down upon. Similarities were complicated, as when I saw them in him, I'd have to either come to terms with a trait in myself I appreciated or hated.

My grandparents were changing with the farm. They walked a little slower now, and they spoke less and with more intent. I decided I would begin going out to breakfast with my grandfather every Sunday.

"I know a good spot to eat. Meet me at 5 AM."

A lifetime of farm work had permanently conditioned him. It was as if his body could tell right when the first light of the day was coming up over the horizon. I would have preferred to sleep a little later on a Sunday morning, but I wasn't going to turn him down after asking in the first place.

The drive was slow in his old F-100 pickup, taking the same winding routes we'd take together to the fair years ago. I'd drive for him, as his vision had gotten worse with age. He'd tell stories about my great grandparents while the sun climbed up over the unkept farmhouses and center towns of old New England. Out in the distance, farmers would already be up and tending to livestock or equipment or crops.

I'd smell the air grow heavy with salt as we traveled eastward towards the Atlantic. We'd arrive at a small, aluminum paneled diner perched in the middle of Rowley, Massachusetts. A sign above its maroon canopies read "The Agawam Diner." The Agawam Diner was a tiny piece of the 1940s that had survived and flourished. Its food attracted people from all over to eat inside its dining car walls and sit at its swivel stool bar with a cup of coffee. It felt straight out of a Hopper painting.

"Howdy Andy."

My Grandfather would tip his cap to a man behind the counter dressed in white with thick-rimmed glasses. He'd wipe his hands on a grease spot on his apron while he shuffled over to us. They talked like they'd known each other for a long time and laughed slow and gravelly as old friends do.

He'd walk us to one of the red vinyl booths by the window and we'd order our food. I'd fiddle with the menu while my grandfather sat quietly with his cup of coffee. Once our food rolled in, he would sit and eat his toast and eggs methodically, cutting piece by piece. He seemed more content than I'd ever seen him. He was beginning to look more like a wise patriarch than an aging relic. He no longer possessed quite a sense of urgency that I once knew in him. When I was younger, sometimes on our way to the fair he'd look out at the farms along the roadside while my mother drove.

"Look at the doors on that barn. Fresh paint. I've been meaning to—"

"Would you hush about that?"

My mother heard it from him often. At first, she tried to reassure him. Our farm was operating on a much larger scale with multiple facets of income. What's more, it looked just as good as the next, save for chipped paint here and there. Much of this was thanks to my grandfather and his endless ventures into different directions and the tight shift he ran his entire life. He gave us everything we had in life, but still, there was always something he'd find that other farmers did better. He'd muse over advertisements in *Dairy Today* for new feed equipment or a tractor. It extended down to the wire on the fencing other farmers used. I'd feel sad for him while I sat in the back seat and I'd want him to talk about the monkey in the cage again. It took me years to understand this self-criticism was in fact what was responsible for his success. I used to think he spent his life running from the prospect of failure, but as I got older, I saw he was only running towards a sense of perfection.

    Of course, he didn't tell me any of that. I wanted him to tell me, though. I wanted to hear it; I just didn't know it yet. I'd toss my fried egg between two slices of toast and stare at him from across the diner table. I'd take a bite and try to look serious while I chewed so he'd let me pick his brain.

  "Hey gramps."

My grandfather nodded once and looked up from his plate. He chewed slowly and clacked his fork.

  "What's the secret?"

    "The secret to what?"

He looked back down at his food and began cutting up his second egg. His eyes stayed on his plate like he knew everything that would be said before it was.

    "You know—*life*. Being happy or—well I guess I don't know."
    "Hmm."

He took a sip of his coffee and looked up towards ceiling in thought as if he was sifting through years of files and information for the answer.

    "I'd say—I'd say work hard and be honest. And If you have to think about whether it's right or wrong, it's probably wrong."

He nodded to himself, content with his proclamation, and took another sip of coffee. I frowned.

"Well, that seems like sort of a cop-out. What's the real answer?"

He laughed and shook his head. I sat and waited for him to answer. He didn't say anything for the rest of our breakfast until his plate was clean. I could hear people laughing with one another, change being scraped from a tabletop, forks clacking. He stood up to go buy the newspaper from a box by the bathrooms. As he rose, he sighed and smiled at me.

"Make hay when the sun shines."

We spent the rest of the morning driving back and talking about when my parents were children. The next day, I told Tommy about what he said. We were in the A-wing.

"What's that got to do with the meaning of life?"

He was painting. He didn't like smocks and brought a long sleeve covered in paint to wear whenever he used oils. I worked on a clay sculpture. It looked awful to me. It was supposed to be a swan, but I couldn't come up with a design that didn't look sloppy and childish. I was beginning to feel serious about the art I created. Every morning and afternoon I'd see the *Thinker* statue out front of the school and think of the passion that must've been behind it. I wanted to create something meaningful and it itched at me constantly. Tommy was more laid back about his artwork, but I could tell he was on the wing of something too. He was beginning to develop his style whether he knew it or not. I wanted that for my work—a style, a voice. When I was younger, I spent so much time infatuated by other artists' styles and now, I was ready to carve out my own. At the moment, all I had was an ugly clay swan. I wondered if Auguste Rodin would know what my grandfather meant.

"I think he didn't want to tell me that he wasn't sure. He still worriesfrets about fixing things and improving things on the farm."

Tommy tossed his brush in a cup of paint thinner and headed for the sink.

"I guess I don't really see a problem with that so as long as you fix whatever's broke."

The sink began to run, and I looked at my ugly swan one more time before taking my gloves off. I was cleaning up tools and bits of clay when I heard Tommy yell.

"That's what he meant by that, I bet."

I sighed and shrugged, walking to the sink. I looked at my hands before I ran them under the water. The chalked clay on them made them look ancient.

Tommy and I had started to hang around with a couple of older kids named Anthony and Lou. They were a bit of a strange duo. Both of them floated around the jock-type crowd of kids. They both played sports and lurked around the top of the food chain but kept a rougher way about themselves. Their hair was a bit grown out, they wore work boots, they talked with more of a growl than the average hockey player. Lou said he just played to fight. Anthony was the more talented of the two. Everybody knew his name, but he clung to Lou to a fault. They both wore their worn letterman jackets while they chain-smoked by the door to the parking lot outside the A-Wing. Tommy met them first in one of his shop classes and introduced them to me. I thought they were both funny. He brought them up to my cubicle.

"Would you look at that."

Anthony peered at a drawing I was working on like it was goldfish in a fishbowl. He reached out and touched the graphite on the paper. It smudged into a translucent streak across the paper, his oily fingerprint ground into the ivory.

"Shit, can you erase that?"

"I'm not sure. It's alright though."

Anthony shook his head and Lou called him an idiot. He shuffled around for a minute.

"I'm sorry kid—still looks pretty cool though. Once we take you out the drinks'll be on me."

I didn't know why he was apologizing but I thought it was nice of him. He didn't seem like the type to dish out compliments, so I felt pretty good about him complimenting my drawing.

The first time we went out with them on a weekend, they showed us the ropes. We lurked around the city in Lou's Pinto. There was a whole infrastructure of spots to party they had developed or inherited from older brothers or friends. I listened to them check off each spot like a grocery list as we drove through town. The car jolted to a stop in the street and sent smoke drifting between the leather interior towards the windshield. I could see the red ember of Anthony's cigarette bob as he spoke.

"Alright, kids. This right here is beer can alley." I looked out at the barren street littered with crumpled cans of Budweiser and 40oz bottles. The road was empty and the forest around it was dead quiet. Anthony flicked his cigarette out onto the pavement, and it let up sparks in the darkness.

"Looks like it's just us tonight. Might as well go to the cemetery."

I sat and listened to Lou talk about why Anthony has lousy taste in music until we came upon a thin dirt road spilling out from the main road. The Pinto's frame rattled and shook as we coasted down into the middle of a cemetery.

When we got out, we stood around in the headlights of the parked car while Anthony rummaged through his backpack. He sat on a larger tombstone with his legs dangling over the name engraved on its face. Tommy and I leaned on the hood and Lou paced and rambled about a girl he saw at a baseball game.

"Found it."

Anthony slung a skinny glass bottle from his bag and then tossed the rest of his things into the car. I pulled my shirt from sticking to my chest. The heat was heavy and struggled to rise, bobbing back down to the earth like an old birthday balloon. Between the branches of a maple overhead, I saw the pink sky of late evening and dug the tips of my shoes into a wet pocket of dirt. The cemetery was small and unlike the climbing rows of headstones around the center of town. There were no tributaries of pavement through the premises, and the whole thing sat on a gently sloping hill that poured out into the forest. It was a little awkward to stand on but digging my feet in and putting my weight against the car's hood felt more comfortable.

The cork in the bottle made a deep *thud* when it was pulled, and the sound fluttered across the cemetery and skipped off the headstones. I watched Anthony take a gulp and then hack and cough.

"My dad drinks such nasty booze."

He handed it down the line. It got to Tommy and he took a swig of it. I watched his face flush red and then he made an exhaling noise as if he just ate a habanero pepper. He nearly threw the bottle into my chest; I didn't know whether he wanted so badly for me to try it or to get it away from himself. I figured there was no use in overthinking and took a big sip.

I'd tasted beer before. I'd stolen sips from cousins at fires or when they drank too much and opened more than one at once and left them scattered around. Jim Beam, which was a favorite of Anthony's dad's, tasted like soap to me.

A few minutes after the second time the bottle circled, I began to understand why people liked it. Each time I'd take a sip, my face and the pit of my stomach felt like they got warmer and warmer until eventually, they were numb with heat. I was a good kind of dizzy, like when you're little and you try to run after being on a merry-go round. I felt dull but excited, and I wanted to talk about things. What was even better was everybody seemed to be feeling the same way.

We talked and goofed around until the air began to cool down. Tommy tripped over his own feet and rolled down the hill and we all laughed until our stomachs hurt. I laid across the backbench of the car and Lou played the radio. The longer I lay in the back of the car, the more that feeling of lightness drifted into a comfortable, tired feeling. My head began to feel like it weighed twenty pounds. Tommy slapped my face until I got up and then he crawled into the seat next to me. The car began to move. Everybody was inside now with loud music blaring and the windows open, the glimmer of the glass bottle striking blades of streetlights as the car slid through the empty streets of the city at night. Somebody lit a cigarette and I smelt its strong flat smell as I leaned my forehead into the headrest in front of me. I watched the rows of brick and pastel paneled apartments drift by, sunken into the gold of the lights. We crossed the bridge into Bradford, and I tried to keep my eyes open.

When I woke up, I was laying on Tommy's couch. It was Saturday, and Tommy's younger siblings were staring at me. I thought they were waiting for me to move. I could smell food cooking. My stomach hurt but I was hungry, and I could feel a marble-sized pain pushing through between my eyes. I sat up and waved to the kids staring at me and pulled myself up the staircase.

Tommy's house was downtown. It was small and crammed between two other houses. The house felt a bit claustrophobic because of his eight siblings and his parents all trying to make elbow room at the same time. Whenever I'd go over, we'd hang out in his room, which was small but cut off from the rest of the family. I rubbed my eyes and banged on the door. When he opened the door there was a mural across the entire wall adjacent to his bed. It was the Boston Celtics emblem, with Lucky the Leprechaun spinning a basketball and smoking his pipe.

I walked up to the wall, avoiding the half-spent tubes of paint and paintbrushes that littered the floor. I wiped away some dust and stared closely at the brushstrokes. The lines were precise, and the plaster of the wall gave the painting a smooth look and texture. It looked like it could be printed right onto a shirt and sold at a game. What amazed me most, though, was that he was brave enough to do it.

"This is crazy."

"Thanks. I just kinda work on it when I got nothing to do."

I turned from the wall and squinted my eyes at him.

"You need to start showing people stuff. You'd have a shot with this if you keep going."

He shrugged and pulled two bottles of Gatorade from under his bed. There was a tiny, mangled TV he kept in his room on a foldout chair. He flicked the television on, and it let out a wisping sound. There was a football game on.

"I feel like shit." He said.

"Me too."

I drank the Gatorade as fast as I could. I didn't know why I was so parched but dug under his bed for another bottle.

"I don't know if I can do that again next weekend." I said.

"I don't know. I'd like to go to a party."

His eyes lit up.

"Well maybe if it's a party." I replied,

At school, I began to win awards routinely for my work. I kept the certificates in my room. My parents said they loved my work, and my mother would display or frame whatever she could. My uncle heckled me over it, but I could see on his face he was happy I found a wing to ride. They'd pile in when I received awards in a big drove and clap. I'd hear my mother talking to Mrs. Paradis about my accomplishments. It made me feel proud.

One day Mrs. Paradis walked up to my cubicle and tapped on the side of the wall.

"You're going to go to college, right?"

"I think so."

She nodded but had a look of surprise on her face.

"To art school, I hope."

I put my brush down and looked up at her.

"Maybe. I haven't thought of what I'd go for."

"Something tells me art would be a good fit."

She laughed and looked at me like I had three heads. I hadn't even thought about school yet. I wasn't even entirely sure you could go to college for art. I wondered what kind of jobs you could get as an artist. I thought of old European artists taking commissions from nobles and royalty. I tried to think of myself doing that and it looked ridiculous.

"We'll start building you a portfolio early. I think you should apply."

I smiled at her and nodded. The idea of going to college just to create art sounded like a dream, but it was one that I had trouble wrapping my head around.

My friends and I began going to parties a few nights every week now and it was becoming difficult to keep my head straight. I went with what they did; I was part of the group. If they were getting wasted right after school, I was too. I saw negative traits in all of us begin to warp and exaggerate. Lou was becoming more violent, Tommy more complacent and Anthony more indulgent. I felt like all three were happening to me at the same time. We'd pull up to Beer Can Alley and there'd be a party happening in the middle of the street. We'd drink up and talk to strangers we didn't know, and Lou would undoubtedly cause a confrontation. It felt like I was listening to a tape over and over and the fidelity was beginning to decay and warp.

One night we were at a house party in an apartment and I drank too much. The entire house was crammed and filled with smoke and spilled booze, so I told my friends I would crash at Tommy's since it was a few blocks down. I woke up on his couch, drank as much water as I could from his bathroom sink, then stumbled out into the daylight.

My truck was at Anthony's house, which was a bit further into the city. I cupped my hand over my eyes and avoided making eye contact with anyone. My hair, which I'd grown out long and I'd begun to comb backward, was knotted and dirty. There were dirt stains all over my shirt and pants. I passed by barbershops full of people stopping in for shaves; past the sub shops and pizza joints with drifting smells of fried food and cigar smoke. If I didn't feel awful it would have been a beautiful walk.

About halfway to Lou's was a mountain bike chained to a fence post. I stopped and stared at it. It looked brand new. Even the tread on it was still fresh. There was a sign draped across the handlebars that read "20 DOLLARS." I fumbled through my wallet and dug out a wad of crumpled bills. I counted them while I waited for somebody to answer the door.

"Are you here for the bike?"

There was an older woman with short gray hair smiling at me. She tilted her head, and her eyes grew out past the edges of the thick lens of her glasses.

"I've only got eighteen dollars."

Her expression immediately shifted to a frown. Nonetheless, she took the money, unchained the bike from the post and I took off.

I hadn't ridden a bike for a long time, and I'd forgotten the way it felt. The sun was soothing with the wind in my hair. It felt so freeing compared to driving a vehicle, and when I'd fly down a hill, I'd feel like a gull dive-bombing into the ocean. When I made it to Anthony's, I tossed it in the bed of the truck and headed home to take a nap.

When summer rolled around, I decided to take a step back from partying so much. My grades had declined, and I knew I needed to get them back to where they were. I took the benefit of being in normal classes for granted and the foggy memory of special education classes made me shiver. I began riding the bike I bought to run errands for my parents or to go hang out with people. When the school year began, I rode it to school and back as well. I wanted to keep myself in shape and I'd gained weight from drinking. If something was happening that night and I knew there'd be nothing to do but get wasted, I'd sometimes just tell my friends I was tired from working.

I also knew life was about to get serious. I was into my senior year now, and the world felt both terrifying and for the taking simultaneously. I'd see my brother at the plant or home, and he'd perplex me. While everybody was either running around the city trying to sort out their future career or just partying the complications away, my brother was calm, almost stoic. He knew he was meant to inherit the plant, and so did everybody else. I was a good worker but the operation of the plant and a capacity to do so came naturally to him. I figured that was just going to be how it was and was happy he cut a decision out of my life for me. Unfortunately, there were a million others to make besides it.

Tommy and I saw Lou and Anthony less since they graduated. We'd grab a bite to eat with them every so often, but they were bogged down at their jobs a lot of the time and I was fretting about college. Something began to feel off about sitting in the A-Wing working on my sculptures. The more I thought about graduating, the smaller the awards and praise I'd received seemed. When I'd go around to parties, I'd hang around with people who had long graduated who still talked about high school. They'd rave about a particular football or hockey game they played, lucid and eternal in their minds but otherwise lost to obscurity. It terrified me to be like them.

Anthony worked at a local grocery store. My mother sent me to buy a bag of candy for Halloween weekend and he was ringing me up.

"You gonna stay in and hand out candy this year?"

"Do I have other options?"

He looked ridiculous in his uniform. He was the type of person that looked disheveled no matter how they dressed. I knew he was going to ask if I wanted to go do something.

"Huge party on the avenues this year. We should go."

"I don't think—"

"C'mon. Why you like acting like an old man so much?"

I rolled my eyes at Anthony. He had a dumb look on his face like he knew he could convince me to go.

"Tommy already said he wants to go."

I left Market Basket with my bag of candy and headed for my truck. He was at least a little right, I thought. I barely went out lately and seldom drank with them. I'd done a lot in the past few weeks and felt good about getting myself back on track, which is why I figured I deserved a night out with them and told him I'd go.

I started building my art portfolio early in the year. I was proud of it, but still, nervousness ate at me. I ended up sending early applications to a few different schools for a degree in General Business. I didn't tell anybody about it. I didn't even tell Tommy, although he was very open about his disinterest in art school and was planning on applying for a different major.

As the night of the Halloween party rolled up to the plate, I became more excited. I thought I owed it to myself, and I missed my friends. We all showed up at Lou's in our costumes. I wore my grandfather's overalls and a trucker hat with a piece of straw in my mouth. Everybody knew my family owned a farm and I figured they'd get a kick out of it. Tommy was dressed like Lucky the Leprechaun and Anthony parted his hair and wore circular sunglasses like Ozzy Osbourne. Lou wore a fire fighter's helmet and we all yelled at him for being lazy.

We drove to the party in the Pinto. The street was lined with cars and I could hear music pouring out the windows from down the street. A few parties were happening at once. The music mingled in the air and made a dissonant noise. Lou walked ahead of us and burned with excitement, a bottle in a bag in his hands and the helmet crooked and draping over one eye. I began to get excited too. The air felt electric and I'd forgotten the feeling of anticipating a crazy night.

The house was so packed people were pressed up against the windows. Lou turned and looked at us with his eyebrows raised. He dropped his cigarette into a jack-o-lantern on the top step of the porch and shouldered the door.

When the door swung open there were two guys dressed as pirates blocking our way through. One of them reached his hand out and kept Lou from going forward.

"Definitely not. You think I don't remember you?"

"Me?"

Lou had his finger pointing at himself in a stupid kind of way. He was already slurring a little bit. I was halfway up the steps, gripping the handrail and scraping at its paint with my thumb.

"Well I don't remember you. Let me in."

He tried to barrel through them, but they pushed him backward. He stumbled and almost fell into me. I could tell he was winding himself up. Out of the corner of my eye, I could see Tommy and Anthony backing up.

"C'mon Lou. Let's just get out of here."

He turned and looked at me. His face was tense, and his nostrils were flared up. I couldn't tell if he was going to fight them or me. For a minute I thought he would spin around and try to hit one of them with a sucker punch, but then his posture relaxed, and he pouted. He kicked the Jack O'Lantern on the way down and I followed after him.

"What'd you do to them?"

He was looking back as if he were watching for something. They'd slammed the door on us, and I could see them through the window talking to a girl. We all sulked and began to follow the sidewalk to the car when Lou hooked a left into the grass. He began to crouch down and walk against the side of the house, tucked away in the shadow cast from the porchlight.

I tried to yell at him but he didn't look back. I looked at Tommy and Anthony. They just shrugged at me and didn't say anything. We ran to catch up with him as he peeked his head over the corner like a spy.

"*Lou. Lou.* What are you doing?"

He scowled and hissed at me.

"What does it look like I'm doing? I'm getting us in."

He peered over the corner of the house again and then waved at us to follow. We were walking casually now. There were a couple of girls by an open bulkhead door. We slipped by them before they could finish their cigarettes. We found the staircase in the basement that led upstairs and ran up. I could hear the music and the muffled conversations through the wall. I got more excited the more I felt it shaking the staircase. Lou was already through the door when I made it up. I followed his silhouette into the wave of noise.

The house was illuminated by yellow interior lights reflecting off of the green and purple Halloween decorations. There was a keg in the kitchen people circled. A group of guys shouted over a game of Forty Fives at a table and an old chandelier swung above the hoard of people beneath it, reflecting faces onto each other. We split up and fell into different groups. I pushed my way through the crowd. I saw a girl I knew from my math class by the living room couches and went up to her. She drank from a red solo cup and smiled a lot. We started talking in the corner of the room and I managed to make her laugh. Eventually, I noticed her cup was empty and offered to grab her a drink from the kitchen. She smiled and said that would be alright and so I made my way pushing through the crowd and sliding between couples and groups of guys lurking around the living room.

I could see the metal keg in the kitchen flashing between people as they shifted around the room. I inched my way forward and tried thinking of things I could say to the girl. From my right, I could see down the hallway of the house. There was a red firefighter's helmet bobbing. Suddenly the bobbing became erratic and I heard shouting. I ran towards it as people followed and flooded the hallway. There were more shouting and thuds. I pushed through people and grabbed the back of Lou's shirt. I pulled him backward and saw a flash of someone's face, their hand and nose bloodied and shaking. Somebody grabbed my shoulders from behind and I dropped the solo cup to the ground. I heard it crunch under the voices of men yelling to get out as a rush of cold wind came from the doorway and I was thrown out onto the porch. I nearly fell down the steps but caught myself on the sidewalk.

"What the hell, Lou."

He was wiping his lip and staring at me, his eyes dulled and drunk. I heard the house shaking and turned around. Tommy and Anthony burst out the doorway. Anthony was yelling at the men in the doorway as it slammed shut.

"Nice going, Lou."

"What? What I'd do?"

It wasn't worth being mad over. It was more of a force of nature at this point than a decision he made. We all walked to the car in silence. Tommy sighed.

"I'm too drunk to go home. My dad will kick my ass."

It occurred to me then that my parents didn't know I was going to a party. They wouldn't be happy if I showed up at home drunk in a pair of overalls. I was about to speak up when I noticed Anthony was smiling.

"What are you smiling at?"

"Well—"

He walked back towards the trunk of the Pinto and opened it. He reached in and pulled out two cartons of eggs.

"I kinda figured Lou would ruin the night so I bought these just in case."

We all yelled at him but agreed to hit some cars. We'd all walked into the night anticipating excitement and it felt like there was a void from things being cut short. We left the car where it was and walked a quarter mile or so down the street. We found an area with a concrete wall that sloped over the street and climbed up. There was a forest behind us if we had to bail out and make a run for it.

The four of us lay on our stomach's like special operatives. We whispered to each other. Lou nursed a bottle while we shifted in the autumn leaves and waited for a target to pass. We each held four or so eggs in our hands.

"There, look."

A Buick came cruising down the street at a lazy pace. It hovered above the street crooked on its shocks and bounced while it went along. Somebody whispered, "Now!" and we all hummed eggs at it. A few caught the windshield and a couple lit up the door panel. The car slammed its breaks. When the door opened a man in a button-up got out and looked like he was about to yell when Lou threw an egg and it hit him in the chest. He yelped and crawled back in his car. We all rolled laughing as he sped off.

We did this for three or four more cars until a Crown Victoria came down the street going fast. It was hard to tell at first but as soon as the light came on, we knew.

"Run! Run!"

I saw the street light up in shards of fluorescent blue and felt my hands go numb. Two men were moving out of the doors fast, yelling something with hoarse voices. I slipped while trying to get up and felt my heart lodge into my throat. My friends whirred by me, scrambling into the trees. I started running. I ran and ran. At that moment an image of the old bull on the farm flashed in front of my face. I remembered the way he'd kick up dust and blow steam from his snout. I remembered how my heart would sink when I saw I was last in the pack running, and I remembered the fence. *Think about making it over the fence,* I'd tell myself. I inhaled deep and sped my pace, dodging tree branches, and jumping over stones in the dark. I heard the sounds of my friends panting fade behind me. I thought about how things would be if I made it, not if I got caught, and I didn't stop until I was leaning over Lou's Pinto coughing. A few moments later Tommy made it to where I was and did the same. We sat for what seemed like forever. I could tell he was thinking the same thing I was.

Tommy asked me if I thought they got caught.

I told him I didn't know as the last time I saw them we split up at a fence and they ran into someone's yard. We both sat quietly for about an hour until one of us started walking and the other followed. We were going to stay at Tommy's place and hope for the best. As we walked, I could see a few people stumbling home in costumes, kicking through the debris of the multiple parties that lit up the area that night. I nearly stepped in a puddle of someone's vomit when I jumped back. Tommy laughed and grimaced at the same time.

"That would've made a bad night worse for you."

I shook my head and tried to laugh, but I felt a weird sensation of anger rising in me.

"I can't wait to leave this place behind."

"I'd like to do the same."

He kicked an empty nip across the sidewalk, the small bottle skipping into the grass. I began to feel another spike of irritation.

"Well, what do you mean you'd like to? Why are you always so passive about things?"

"I mean—"

He took two long strides ahead and stopped me.

"I'd *like* to—which is exactly what I said. You're always complaining about being unsure about your future."

"What? You're telling me you're not?"

My voice was rising to match his, but I took a step back. He stopped and stared at me, his eyes darkening with anger.

"I'm sure as shit about my future. I've got no grades—no one looking out for me. I barely have a dollar to my name and whenever I do it either gets spent on a bill or a hot meal. So, if you're asking—"

I began to look at the pavement. He started walking.

"I'm pretty sure I'll stay right here whether I like it or not."

We walked back to his house most of the way in silence. When we got into his living room, he tossed me a bottle of water and he sat on the couch adjacent to me. He looked tired now and a little melancholy.

"Sorry I flipped out. I just know you have a shot at doing what you want—whatever that means. Make sure you do get out into the world, instead of just talking about it all the time."

He punched me on the shoulder and headed upstairs to his

room. I tried to sleep, but I felt like there was a crushing weight on my chest. I left his house and began the long walk through the night to my home over the Merrimack. When I finally made it home the sun was up. My mother was awake, sifting through bills and financial records as a pot of coffee steamed. I lied and told her Tommy dropped me off close by. Before I headed to bed, I looked at her. In the morning light, I could see the true immensity of stress and worry she dealt with for the first time. I asked if she was alright and she grabbed my arm with her hand and sighed. I could feel the callouses on her palm and fingers.

"Of course, honey. Just a bit tired."

I nodded and walked up to my room. For hours, I still couldn't sleep. I laid up forever thinking about how'd I make money in life. It seemed wrong to care so much about art now; disgusting, even. My mother and father hadn't even had a moment to think about what they wanted to do. My best friend didn't even get to have a say in how his life went. It felt like a vice, like drinking with my friends or egging cars. I felt embarrassed about considering something that was such a gamble. I vowed to leave all of it behind and move towards something that could get me out of the trap I saw closing around me.

6

My acceptance letters came in. I'd gotten into a few schools; at least half were art schools. I folded them and put them back in their envelopes. At graduation, I knew I wouldn't see many of the people in front of me ever again. It didn't bother me much, except for one particular interaction as I left the ceremony. I bumped into Ms. Paradis.

"Dale! There you are. You still have sculptures in my classroom! And you never told me which school you picked!"

I froze up and stared at her for a moment. I thought about lying or making a run for it, but I had a feeling she somehow already knew the truth.

"I'm not going to be an artist. I don't want to be one."

"What? What will you go to school for then?"

She looked hurt and it made me feel lousy. I tried to seem preoccupied with looking for someone that didn't exist.

"I don't know. Business, I think—or marketing."

I began to step backward, shrugging.

"I just never heard anybody use the word starving before any other job title."

When I said that she tilted her nose up and I saw a defensiveness come over her. I didn't mean to offend her if I did. I felt ashamed for some reason; like I was staging a double-cross.

"Well if you aren't willing to take a chance, then maybe you're right."

Nonetheless, I buried any heartache deep and geared up for my first year at Southern New Hampshire University's business program. I figured the school was close enough to come back if the farm really needed me but far enough to get away from The Merrimack Valley. I was ready to go talk to some new people and hear a new perspective; I'd been kicking beer cans with the same couple of people from the same little city and we'd run out of things to talk about.

Move-in day was exciting. Everybody wondered around the dorm buildings with a beaming sense of self-direction. My parents dropped me off and helped me move some things in. They told me to make smart decisions and drove off back to the farm in my father's truck.

At first, I loved living there. Independence was exciting and made me feel like I was carving my way. I spent a lot of time just walking around the campus exploring where everything was. My roommate was a nice guy and we got along fine. He liked football and hung all kinds of memorabilia all over our dorm.

In terms of classes, a problem arose almost immediately. I found out very quickly that I was underprepared for a college classroom. The classes I took at Haverhill High were very easy to coast through. I'd spent so much time trying to appear that I was proficient in reading and writing that I didn't improve much from the baseline required to keep me out of special education classes.

At first, I tried to take notes. The professor would shout in the lecture hall and I'd hear the sound of pencils scribbling around me. It was hard to focus on what he was saying; his voice was echoed and muddled by the time it hit my ears. My hands would shake, and I'd work up a sweat trying to get my brain and hand to move at his pace. At the end of class, I'd look at my notes and there'd be the first two words of a hundred different bullet points. When I realized that wasn't getting me anywhere, I tried to go back into the textbooks I bought and write my notes. They were abysmal. They couldn't have been filled with anything larger than an eight-point font and the paragraphs stacked up over each other in double columns on every page. I'd stay up for hours trying to write up a single page of notes and then show up to class late. My dyslexia had finally caught back up with me.

In elementary and middle school I didn't know my official diagnosis, but in Highschool I finally learned that I had dyslexia. It didn't seem to matter much then as I spent most of my time in the A-Wing, but it became increasingly clear that it would be a much bigger problem in college.

I failed my first quizzes for each class. I walked back to my dorm with my head down and threw them on my desk. The red scribbles and circles the professors made stared at me like an angry mob. I wondered how much money I'd end up blowing if I flunked. Even worse, I wondered what it would be like to tell everyone at home I flunked out my first semester.

I became furious and paced around my room. I didn't have any time to get better at reading and writing; that was out of the question. I stared at my statistics textbook. Everything about it made me mad. All that money for something I could barely read. The price tag was still stuck to the back cover. Eighty-nine dollars and ninety-nine cents. I wondered why a book cost so much. I was about to scratch the price tag off so I would stop staring at it when a light bulb sprang on in my head. Multiple people in my classes had yet to buy their books. I'd watched the professor scold them while they tried to explain themselves.

I brought my book to class the next day and pretended like I was taking notes until the class ended. I picked somebody out in the crowd I had seen get yelled at earlier in the week. He was still sitting at his seat in the lecture hall with an empty desk. When everybody flooded through the exits, I weaved through the crowd to catch up with him.

"Hey! *Hey!*"

People turned around and looked at me. I flew by them until I got within arm's reach of the bookless person and tugged the back of his backpack. He jumped a little and turned towards me. He looked perplexed and annoyed.

"I noticed you haven't bought a book."

"That's right."

He tilted his head back and looked at me. I scrambled for words to explain.

"Listen—this stupid thing was almost a hundred dollars. Do you want it?"

"What do you mean? You want to sell it?"

"No, no. I don't want any money."

I handed the book his way.

"I just want all your notes for this week's quiz. I'll bring them back next class."

He looked at me like I had three heads. He reached his hand out with caution and took the book from me. He began to open his backpack.

"If you say so."

EXIT 48

Once he gave me the notes I ran straight to the copier. I printed out a stack of copies and took them back to my dorm. The next time we had class, I gave him the original notes back and sat close to the exit. When class was over, I sped out and positioned myself towards the end of the hall. Right behind me came the crowd of kids piling out.

I stopped whoever would let me talk to them and offered to trade a copy of the notes I had if I could borrow theirs for the night. I got three or four people to agree. Then, I asked a fifth person if I could give them a copy of *all* the notes if I could copy their notes next week. They agreed.

That week, I had plenty to study from. I did pretty well on my quizzes and knew I struck gold. Eventually, I worked out a weekly system. If I could manage to get one person's notes, I could exchange it with someone else for a second set. People would exchange bundles of different notes for more valuable things, like graded assignments. If I got my hands on one assignment, I could turn it into seven or eight completed assignments by pitching it right to classmates. I'd wake up early and print copies for whoever donated to the cause. People would meet me after class, and I'd pass them around. There was always at least one kid who was in another class with me and I could cross into that class through them. I didn't feel too bad about it. I figured I was learning just as many useful skills running a homework ring as I would with my nose in a statistics textbook.

Being the note-merchant gained me some new acquaintances. I started going out to parties with some people I met during my trades. I'd get ready in the floor bathroom on weekends just to walk down the hall or to an apartment near the campus. It was exciting at first. It felt like I was living a little chapter of the American Dream. They were a little more refined than the parties back in Haverhill, but not by much. I'd hover around a cramped suite or frat house with a cup of beer and mingle with different groups of people.

Something was burning in me and I wanted somebody to tell me the same thing. The more I looked, the less I found. It seemed like I just kept finding things that reminded me of home. Everybody either wanted to drink until they couldn't talk or sit on a couch and talk about nothing at all. I even tried to talk about people's majors, and most of the time I was just met with indifference. It was starting to feel like I was back in high school. I was pretty sure there were even kids from my high school at the parties. The idea of moving away from my hometown to live somewhere just like it began to gnaw at me. I wasn't learning much, and I hadn't met anyone interesting, so why did I go away in the first place?

I was at the copy machine one morning making the rounds. My system had gotten too big to fail and I had to wake up earlier and earlier to accommodate. While I organized stacks, I could smell coffee from the doorway and heard a pair of shoes clunk over the linoleum.

"Pretty smart thinking on your part."

It was the guy I got my first set of notes from. He was holding my textbook in his pajamas. His hair stuck up wild in one direction.

"I respect it. Nice to see somebody using their brain."

I laughed. I hardly thought what I was doing was very respectable. It was more a means of survival than anything. I fumbled through a box of paper clips.

"Just trying to keep my grades up. I can barely read so I don't really have an option."

"You're serious?"

I nodded at him. I don't know why I told him. He looked

more surprised than anything.

"No kidding. Sounds like something that's got a good backstory. Want to grab food after class?"

"As long as you wait up for me to deliver notes."

He laughed and put his hand out.

"I'm Gene. Thanks for the book, by the way."

He waited for me after class to make the rounds with my printouts. We got food at the cafeteria and after that, he didn't waste any time breaking the ice. I watched as he struggled with a scalding piece of pizza and started talking about the printing scheme. I thought he was blowing it out of proportion, but he insisted that the entire world works off the steps completed to get that paper scheme running.

"From trading notes to trading stock."

He laughed at his joke and then took a sip of coffee.

"But you can't read?"

I explained the whole thing to him. The farm, the short bus, the climbing up and out, and manipulating different systems to find a different route around it.

"That's smart business, right there. You don't even realize it. It trained you."

He raised his eyebrows up and down and pointed at me.

"I don't know. I've been trying to learn but it seems like I have less time for it the longer I'm in school."

Gene shrugged and took a bite of pizza.

"I say if you made it this far, you're doing something right."

I wondered if he was right. I hadn't thought about it like that. He tossed the pizza forward, so it fell to his plate with a *thud*.

"Probably learned more from not knowing. It's about mentality."

He tapped on his temple with his pointer finger. I could already tell he was a strange guy, or at least someone that wasn't like anyone I knew back home. He talked rough and with intense electricity; like you'd think he was angry if you didn't know the context of the conversation. His speech would be poised and intelligent and then degenerate into swearing and hand movements the more passionate he got. He was dressed nicer than the other kids around the cafeteria, with a trendy professional kind of look. He was down to earth in his speech but seemed to only want to talk about things larger than life.

"I'm from the city. New York."

He told me little about his actual life; only about schemes he was chasing and schemes he'd caught or lost hold of. Now and then he'd stop to tell a good story or criticize something about people.

We walked back to the dorm building and stood outside by the front door. He fumbled with a packet of gum.

"I'm going home to New York this weekend. Can't stand to sit around here doing nothing. You wanna come?"

I stood for a minute and stared. He stared back at me like I was wasting time.

"Well, I—"

"Yes, no?"

"Sure."

He offered me a piece of gum and I accepted. I began to unfold it from the foil while he tapped his foot and looked off.

"Cool. I'll see you here tomorrow at eight A.M."

He walked off without a goodbye. The next day, I was outside before him with my bag. I'd gotten good at meeting people on time

EXIT 48

bright and early from my grandfather. There had been a few times before our weekly trips to the diner that I ran outside four or five minutes late and he was already gone, probably already halfway through the North Shore. I never understood that about him, but I figured it ended up teaching me a good lesson about life. I waved when I saw Gene come outside. He walked with a bag in his hand and his keys jingling around his finger.

"You're not kiddin' around. Ready to go?"

"You bet."

We walked to the parking lot his car was at. It was an older station wagon, but it was in good shape. The interior was meticulously clean and smelt like detergent. We drove south through New Hampshire, Massachusetts, and Connecticut to New York City while Gene played the radio and pointed out things along the way. My eyes were glued to the window. I could barely remember what Boston looked like, never mind the rest of New England and its little differences that carve each area into its own identity.

After Hartford, the land grew back in for a bit until the world began to shift into a concrete maze. We drove into tunnels with bright orange lights and four-lane bridges. The New York skyline cast up above us with its glass and concrete walls. The empire state building stood as an old relic, slowly disappearing into novelty around the monstrous modern structures that cast shadows over it.

We made it to Gene's apartment. It was a nice place. There was a couch I could stay on and I threw my bag there. We werent there until Gene said it was time to go meet the city. We walked to a subway station and caught a car to somewhere he knew. The subway car was overflowing with people and I practically hugged the railing while a couple near us argued and Gene tried to yell over them at me. I couldn't hear what anyone was saying. Somebody had told me once that New York had rats the size of dogs and I was scanning the ground for any glimpses of one.

It was dark by the time we got to a bustling strip of bars. I looked up and could see the outline of smog splitting against the tops of buildings. It was cold, but I could feel the heat of the thousands of people cutting through the city streets. Some wore suits and weaved between people with their lapels folding in the wind. Some others huddled against walls or stumbled drunk with a friend. Between the waves of bustling people, I saw some doing the same thing I was, looking outward in awe at the ocean of individual lives being led by a rope in different directions. It felt strange to know what they were thinking without ever meeting them, and I wondered if all of the people around us traveling at a hundred miles an hour had their foot on the gas or the break.

"Over here."

Gene waved under a rickety neon sign against a brick hideout. The deep reds and greens of the Irish bar's logo poured down and lit up his hair and glasses like they were on fire. I jogged to catch up and scrambled through the door with him. Inside, it felt like it was a hundred degrees. The heat of people's breath lifted the old smell of mahogany from the floors and walls. Glass rattled and roared as it slid down the varnished countertops. I nudged my way through whispering people and people erupting in laughter to catch up with Gene as he threw his elbows onto the bar. The bartender was an older girl with her hair pulled back tight. I couldn't hear what they were saying but it was strange to me that Gene looked comfortable. I'd never been in a bar and I was half expecting somebody to drag me out.

EXIT 48

By the time I made it over, he had two cocktails in front of him. He slid one to me and I took a sip. He took a sip too.

"It's not cheap beer but it'll do."

I laughed and the citrus in the cocktail stung my nose. It felt good. I looked down at the molded glass. It could've been cheap beer and it would've tasted better than anything I ever had back home.

"You know her?"

"Yep—old friend. Nobody'll mind us so as long we don't ask them to."

I pulled up a stool and worked through my drink. Gene ranted about all sorts of things I'd never heard of. He would become invested in a topic immediately and speak loudly and with conviction. I'd find myself trying to catch up on *why* exactly things will change in the next few years or *why* a particular trend fizzled out. He knew I didn't understand certain things or words about investing or economics, but he wasn't being pretentious. I learned quickly trying to catch up in conversation; much quicker than from a book or lecture. There was something about the urgency and organic nature of talking with a friend that burned things into my brain. It felt real; like the things we were talking about were in play around us instead of dead on a laboratory table.

After a couple of drinks, we kicked around the bar working our way into conversations. People were eager to talk. Some wanted to talk about themselves; others wanted to talk about the things they cared about or did. I listened to all of them intently. There were groups of young marketing hotshots with their ties undone. Kids from the art schools sat around in knit sweaters and denim coats and discussed

projects of artists I'd never heard of. They'd roll their eyes about something political and smoke clove cigarettes. I liked the cinnamon smell and I liked talking to them. It was as if they inhabited an entirely different world than me and they made me think I might've liked art school. There was a girl in one of the circles with a white overcoat and dark hair. She kept referring to her artwork.

"What's your art like?"

"Me? I mostly do installation stuff."

"What's that?"

Her eyes lit up even brighter. She looked as if she was excited she found the first person who asked. It made me feel a little out of the loop, but I didn't mind.

She went on about it. It was difficult for me to grasp the concept completely. I never thought about rocks being put in the corner of an empty room as art, but I figured she was the one in art school and not me. Besides, any opinion I had about what she was saying was outshined by the excitement of learning about this little corner of the world. I'd always thought about art as a display of skill; things artists created were meant to put people in awe. It was a way of telling others you were significant in some way. I thought back to when I first met Anthony and Lou and they were impressed by my art; how they'd said they couldn't do what I did. The way this girl talked about art was something entirely different. It was all kinds of different things. Some of them were very vague, like that it was an "imitation of life." Yet, at other times some definitions of it were painfully specific.

"Are you an artist?"

"Me? No, no. I just like hearing about it."

She smiled at me and I didn't know what to say. I was racking my brain when Gene grabbed my shoulder and leaned into the discussion.

"Time to wander."

I nodded. I waved to the girl as I walked back toward the door. She waved back.

"Everyone is an artist you know."

"Not me."

I watched her laugh as I stumbled back out into the New York sidewalk. The wind compressed as it traveled through the glass laden buildings and blew cool air through my shirt and hair. I looked around and noticed the streets were a little more thinly spread. They bustled nonetheless; it looked as if all the levelheaded people had returned home to their quiet lives and now the street was filled with the eccentric beating heart of New York. I grabbed a hot dog from a food stand and walked with Gene past nightclubs and fluorescent white convenient store windows.

"If you remember anything about the future—"

He stopped to compose himself. He was drunk now; wild-eyed and waving his finger like he was an old prophet. He wobbled a little and then leaned in close with a serious look.

"Make sure it's the internet."

I wasn't sure what he was talking about at the time. The internet was something that I heard about, but the wasn't a part of the mainstream in 1990.

He did a spin and began to walk forward towards a crowd of yelling people outside a nightclub. He walked crooked while trying to wipe his hair into the shape it started the night with. I stood feeling confused. Here he was telling me this after stumbling out of a bar and we'd never spoken about the internet. I never really thought much of it. I didn't even have a computer in my house.

"What are you talking about?"

He stopped and stood without turning around. I couldn't tell if he was trying to be dramatic or forgot what I said.

"I don't get what you mean!"

He swung around and almost lost his balance. He was pouting and looked annoyed he had to explain himself.

"I don't either—but I know I'm right."

I shrugged. I figured he'd gone haywire for the night and decided I'd pry him about it some other time. We spent the rest of the night exploring the different veins of the city. We couldn't get into anywhere else; Gene couldn't remember if he knew anybody that was working at other clubs or bars. I began to feel myself slow down. The excitement had spilled over into overstimulation. I thought living in New York every night must make people exhausted. I waved a lonely taxi for us and we took it back to the apartment.

We bombed back to New Hampshire the next morning. After that first night in New York, the city became the centerpiece of our lives. We both managed to plan our semester schedule so that we'd have three intense days of classes and then a four-day weekend. I alternated between going home to help at the farm and then spending the money I made in New York. Gene did the same. He always had a side hustle. It seemed like his hand was always dipped into three different small ventures. He was a natural-born capitalist. He was undeniably logical; sometimes to a fault. It could be perceived to people as cold sometimes, but he got away with it because of how well he had honed and refined those very traits. I thought about myself whenever I noticed that about him. I couldn't quite figure out exactly what trait I should focus on. Strangely, I felt like only half of me could relate to him. The other half was completely at odds with any of the qualities that help people navigate the professional world.

EXIT 48

Our expeditions in New York kept me going while I worked my way through school. I couldn't stand to be in a dorm. If a plan to head to New York fell through and I had to sit around and watch people drink beer and complain in our common area, I'd retreat to my room and occupy myself with something else. The other issue was the time we were forced to be in our actual classes. Gene and I had both agreed that the payout for the time we spent in classes wasn't worth precious time on earth. Neither of us had felt like we learned much and Gene would often complain about how dismal it is to sit through school to come out with a degree and nothing else.

One morning we were headed back to college from New York. It was my shift driving and I was trying to keep my eyes open by spelling the names of towns in my head. We were passing Hartford, Connecticut on the highway and Gene was looking for gum in his coat.

"What the—"

He pulled out a piece of paper folded meticulously into a fat square. He began to unfold it and I was intrigued; better than spelling "Hartford," in my head."

"I completely forgot I met that kid."

"What kid?"

The night before seemed hazy. We'd managed our way into a nightclub that would've even been a blur sober. I couldn't remember many specifics besides that it was hard to talk over the music and the lighting was blue.

"Some long-haired artsy kid. We were talking outside and went looking for a flyer stapled to a light post; this must be it."

He squinted and pushed his glasses close to his face.

"Semester at sea—huh. This school is giving credits to go travel on some boat."

He read to himself for a few minutes. I heard him whisper the names of a few countries

"India, China, and Nicaragua."

I couldn't even think in my head what some of the places looked like.

"If I fill out your application and we get in— will you go?"

I was about to say no. Then I stopped myself once and almost said that I'd think about it. There were reasons for me not to go. I thought as quickly as I could about all the excuses to not go. Then, I wondered if I had any. I had been in Haverhill my whole life and just begun to explore different states. Now Gene wanted me to go on a boat to Central America and Asia.

"Sure."

I said the word before my whole brain agreed with itself. Gene was already clapping and cheering for us in his seat. I couldn't back out after so many nights of complaining about people that would never do this—so many nights of saying we would.

"I'll send the application in tomorrow."

"You're kidding."

"No way."

A few months later, the semester was ending. The letters came in and they'd said we both got in. Gene called me when he got his letter.

"It's really happening!"

"Yeah—I think I'm just still taking it all in."

"You're not getting cold feet on me, are you?"

I let the static run on along the wire. I was nervous about the entire thing. I'd been avoiding thinking about either outcome until the day the letter arrived.

"Listen man—I've listened to you complain about how trapped you feel since I met you. Now is your chance to get out."

"I know. I won't back out. I promise."

I talked with Gene on the phone for a while about it until we ended up getting ahead of ourselves. Afterward, I told my parents at dinner. At first, they were apprehensive and shocked but as I explained they settled down. They both were weary; the places on the itinerary were mysterious to the typical American. I didn't know anything about the countries myself, but I tried to talk to them about it as I did. I reminded them it was for college credits and that I'd practically be able to graduate when I got back.

It might have been the word "graduate," or maybe it made them happy to see me so interested in something involving my education. I had been cynical and half-hearted about it lately. I even told them at one point I was disappointed.

Whatever it was, my father's demeanor changed, and he seemed on board. I could tell he didn't understand it that much but understood it might be useful for me. My mother looked worried but understood.

I spent the months leading up to the trip at the plant. It felt good to be there. The idea of leaving it all for a bit made me cherish things I didn't notice before. I had conversations with some of the other guys I never thought I would. They nagged me a little about leaving but I knew it was in good spirit. I'd be back eventually.

I saved as much money up as I could. I packed what seemed to make sense at the time: a few sets of clothes, a toothbrush, and a couple of pairs of shoes; I couldn't think of much else. The day I left, my parents drove me to Logan airport out of Boston in my father's truck. I watched them from the back seat as we drove. I felt like a little kid. They nervously made small talk and my mother reminded me about all sorts of things to take care of myself. When I waved to them in the terminal it already felt like something unchangeable and separating had begun to make a forward movement.

7

The man sat at the desk scribbling on a yellow pad of paper. His collar was stained from sweat and slumped to one side. He looked up at Gene and me through his clouded glasses and wiped his forehead.

"I can do two-hundred for the day. For the two of you."

"We'll take it."

He was nodding at the man, the muscles in his neck rigid. He fumbled with his wallet in his lap.

"My nephew will take you."

The man yelled something in Portuguese down the hallway behind him. A younger guy came shuffling out to greet us. He smiled nervously and waved. I waved back at him while he picked at his shirt and leaned over to shake our hands.

I said "Hello, how's it going? The boy straightened out and stood behind his uncle. He sighed and shifted his feet. The uncle was moving quickly now, packing his things up into a neat corner and looking up at us now and again. Gene had stopped picking through his wallet and was squinting at the boy. He pointed towards him.

"What's a good place to eat around here?"

The boy's Adam's apple bounced in his throat. He smiled and let out a shaky laugh. There was an awkward silence for a moment when the uncle jerked his head and began to speak up. Gene interjected him first.

"He can't speak English?"

"No, but he—"

"No-no-no. We need a guide that can talk to us. Thanks, but no thanks."

Gene stood up and began to walk out.

I followed him out to the street. The corroded creams and whites of Rio's apartment buildings loomed overhead as people rushed between meal-carts and shop stands. Car horns and whistles honked in between alleyways. I smelt batter frying in the air. I was hungry. I wished for a moment we paid them. There was so much food around us, and I didn't know how to order any of it. Small clusters of buildings peaked against the rest, painted in distressed coats of soft pinks and greens. They reminded me of the apartments at home in Haverhill.

"Well, I say we try another place." Gene suggested.

Gene began to walk into the flood of people when I heard someone yelling behind me. It was the man from inside. He was rushing out the front door, covered in even more sweat than before and panting.

"Espera!"

The man caught his breath as Gene swung around.

"I will take both of you. My English is fine. Pay upfront and we will head out."

"Obrigado."

He nodded as I reached for my wallet. I was too hungry to discuss details. We both coughed up our money and crawled into his sedan parked on the street. He took off driving fast through the city, holding the horn down with one hand and burning through a cigarette with the other. He hooked a hard left and I gripped the handle of the back seat. Gene laughed and held onto the handle upfront.

Our guide took us to a little hole in the wall where he knew the owner. We ate *Feijoada* while he talked about the area. At first, he seemed annoyed with us but the more we talked the more he settled in. He turned out to be a pretty funny guy and the day flew as we drove from spot to spot and he pointed out the different things and told stories. At the end of the day, we thanked him, and he dropped us off at the port.

Our trip around the world was a quarter over. We departed from the Bahamas and traveled south into Central America. From there, we would cut across the ocean and stop in South Africa. From South Africa, we'd head towards East Asia.

We were traveling on an old 1970's cruise liner with a group of kids we'd never met. There was a bar on board and an old seawater swimming pool. Whenever it was filled, we'd sit around it through the night and talk about our lives at home. Our rooms were typical of a cruise liner. They had double beds, hotel-style bathrooms, and showers. Besides that, everything else was stripped down and made cost-effective. I liked being in the simple living spaces because it kept me from wanting to board myself up from people.

The atmosphere on board was a bit strange in comparison to my prior experiences in college. Professors and crew members mostly kept away from all of us, and the academic requirements for the trip were loose and vague. I sometimes felt like someone should be breathing down my neck and telling me what I can and can't do. I could tell other kids on the boat felt the same. Some of them responded to it negatively, practically self-destructing from the freedoms dropped on their lap. They were never sober, and many of them behaved dangerously and erratically in countries we went to. It was difficult to juggle the different dispositions we had to keep. On one hand, we were given a week in one spot to do whatever we wanted, besides the small requirements and tasks on our syllabus. At times it almost felt like being home, but after some of us were mugged or beaten badly most of us made it a point to be more cautious.

The months ran by and I eventually stumbled upon one of the most beautiful places I'd ever seen. I was on the deck when India began to emerge through the haze, momentous and bustling and gleaming like a bouquet of razor blades and flowers out across the ocean air. I ran my hands through my hair. The entire deck was salt swept and so was I. I was smiling; I must've looked like a crazy person. There was something about the architecture, old and new, that ignited something in me. It was different from the buildings I saw at home. Even in New York, there was an old shadow beneath the stout brick buildings that encompassed me my whole life.

Many of them garnered the same colors of much of the cities I frequented on the east coast: oranges and reds and browns. Yet, at the same time, they looked fresh and new to me. It was something about their slopes and curves. As I hung over the railing, I tried to look as far ahead as my eyes could see. I felt a way I hadn't in a long time, and I couldn't begin to figure out how to explain it to anyone, so I sat there until we made our way to the port.

Gene and I split up during our week in India. I wanted to learn as much as I could before we left. We both took tours of different things. I took a tour of the architecture and a few historical sites. I couldn't get the buildings out of my head.

Halfway through our stay, I tried writing on a postcard to my parents. I thought they'd get a kick out of a postcard from India. When I tried to jot down a few words, I couldn't focus enough to start. I started doodling instead, sketching out the city skyline. In my peripheral, Gene was being strange, shuffling around and looking in the mirror over and over again. He opened his duffel and began to throw clothes and bottles of shampoo onto the floor until he pulled out a bottle of cologne and sprayed it on himself. I finally gave in and laughed at him.

"You got a date tonight?"

"Kind of."

He lifted the collar of his shirt to his nose and sniffed. He made a frown and then reached for the deodorant on his nightstand.

"I met a girl on a tour today. She's Belgian."

I put my paper and pen next to me and sat up. Gene was raising his eyebrows up and down at me.

"Crazy good looking—speaks good English too. She said I could tag along with her and some friends tonight."

"Does this mean I'm on my own tonight?"

His eyes darted away from mine.

"I could see if—"

"I'm just kidding. I'll figure something out. Maybe I'll Just go out with Mike Regan and Jamie Munson then."

Gene laughed and threw his clothes back in his duffel bag and said

"Be careful, last time we hung out with those guys we almost missed the boat." Once he left, I looked down at my little drawing and sighed. I folded the postcard into my pocket and went to find a way to give my parents a call.

The sun was beginning to go down when I left. It painted everything magenta, and I wandered through the city's smoke and dust, past the markets and pop up stands. A boy flew by me on a bicycle and continued to glide into the rolling crowd of people. I could hear a rooster crowing and rustling steel crates. Above me, men worked on buildings, hoisted up and yelling to one another while suspended in the air.

I began to get lost in the moment. Everywhere I looked something different was happening. I walked up to tables filled with large baskets of fragrant spices and curry. Above my head were brightly color shawls strung booth to booth. I went into shops and played with strange trinkets. A few times, I just hugged a wall and watched people's interactions passing in the street and bartering goods. It never becomes less surreal being surrounded by thousands of people, hearing their voices all at once and not understanding a single thing they are saying.

I completely forgot about the phone call. Before I knew it, the air had cooled to blue and then to black and many of the shops were folding up. I'd lost track of time and didn't know what to do with myself. Down the street, I saw a small shop with its golden light still glowing out into the darkness. I walked towards it and greeted a small old man slumped in a lawn chair and chewing *Gutka*.

I leaned against the window counter and pointed at the beers in the fridge. He nodded and pulled them from the fluorescent shelves. As he was opening them, I put the money on the counter. When he gave me them, I slid one his way.

"Me?"

The man was pointing at himself with his eyebrow cocked. I nodded and he smiled and took a sip. I sat there for a long while buying beers for us. His English was very sparse, but we managed to talk into the night. He told me about life in India and life in a pop-up shop. I told him about the boat I was on and about Massachusetts. I told him about Gene and the Belgium girl and whatever else I could think of while I drank.

We quieted down and he began wiping the refrigerator windows and organizing the shelves around him. I pulled a folded piece of paper from my pocket and looked at it. I'd forgotten I'd drawn it earlier. I realized I couldn't remember the last time I drew something before that. I looked up and the man was peering over the edge of the paper at the drawing.

"Artist?"

He was pointing at me, standing in the center of the old fluorescent lights with rows of candy and cigarettes around him.

"No, no. I—

"Artist."

The man smiled and winked. He went back to wiping counters and organizing bags of chips in neat rows. I smiled. For some reason, I didn't want to argue. I looked out at the street. They were close to empty. Car headlights lit the steel of barred windows and doors. A moped sped by.

"What time are you open until anyways?"

"Until you go."

We both laughed. I drank the warm bottom of my beer and thanked the man. He waved smiling as I left, and I listened to the city fall asleep while I walked with a sway in my step.

When I woke up, Gene was still gone. I laughed a little to myself and shook my head. It was noontime. I held my head with one hand and walked to the cafeteria on the ship. I made myself a cup of coffee and watched the gulls drift overhead.

When I got back to my room Gene was home.

"Let's hear it."

"Nothing to hear yet."

"What? Where have you been all morning?"

He had a look on his face like he'd invented the wheel. He pulled a massive cardboard box from under his bed and pried the top open.

"Five grand in silver."

"What?"

The box was filled with innumerable rings, necklaces, bracelets, silverware, and random knick-knacks.

"The Belgium girl is a merchant. She's in India to pick up jewelry to sell back home.

"Okay. Why do you have it?"

He looked at me like I was crazy.

"What? No—I bought this. I told her I was here for the same reason.

This trumped all of his antics I'd ever witnessed. He was standing in front of me with five thousand dollars in silver trinkets, hair disheveled and eyes wild.

"Well, I sure hope she believes you."

As far as I know, she did, and his master plan was a success. The day we departed from India I watched him put the box of silver back under his bed. I wondered if he thought it was worth it, and I wondered what he would do with five grand in silver once we got back besides put it under his bed at home.

The rest of the trip seemed to pass by before I could get my head around it. We stopped in China, Japan, and Malaysia. People on the boat continued to party until we were bound for Seattle. I tried to join in, but something was eating at me. No matter what I tried to do or where I tried to go, I couldn't escape this feeling like I was being dragged down by something. My desk lamp fluttered from the rocking waves while I lay up in bed. I'd seen the other half of the planet and still felt boxed in. I thought about the time I spent partying with people on the ship or in different countries. It made me angry. It was exciting and led to all kinds of wild things happening, but regardless it felt like there was a storm cloud over me when I did it. It wasn't much different from doing it in a dorm in New Hampshire or a party in the woods by the family farm. It all felt cyclical and made my head hurt.

Our last stop before home was Malaysia. I found a payphone near a ring of shops by the port and called home. I listened to the phone ring as I leaned against the booth. Suddenly I heard a rumbling static and voice over the other line.

"Hello?"

"Hi, mom."

I didn't call as much as I'd have liked to. It felt strange to hear her voice over the phone line.

"You and Dad are still meeting me in Seattle, right?"

"Well of course!"

I had a dream the night before. It must've been the boards of the boat moving beneath my feet or the sound of the air rushing against the steel side of the ship. I was in high school again, pedaling my old bike through the streets of downtown Haverhill towards home. The sun was shining strong and profound like it does when the day comes to its crescendo in the noontime. I could hear my friends behind me yelling. Tommy and Anthony waved their hands and their voices rose higher and higher into the atmosphere. The louder they yelled the harder I pedaled away towards the outskirt of the city.

I didn't know what they were yelling. I didn't want to look back again. Maybe it was about Lou; how he'd died drunk in a car crash months ago and how I didn't call—how I never called on any summer back home or in between and how I probably never will. Maybe they were yelling for me to keep moving, to look down at the tree line, and head for something they couldn't see or couldn't reach for. I hoped it was the latter.

"Can you bring my old bike?"

"What for?"

I paused for a minute over the phone line.

"I just figured I could use it to help me see the sights."

"Alright, love. I'll tell your father."

We talked some more, and she went off to bed. I hung up the phone. I walked out to the deck to stare at the ocean before trying to sleep.

When we arrived in Seattle, my parents were waiting at the cruise terminal.

I walked with Gene, our clothes dirty and hair long. After I hugged my parents, I looked over at him.

"Want to stay a few days with us?"

"No, no—I already booked my flight. Thank you, though."

I patted Gene on the back and nodded. His bag jingled as he hoisted it over his shoulder.

"I've got to figure out how the hell I'm going to get rid of all this silver."

He was laughing and shaking his head while he turned and split from us. He waved as he headed from one terminal to the other.

I walked with my parents to a rental car and breathed the air of the American Northwest. It was heavy and cool, and I could see the snowy top of Mount Rainier looming over the city skyline.

I spent a few days with them exploring the city and telling them about my travels. I was elated to see them but felt restless sitting in restaurants and talking about what I just did for months. I felt happy for them. They seemed wrapped up in their adventure, taking the city in as they floated through each day.

Halfway through their stay in Seattle my mother found me outside our motel, attaching a rack to the back of my bike. My bike was set on its kickstand, the dust wiped from its frame.

"What are you doing?"

"I was going to tell you, but I didn't think you'd bring my bike. I made plans on the boat to ride bike back home from Seattle."

She moved forward with her hand out.

"Now wait a minute, you must be joking"

She grabbed my arm and began to talk at a mile a minute about all the things that could happen to me. My father found us outside the motel as I tried to calm her down. I explained to them I'd been planning it for the last two months and showed her the special bicycle route maps I'd purchased and marked up with a detailed route home. I was beginning to worry it would be a more difficult departure than I thought when my father finally spoke up.

"I don't think he's going to budge, honey."

I gripped the handlebars of my bike and looked at both of them. My father laughed.

"Good or bad, he won't listen to either of us until he goes and does it." he said.

I smiled at my mother and she sighed and hugged me. We spent the next day purchasing supplies that would help me on my trip. Soon after I started pedaling. I carried specialized maps designed for bicycling cross country but didn't bother to take note of the textured land east of Seattle. It turned out to be the Cascade Mountain Range.

I quickly dumped most of what I brought besides a few necessities. My extra clothes and cooking supplies all went over the guardrail early on. I nearly turned back but couldn't imagine pedaling uphill past the same thing twice.

It took months. I had just enough money on me to buy canned food and cheap supplies until I got home. I'd wake up early by the road in the woods or a field and drag my bike to the endless snake of concrete spanning the United States. Now and then I'd meet a stranger. We'd sit and talk through a bit of the day. Sometimes, they had a place for me to sleep. I'd say yes and I'd say no. More than once I had to sneak out of an apartment in the middle of the night and continue. Some people were more dangerous than others.

The Midwest seemed like an endless ocean of wheat. The current of air that followed cars was strong and oppressive. Several times, a camper or tractor-trailer blew me off the road, and I had to scramble to get up and keep going. Still, the landscape was undeniably beautiful. I especially loved watching storms form in the distance. I could see the clouds circle and swell, bursts of lightning splitting the air and illuminating the gray backdrop.

I sat up in a field one night and watched the long grass blow like a tide across the endless expanse of land. The air was cool at night and I ate soup from a can I heated with fire by the road. There was something about the moment that brought me above my entire life beforehand. It was as if I felt content for the first time. Whatever I previously worried about seemed arbitrary and fleeting under the massive, untouched sky and the millions of stars poking through the inky black like pinholes to heaven. All I had to worry about was keeping food in my mouth and heading where I had to go. I knew the way. It was a simple path eastward. I took my sock off and rubbed the arch of my heel. Both my feet were covered in blisters, the majority of my skin worn off and scabbed over. I was filthy, dirt staining my face and clothes. I didn't care. On the inside, I felt purer than I ever had before.

I realized then that it was the orbit of other people that kept me falling into dark pits. I couldn't separate myself from them. For so much of my life I tried to run with a crowd; I never realized I was meant to go my own way. It wasn't anyone's fault but mine. I couldn't manage the two sides of myself, and one half-swallowed the other. I needed a way to box myself out from the world and lead my own life. I needed something like a cubicle outside a classroom, or a fort away from the prying eyes of the world.

I shook my head as I thought about the last few years. I hadn't moved in any direction integral to myself. What would a career in finance or economics—even politics, do for me if I spent the whole time miserable? I'd taken a boat across the whole world and couldn't find happiness living the lie that I was fit to pursue a conventional life. I still didn't know what I wanted to do. I just knew that then and there, sitting alone in a wheat field a thousand miles from home and making my way, I was happy. I couldn't stop thinking about my old art teacher in High School, Ms. Paradis. I knew why she looked at me like I hurt her feelings that day. She knew what I might miss out on for the rest of my life, and it was this.

I trekked the open road in the coming months, all the way back to the hills of New England. I'm not sure what I expected to return home to. At first, people wanted to hear about the things I saw. I had so much to tell everyone—what's more, I felt like I finally understood myself and others and wanted to scream about it. It was all things trivial to their daily life.

I finished my degree part-time at a community college. We went out for dinner after I graduated, and it made me happy to see my mother beam with pride when she framed my degree. As life lurched forward, I felt the glow fade from all that had surmounted and fell back in line. A degree is only worth what you do with it, and I'd put little thought into what I would go out and do. I only knew what I wouldn't.

I hopped back on the crew at the plant. My brother was in control of things and they were moving faster than ever. His demeanor had changed since I left. Something more urgent and competitive possessed him since he'd taken charge of the plant. It reminded me of my grandfather, and I admired it.

There was an absurdity to being back. I'd spent years at school, traveling the world and biking across America. Yet, here I was filling crates with bottled water. I

felt like I'd gone in a big circle. As the months passed, I felt dull and I fell into a rhythm. The constant ache of not having a direction ate at me and consumed my energy.

I wasn't concerned with going out and partying; I knew it would drive me deeper down into whatever I was trying so desperately to climb out of. I felt bad for my old friends from high school. A part of me missed them, but a bigger part hoped I wouldn't see them around. I didn't know how to address the things that had happened since, and I didn't want to be a part of any further tragedy.

The equipment at the plant was getting old. Everything felt old the more I looked at it. All the kids I once ran from bulls with were grown up, toiling through the workday, falling in love and building lives. The adults had all grown into the sunset of their lives. Even my uncle walked with a little less pep, although he still never stopped working.

I stood in the plant after work with my brother one day. He was looking down frowning at the conveyor belt. A split in one of the steel curves had begun to widen. We were both stressed and racking our brains. Parts were expensive in the bottling industry. It often required a specialized company to fabricate a new piece or even replace the entire conveyor system.

"I wonder if I could find someone to weld it."

I shrugged at my brother. Lots of people could stick weld. It was a secondary skill in a farm environment. My uncle had an ancient stick welder in his shop, but I wasn't sure how often he'd used it.

I went back to the bottling plant that night and looked at the split. It was the weekend and I had nothing to think about. I spent time now trying to fill my free nights with things besides drinking and going out to bars and parties. I wondered if I could fix the piece. I had a basic understanding of welding but had never done it before.

I unbolted the broken piece from the rest of the platform and carried it out past the cattle barns. My uncle's shop was attached to the barns, down a little corridor and tucked away near the milk pumps. The room was small but efficient, its walls covered with tools old and new. Some of them looked a hundred years old, crusted over with deep red corrosion. I always loved rummaging through them and looking at old archaic things. There was some type of appeal in old tools and farm equipment similar to classic cars. They aged with elegance in the same way, with their yellowing paint and chrome branded badges.

I wandered through the light of a dusty shop lamp and made my way to the welder. It was old; probably outdated even when my uncle first bought it. It was a faded, army green with large carbon steel levers and bolts. The hose sat coiled on top of what looked like a massive oxygen take.

The concept was simple enough to understand, but I underestimated the muscle memory and skill required to make clean, strong welds. I spent the night learning on scrap until I mustered a little confidence. I could still barely do it, but I felt impulsive. The anticipation overrode my judgment, and I went for it.

When I held the piece from the conveyer belt up to the light, I was embarrassed. The weld would probably work, but it was just about the ugliest thing I had ever seen. Outside, the sun was beginning to come out. I ran the piece back to the plant and bolted it in.

When I woke up later in the morning the weld looked even uglier than I remembered. I stared at it with my brother. He wiped the sweat from his forehead.

"It isn't the prettiest thing in the world."

I felt proud and embarrassed at the same time. I knew I could get better. I felt an impulse to practice. It was a skill nobody else around specialized in and I could make myself useful whenever we needed someone to fix a piece of metal. I began spending my free time practicing on scraps of steel. I came to admire the clean welds on pieces of old equipment. I constantly compared pieces of scrap I welded over the coming months.

Beyond feeling useful, there was something else that drove me to keep practicing. When I first began to make clean welds, I'd feel a sense of euphoria when I looked at it. It felt like I was bringing something to life; like I was *creating* something. One night I sat up alone in the shop with an old bottle of wine I found kicking around. It was left over from when I was in college, stowed away in my old dorm locker that sat forgotten in my closet. I was looking out at the mess around the shop. There were scrap pieces of metal everywhere, welded randomly together into unusual shapes.

I looked at the label on the bottle. I felt goofy drinking wine; I seldom did. I was trying to remember the last time I drank some. It must've been a night in New York with Gene. I could vaguely remember going on a double date to somewhere nice and ordering some for us and the girls. The restaurant had their wine on a massive display by the bar, with the bottles peeking out from racks for the waiters to grab.

I picked up a few bars of steel and some wire. I spent the night carefully welding the cuts of metal into a small platform, then bending and attaching the wires so they jutted out like coat hangers. When I was done, I stood back and couldn't help but smile. I thought maybe I'd give it to someone as a Christmas present. I was a bit afraid of doing so. I wasn't sure why, but I tucked the wine rack away and decided I'd worry about it at a different time.

I was happy to pick the phone up one day and find Gene on the other line. I hadn't seen him for months and we'd gone our separate ways. He seemed in high spirits and I hoped he was doing well.

"What've you been up to? Any master plans?"

I tapped my foot. I felt like the gun was on me for the first time in months. I wondered if I should make something up.

"No, not really. I don't know what I'm going to do."

"Same here. You sound down in the dumps."

I felt dull; like life was passing me by. Sometimes I wondered if it was worse than acute pain or sadness. It sneaks up on a person, and before they know it a year has passed, and they can't get it back.

"No, I'm alright—just dealing with being back home. I've made some cash, at least."

"Hey, speaking of, what are you up to this weekend?"

"Nothing whatsoever."

"Well get this—"

I smiled and thought of the first time he asked me that and we ended up in New York.

"All that silver I bought—I stared at it for weeks trying to figure out what to do. Finally, I found a trade show in New York and said what the hell. Sold everything like hotcakes. Hell, I flew back to Asia and bought *more*."

I shook my head laughing. I wasn't even surprised. He was born to sell things—born to make money with whatever he got himself into.

"You wanna come to one this weekend? Drive out."

"I'll have to—"

"Great. See you then."

I heard his phone click and hang up. I missed the days of driving out to New York and decided I'd go.

When I made my way out and met him, he was struggling to load a massive box into his car. He looked up and tossed it into his trunk and I heard metal rattle inside the cardboard.

"That's all silver?"

"You bet."

We drove upstate and he explained the entire story since we last met. He sold his first bout of silver and made thousands. The markup was ridiculous compared to the street price in Asia, and he said he was still selling cheaper than most people in the same market. He went back and bought the massive amount that sat in the trunk behind us; pounds of rings and necklaces and knickknacks all marked up for the American marketplace. The numbers he was talking about made me want to do it too. I wouldn't mind going back.

The show was outdoors. Gene had a tent he lugged around, and we set it up together. After that, we kicked back and talked the day away. To my amazement, person after person came to the tent and Gene sweet-talked them into buying whatever was in their hand. It got me so excited I started doing it too. I was surprised by how natural it felt. A person would come up, and we'd begin talking about anything that was on each other's mind. The key was to hook it back towards whatever they were holding. I managed to make a few sales for him, and it felt good. He tossed me some of the profit; "commission," he'd call it, and then we'd laugh.

His attention span outlived mine. I told him I was going to grab food and check the other booths out. I used my commission money to snag myself a slice of pizza and wandered through the different stands and booths. People sold everything. Gene said it was mostly a "craft" show so most of the stands were small little knick-knacks.

I found a stand with someone making metal jewelry on the spot. It didn't occur to me that people here made things to sell; I thought they were like Gene and just vendors. She was using pliers to twist old pieces of scrap into jewelry. I thought about my wine rack sitting in the shop at home. I couldn't help but go up and talk to her.

"Is this your job full time?"

"For the most part."

She looked like she didn't know whether to be offended or not. I picked up a bracelet she made. They were very cool. All of them were unique to each other but looked like they all came from her.

"I like your style."

"Thank you!"

She smiled at me. The word "style" reminded me of high school;

all those hours obsessing over that word with my paintings and sculptures. I suppose I never thought about things like jewelry or picture frames or cups like that. I liked the idea of it. This was a whole avenue of art I never even cared to think about. I could remember thinking about how unimaginable being an artist was. The concept of standing in a studio in a smock seemed ridiculous. This all looked closer to something I'd do on the farm. It reminded me of vendors at the fair, trying to sell roasted turkey legs or toys.

"I wish I could buy something. I like it though."

I sped away before she could answer. The more I looked around the more I noticed people working on things they were selling, all of them making money off of it. I was baffled.

I listened to Gene talk about the internet on the way home. He was right, I could see it now. I could see so much more too. I didn't bring it up to him. My thoughts were too jumbled to translate to another human. When I got out of the car at his place, I headed for my own.

"I want to go to the next show. India too—maybe."

He tilted his head and looked at me funny. Then he shrugged and fixed his glasses.

"Hey, sounds good to me."

I drove home as fast as I could. I wanted to practice my welds. I wanted to make plans for the future. For the first time in a long time, I wanted to draw with purpose. I tried to remember where my old sketchbook was.

The next day I was exhausted at work. I'd been up all-night drawing like a crazy person and practicing welds. I'd bounce between my sketchbook and pen and over to the welder and scraps of metal. Then I'd bounce back. I didn't get anything done. My sketches made no sense, my welds were just more scraps welded to other scraps. What mattered to me was I felt like I was moving towards something. It was a different feeling than partying or going away to college or traveling the world. All of those things, I realized, were about running away. What I was looking for had been stowed away in my Uncle's tool shop. I had an outline now, a rough draft of where I'm supposed to be. I just had to fill in between the lines and let life come through the paper.

I practiced every night and branched into other aspects of metalworking. I learned how to cut metal, shape it, polish it. The things I drew came naturally to me. It ignited a part of me I abandoned long ago. The math involved in sketching out rough blueprints came easy to me, too. It was like a language I was meant to speak.

Nobody around the farm questioned me. I was glad. I didn't want them to know I was drawing things or building through the night. As I became a better welder, I became more useful around the farm, so everyone seemed to leave it at that. When I'd fix a piece of metal, it further invigorated me. It felt great to be useful in a way unique to what I was before, and it felt great to see genuine gratitude in people's faces. It was the type of validation I'd been looking for in all the wrong places; a sigh of relief to a lifetime of trying to just stay out of the way.

Out of the mess came a design I was proud of. It was made of sheets of steel cut into a curve like a "C." I welded the sheets together and cut a set of large holes down the side. I hung it on one of the shop hooks then looked around the floor. I got on all fours and dug my hand under one of the benches. I found the empty wine bottle I left there weeks ago and placed the bottle in one of the holes. I stood back and looked at the thing I created and smiled. I wasn't giving anyone that old piece of junk I hid for Christmas.

8

I was in my garage. I'd just bought myself a CNC plasma cutter kit from an ad in *Popular Science Magazine* and fumbled with the manual in the dim glow of the bulb overhead. I'd put an old radio in there to listen to while I worked. I put the manual down and turned the dial until I heard the *Howard Stern Show*. His voice burst through the static with tension. I stared at the plasma cutter's parts strewn across the floor in disbelief as he described the smoke pooling from the New York skyline. He fumbled his words as the second plane struck and ripped through the beams of the second tower.

I called Gene and made sure he was okay. I couldn't help but think about all those nights in New York. I thought about the brief friends we made as we jumped from bar to bar—from the nightclub to late-night diner. We were all the same back then, stumbling into the rest of our lives with only tiny fragments of direction and passion to guide us. One of the towers began to collapse, plummeting to earth with the weight of thousands of past and future lives. I thought about the business major hot shots that would frequent the spots we went to. I hoped they weren't working inside.

I thought about the girl I met years ago on my first trip to New York. She was an artist. I wish she could ask me again if I were an artist; I would say, *"yes,* it just took me thirty years to figure it out."

The collapse of the world trade center was horrible to listen to.

The coming months, however, were worse. The markets crashed and dragged the economy down with it. Politicians yammered about war endlessly. Everybody everywhere was on the edge of their seat for a hundred different reasons and I had inherited the awful timing of just quitting my job at the farm.

For all of the turmoil that followed the attacks on the world trade center, it fortified my determination to be an artist. I'd finally taken the plunge to pursue a full-time career sculpting metal, and watching the economy fall with the towers showed me how fragile everybody's financial security was. If I had sold out and pursued a career in something more lucrative and stable, I'd be in the same spot I was right now—dead broke.

So much had happened since I welded that first rickety wine rack in my uncle's tool shop years ago. I was married, bought a house and was hoping to start a family. My grandparents had passed away, along with many old friends, and my cousins and brother had started their own families. Gene and I stayed in touch but he was off carving his way just like me. We rarely had time to even speak over the phone between both of our lives.

I'd spent the years working at the farm by day and sculpting through the night and weekends. It became increasingly apparent to me the older I became that there was no place for me at the farm. My brother had it all under wraps. I knew he could run the operation just as well without me. I'd begun to feel as though I only had a spot there because I asked; that I ate more than I cooked. All the while I was becoming more obsessed with sculpting and the notion of selling my art. After I went to my first trade show with Gene, I tried to go to everyone I could with him. I'd meet him out in New York, and we'd drive to whatever state and set up. Once we got there, I'd wander from tent to tent, asking as many questions as I could. I was trying to compile as much mental data as I could about the lifestyle. It was immediately apparent it was a difficult life. People of all walks were part of the trade circuit. Some were entrepreneurs and business moguls like Gene, some were passionate artists dedicated to their work no matter the financial hit they took. Most were drifter types, reselling whatever art or merchandise that fell into their hands and living nomadic lifestyles across America. I was jealous of all of them. I wanted to create art that was admired and feel fulfilled. I wanted to travel to strange places, meet people of all sorts, and then tell them about my work. I also wanted to make money, of course. Money was what was holding me back. The notion of shame and professional failure held me back time and time again.

Nonetheless, I was getting good with metal. I'd perfected my wine rack design. I was welding them from sheets of brushed stainless steel, the structural design perfected to hold bottles secure in a way I deemed elegant. They were robust but hollow and light enough to hang on a wall. A few I built were larger and stemmed upward in an "s" shape from a thick steel sheet on the ground. Some had glass or steel tabletops bolted to the top.

I'd also begun to experiment with building clocks. I purchased a stock of quartz movements and fabricated each component for them. At first, I focused on purely geometric designs, such as triangular or hexagonal steel clocks, but as I got better at metal fabrication, I began to work on more intricate designs.

Gene convinced me to go back to India on a run to buy jewelry. We were going to leave from Logan Airport. I told Gene to drive to my house and then we'd take my car into Boston. I was in my shop when he walked in and he flapped his arms.

"What the hell is all of this?"

"I told you I've been working on sculptures."

He laughed and walked up to one of the clocks on the wall. He touched one of the steel hands as it made its orbit and nodded his head. I'd told him I had been working on sculptures but downplayed it the same I did to everyone. For some reason, I had so much trouble telling people about it, even though it's all I wanted to talk about. My family had a vague idea since I was beginning to accumulate so many pieces and supplies that they spilled into their everyday lives. I gifted things to them and chalked it up to a hobby I do to pass the time. They didn't ask much further. I seemed happier and they were happy with that.

"Well gee, I see what you mean now."

I showed him how I built them and then we got lunch downtown at "The Tap", an old bar in Haverhill. Afterward, we headed for Boston. It was routine to him now, flying out and bartering large sums of silver and other goods to flip in the United States. To me, it was exciting as the first time we studied abroad. I'd wanted to go back to Asia since I left. India and China were my favorite places we went to. Being invested in my art made it all the more exciting. I loved East Asian artwork and architecture. It contains everything I'm drawn to in reagrds to aesthetics, and I realized soon after beginning to make my sculptures the feeling I felt when I first saw India's buildings was inspiration.

It was all how I remembered it: bustling and filled with chaos and beauty and scorching heat. Gene and I took a cab from the airport to a hotel. He went off about the internet; how someday what we were doing will be cut out of the equation. He said it'll be the great leveler—that people like us, and the big companies will be on the same mailing list. He'd been talking about it for years and I believed him now. The internet was beginning to cause a shockwave throughout humanity and the wise could see what was ahead.

The next morning, we met with his supplier. They knew him there, and after some bartering, it went smoothly. We left with several pounds of silver goods. Afterward, we hit a couple of other spots for tapestries and knick-knacks, then we stopped at a bar and got drinks. As the light began to shrink from the windows I burned through a few beers and finally cracked. I told him how badly I wanted to be an artist. Once I started, I couldn't stop. I dumped the years of lying to myself and others out on the table and spoke a thousand miles a minute about what I wanted my life to be like—how I wanted to create things from metal and make money that way and how nothing else would do.

After my rant, he took a sip of his drink and looked off. I wondered if he was paying attention. I was about to wave my hand in his face when he snapped his head towards me and gave me a death stare.

"I don't see the issue."

"The issue is I—"

"No. Don't be stupid. You've wasted years being afraid—cooped up on a farm."

I didn't say anything and looked down at my drink. When I looked back up, he was still glaring at me. He put his hands up in front of him and shook his head at me.

"We go to trade shows. I sell things *at* trade shows. Bring your shit and set it up at my tent next time."

We finished our drinks. I dug through my pocket and Gene put his hand out in a stopping motion. He flicked through the bills in his wallet, his glasses perched on his nose.

"You know—you always talked the talk."

He placed the bills under his empty glass and began to stand up. I stood up too and we headed for the door. He grabbed a handful of *Mukhwas* on the way out and held the door for me, the seriousness rising back into his face.

"But it's too late to walk the walk. You better run."

I felt a seed pelt me in the back of the head as I walked down the sidewalk. I turned around and thought about yelling at him, but I knew he was right. The window was closing and if I was going to shoot, now was the time to take aim.

We returned to the United States a week later. The next time I saw him, my truck was full of wine racks, clocks, and a new stool I'd designed. The stool was composed of a single beam that twisted into a minimalist, but comfortable shape. I sprayed it with thick red enamel paint.

"Welcome to the lifestyle."

Gene had his arms out while he leaned against the hood of his car. I trailed him in my truck through upstate New York and into Pennsylvania. I couldn't keep myself from checking the rearview over and over and again. Moving a bunch of sculptures across states and highways was more stressful than I anticipated. It wasn't like moving equipment or lumber or raw steel; nothing about them was uniform or very stackable and consequently couldn't be ratcheted down very well, if at all. I winced every time I took a turn or hit my breaks. I didn't want to show up with a bunch of broken clocks and dented wine racks.

The show was inside a massive, decommissioned armory in Pennsylvania. It was typical for trade shows to take place in peculiar locations. They were sometimes outside, but most often inside some large, rented space. Each vendor set their booth or tent up like a little storefront installation. Gene's vending area had evolved over the past couple of years to have a vaguely "eastern" look to it. This was partially why he made an effort to buy furnishings as well as jewelry; he could furnish his storefront in a theme-specific way and sell the decorations right off the wall. It was difficult to do that with only rings and necklaces.

When we showed up, we set up shop like we always did. After we got all of Gene's stuff where it had to be, we began to lug my pieces off the bed of the truck and inside. I felt a little bad; my pieces threw off the look of his booth. My pieces didn't match the trade show in general. I was learning there were many different types of trade shows, and Gene picked one's where he knew he'd flip the most jewelry.

I tried to display my pieces in a way that wasn't intrusive, but I still wanted people to notice. He didn't seem to be bothered.

"They sorta fit the look. Works for me."

He shrugged and leaned back in his chair. Eventually, the onslaught of people arrived and flooded the corridors between booths.ABut this is Gene was almost immediately swamped with interest and the cash began to roll in. People stopped and looked at my sculptures. I was timid at first and would only smile and wave. They'd wave back and then be on their way. I kicked myself over it; I knew they were customers lost. I didn't know why it was so easy to help Gene with his jewelry but so difficult to talk about my sculptures to people.

I racked my brain and thought about all the mental notes I took at past trade shows. I tried to think of how people had reeled me in before and convinced me to buy something. I remembered back to when I studied abroad there was a teenage boy in Venezuela selling ponchos from a clothing rack on the side of the road. He cornered me as I passed by and hammered me with questions and conversation. Somehow, I left with a poncho on.

I noticed an older woman looking at one of the wine racks. I waved and smiled at her. She smiled back at me and I hesitated for a moment. I took a step forward to force myself to engage or look weird trying.

"How has your day been?"

"Good, thank you for asking."

She smiled at me but didn't say anything else. I already hit a brick wall. I took another step forward.

"Are you looking at one of the wine racks?"

"Yes, did you make them?"

I told her everything. I told her how I make them, how I got the idea. I told her where I'm from and what my house looks like. I told her I grew up on a dairy farm and that we bottle water now. I told her I used to be horrible at welding but practiced and started building things in a barn tool shed. Then, I asked her what type of wine she likes. I didn't drink wine; I didn't know the difference between any of it but tried to act as if I did. She went on about different wines she's tried, then started talking about her daughter and granddaughter. I listened intently and chimed in whenever I could think of something nice to say. I was about to tell her that I imagine her granddaughter was a wonderful person when she cut me off.

"I don't see a price on any of them."

"A price?—Oh, a price!"

I wanted to slap myself. I hadn't even figured out how much I would charge for anything. I was too worked up about even bringing them to a show to consider thinking about pricing. I couldn't tell her that; she might think it was strange—lazy even. I tried to think about how much I'd pay for a wine rack if I didn't already have a truck full of them.

"That one—that one is $225."

She tilted her head and raised her eyebrows. I couldn't tell if I said it cost too much or too little.

"I'll take it if you can move it into my car for me."

I nearly gasped. Instead, I nodded and smiled and moved like lightning to take it off the wall. Gene watched the whole ordeal out the corner of his eye and grabbed her money for me. I threw the wine rack over my shoulder and followed her out into the parking lot. The sun was shining down hard and reflected off the paint of the cars that sat in neat rows all about the pavement. I felt the heat of the sun reflecting off the wine rack burn my neck as I marched it to the woman's Mercedes. I stowed it across her back seat and shook her hand.

"Thank you. I hope your granddaughter gets into the college she wants."

The woman smiled at me.

"Thank you. Good luck with the water bottles."

I ran back to the booth as fast as I could to bask in the glory of a sale. I wanted to jump up and down and shake Gene. I was about to shout to Gene once I was within earshot when I saw him discreetly pointing behind himself. More people were looking at the wine racks.

It felt like someone was playing a joke on me. I straightened out my shirt and composed myself then engaged with the people looking. I'd broken the seal now and understood what I had to do.

First, I'd make contact with someone and then corner them into talking. It was a little more difficult than selling jewelry to people. Getting somebody to try a piece on and hyping them up was often all you had to do to make a sale. I couldn't do something like that for a clock or wine rack, so before I even brought up the sculptures, I'd try to get them to talk to me. Some wouldn't talk much, but most would talk a whole lot. The conversations would be tangential, spinning out into directions involving people's loved ones or college days or their awful morning they had before they arrived; but it didn't matter. I began to realize that's what people wanted to talk about. If I tried to explain to them the process of building sculptures most of the time their eyes would glaze over, and it'd work against me. They didn't want to learn how to shape a sheet of metal or make clean welds—they wanted somebody to know them and they wanted to know somebody. The art came second; it was an extension of the connection they just made.

I only sold the first wine rack that day, but the two hundred dollars in my pocket felt like a million. People had taken an interest in my work, and although I didn't sell much, I could tell it was on people's minds. My stool didn't have a single bite, though. Gene loved it, and so did I. I figured stools are much more universal and useful than a wine rack, so I was a bit confused at the lack of interest. I asked Gene what he thought, and he just shrugged. I was in an afterglow and didn't care to ponder it anyways.

I loaded my wine racks, clocks, and stool into my truck. I grabbed the handle of the driver's door and heard it click. The old hinges of the door squealed as I swung it open. I'd had my father in the back of my head all day. The more I spoke to potential buyers, the more I couldn't stop thinking of what he told me so many years ago. .

"No matter what you do in life, there's nothing wrong with brightening someone's day."

I could see Gene through his windshield and could tell he was flipping through the profits of the day.

"Saves you a little money too."

I thought about how he spoke to people on his daily milk deliveries and thought he'd be a good salesman at a trade show.

I drove home singing along to the radio, patting the cash in my pocket to the beat. I made far less than my regular paycheck at the farm, but the money in my pocket felt so much different. I'd felt like I truly deserved it—that it was the fruit of something I did for more than a paycheck. It made me smile to think of someone hanging up their new wine rack. It would bring them a little happiness and use, just as building it brought me happiness and the money I made will be of use to me. I daydreamed about them becoming coveted as I climbed the rungs of the sculpture market. Even if they never became worth anything, it made me smile to know if I died on the car ride home a little piece of who I was would remain somewhere long after I was gone.

I saw Gene pull off the highway towards a sign for a Sunoco. I figured I'd grab gas too. We stood at our pumps and shouted to each other over an onset of rain.

"Hey, I was just thinking about the stool. You know—how nobody liked it."

I flipped Gene off and he laughed while he hung the pump up. He took off his glasses and began to wipe them on the collar of his shirt.

"Seriously, though. That thing belongs in a loft in Manhattan."

"Isn't that a good thing?"

"Well, yes, but—"

He jogged over to me and put his glasses on.

"It's about the market. Who is your customer? Your audience—you know; Nobody in suburban Pennsylvania wants to sit on a piece of mid-century art in their McMansion."

I nodded. I hadn't thought of it that way. Just like the price tags, I didn't consider I'd be having to worry about my *audience*. I just made what I liked.

"Something to think about. You killed it today, though. Looks like you'll need your own booth soon."

Gene waved backward as he jogged back to his car and drove off.

When I got home it was late into the night. I brought the stool to the tool shop and sat down. I counted the money out on the table then looked around. I did some quick math in my head. Accounting for the price of the steel, welding gas, and other suppies I barely made a profit. I scratched my head. There was so much I had yet to think about in regards to selling art. The mountain grew larger the closer I got to it, but I didn't mind. I shrugged it off and told myself to be glad I didn't take a loss.

I started building new things as quickly as I could. A million ideas were running through my head. Each one branched into a thousand others, and those ideas all required choices. How large would the sculpture be? Would I paint it, leave it raw? It was overwhelming before I'd even begin something.

I had shown my family the money I made. I was proud of it, and I could tell when they saw I sold a piece they were surprised but proud. It made me happy, and it appeased a part of me that yearned to prove I could make my own way. A person saying they enjoy your art is one thing, but a person witnessing others enjoy your art feels even better.

I kept up with the trade shows with Gene. Eventually, I built and designed my booth so I wouldn't have to keep stealing Gene's space. I designed my booth with the feeling of a rustic lifestyle. I decorated it with colors that were familiar to me: browns and deep reds and oranges and golds. I hung the wine racks and clocks around the booth and displayed some furniture and exclusive pieces I'd built in the foreground.

Life began to fly by. A new century bloomed, and I began to feel a great sense of urgency. I hadn't been to a trade show in a while; I'd been focusing on refining my designs and trying to come up with something fresh. Over the months I diversified my work as well. I ended up with a unique accumulation of clocks, lights, wine racks, chairs, and tables. I was proud of them, but much of their fruition was from the logical facet of my mind. They were things I knew would sell. In between, I began to fulfill a growing ache to create something bigger and more akin to my aspirations.

I knew there was a big show coming up and called Gene to see what the move would be.

"Hello?" he answered.

"Hey stranger, you going to the show in a couple of weeks?"

"Did I not tell you?"

I sat quietly on the phone trying to think back to my last conversation with Gene. I hadn't spoken to him in a while.

"I'm parting ways with the lifestyle."

"You're what?"

I could feel the panic rising in me as he spoke.

"Did you think I'd do this forever? I only kept doing it to bolster bigger plans."

"I guess I never really thought about it. Why now?"

Gene laughed through the phone line.

"Do you think I just liked to talk about the internet? I've been investing profits from the silver in startups for years. I need to start planning the next step."

I laughed too. I never paid attention but realized now he'd been banking on this. I thought about congratulating him, but it felt silly to congratulate someone for something they were so sure of happening.

"But you—" I stopped laughing. There was suddenly a seriousness in Gene's voice.

"You need to keep at it. I just sold cheap silver to make a quick buck, but you're doing something real."

"You think so?"

"Of course. Don't get trapped in those flea markets, either. They're a steppingstone. I've got to go, though. I'll talk to you soon."

He hung up the phone. A part of me was sad. We were getting older and becoming adults. Now was the time to pave ways. I knew I needed to start going to trade shows that suited my work better anyway.

The trade show circuit was challenging to navigate. The nature of trade shows covers a vast array of purchasable goods. "Craft," shows, like the ones I'd been to with Gene focused mostly on jewelry, silverware, glasswork, and other small items. They had a strange vibe, as everything there was either cheap and mass-produced items akin to a flea market, or they were painstakingly crafted by hand. Some trade shows focused on equipment and some were entrepreneurial. Some weren't for goods at all, but rather services. I needed to begin honing exactly what type of trade shows I wanted to set up at.

I thought about what Gene had said on the phone. I could already see how people get trapped in the lifestyle of selling goods at trade shows and never progress forward. Taking the first plunge into selling my creations caused my dreams to expand outward and inflate. I knew I didn't want to make wine racks forever. The more serious I became about my work the more I realized I didn't want to make something that hangs on a wall. I wanted more of me in my work. As I built my shop in my garage at the turn of the century, I dreamt of the same dreams I did when I was in high school. I could care less about the wine racks; I wanted to make *Artistic* sculptures; the things I dreamt of creating as a kid.

For a while, I stopped focusing so much on trade shows. I turned my focus towards the upper levels of the art community. I printed pamphlets of my work and drove around New England leaving them in the lobbies of art galleries and businesses. I'd pack my truck and corner gallery owners, pitching them my work as a door to door salesman.

Meanwhile, I began working on new designs. I wanted to create something reminiscent of an older time, but fresh and contemporary. I hatched the idea to build sculptures out of steel inspired by the vintage pin-up girls painted by Alberto Vargas. The old pinups of the twentieth century stirred something in me. There was something mysterious and classic about them and the fact their time was one before my own. I could still remember being young and seeing them painted on the nose of fighter planes in photographs from World War II and Vietnam.

The world was moving fast, and although many people reeled with excitement for the future, they also stared nervously into it. I'd find myself walking around the farm looking at the aging equipment and structures seeping into rust. There was a cultural desire to seek comfort in the past and forget it at the same time, and I felt compelled to reimagine the old pinups. I plasma cut them from thin sheets of stainless steel and layered the sheets on top of one another. I brushed some of the layers and polished others to create a sense of depth. The final touch was something I pulled from the comforts of my past. From my childhood, I could remember the sight of boxcars traveling across the bridge that runs over the Merrimack. They were always covered in deep, russet corrosion. I had always wondered how they rusted like that; why they didn't rust the same way an old bicycle did when it was left in the rain. There were no deep runs across splotches of steel, no large, peeling chunks bitten out of their frames. The bridges that clung above the river looked the same, coated in that deep reddish-brown. Years later in my travels, I noticed buildings utilizing that same type of corrosive element for aesthetic purposes and immediately knew it had to be a specific type of material. I did some digging around and learned about COR-TEN, or weathering steel. I learned about its development by the railroad companies and its unique ability to corrode thinly on its surface, forming a protective layer for the rest of the metal.

 I immediately acquired sheets of it and used it to complete my pin-up sculptures. I used the weathering steel for their hair, so that when it oxidized it would turn a beautiful reddish color and contrast excellently against the more sterile look of stainless steel. I learned how to expedite the oxidation process with chemicals and ensure the most uniform and appealing finish with stabilizing sprays.

 It looked beautiful to me and I felt myself burst with pride. I began utilizing the concept for the rest of my work and they began to come to life as if it was the piece of the puzzle that was always missing.

 I'd also begun to build much larger sculptures than I ever had before. Like the pinup girls, they were different from my previous pieces in their lack of utilitarian purpose. I'd stepped further away from validating my work by ensuring it had some type of "practical" use. These sculptures existed solely to be sculptures, and nothing else. It was a more difficult step to take for me than it may have been for others. Much of my life instilled a sense of practicality in me. Life on a farm was about practicality; everything served an essential purpose. A person did not buy a fence because they liked the way it looked, but rather to keep cattle or chickens where they had to be. They bought a tractor to plow their fields, not to display it on a lawn. I had to, in some sense, work that impulse out of me and I knew it.

The sculptures were very geometric and post-modern. They resembled the aesthetic appearance of my wine racks and clocks in many ways but ventured further into the abstract. Many of them were designed to appear as impossible feats of physics. They utilized crafty metalwork to bind large round shapes to snake-like coils of steel structures sprouting up from the ground.

For all the inspiration I felt illuminating the dark garage I toiled in every day, it was just as quickly crushed by the responses I received from galleries. I never received any calls from the places I left pamphlets, and the times I was rejected in person left a devastating mark on my confidence. The first time I was rejected I was met with hostility, the gallery owner swatting me away like an insect buzzing in his ear. I left furious and hurt, clenching my teeth the whole way home. When I pulled into my driveway, I rested my forehead on my steering wheel and sat in the dark alone. I'd never been met with negative feelings over my art. It was a difficult pill to swallow. Art had been my escape from the harshness of reality my whole life. Now it was driving me headfirst into situations that made me feel small and insignificant. I wasn't equipped to deal with the rejection. The rejections in which people spoke politely to me were almost worse. They spoke with some type of manufactured pity in their voice; the pity a person hears as a child when their schoolteacher thinks they're doomed.

A version of myself years earlier would have thrown in the towel and concluded I was unfit to create art; that I was a person born to shuffle into my place and ride out a lifetime. My saving grace was the fact I'd fallen too deep. I felt as if a strong current was pulling me by my ankles outward into a new chapter of my life, and resisting would only lead to treading in place. I was in too deep to run away, and the only option was to trudge forward and through it.

As the rejections piled up from week to week, I felt the sting of the hole I'd burned through my wallet. The money I accrued from selling smaller pieces at trade shows was running thin, and my pinups and larger sculptures had cost considerably more to build than a wine rack or lamp. The thought of encroaching bills I had to pay drove me into a panic. I looked around at the amassed sculptures piled about my garage and began to grow angry with myself. I felt the utter lack of space amongst them. My tiny garage piled up with equipment and half-finished projects until all that remained was a thin passage to either doorway. It became so claustrophobic I felt like I couldn't breathe. I stepped outside into the cool night air and took a deep breath. I told myself to calm down and think. I had to make money, someway, and somehow. I couldn't cave in; there would be no way out.

Once I calmed myself down, I concluded I'd focus on trade shows again. I needed to pick wisely where I set up shop; time felt more of the essence than ever. If I ever wanted to expand past the trade show circuit, I knew I couldn't kick my feet up at anything that was in town for the weekend. I needed to make strategic decisions that would ensure I'd profit to get money circulating back into my life and continue trying to push forward.

I walked back into my garage and picked up a stack of notes and flyers I had on a workbench. I grabbed information for trade shows wherever I could, whenever I could. I flipped through them feverishly. Most were duds; flea markets at best. At the bottom of the stack, I stumbled upon something I knew I could sell something at. It was the Boston Wine Expo.

'*Okay*,' I thought.

"Let's do it."

9

I attended the Boston Wine Expo and gave it one hundred percent of my effort. I bought lightbulbs to illuminate my booth and sculptures with a golden shimmer. It went nicely with the oranges and danced off the stainless steel. I practiced my pitches and dressed nicer than usual. My hair had grown out longer, so I pulled it back neatly. It was a rare and golden opportunity. I fit the trade show theme but offered an alternative product from many of the stands who sold wine and competed amongst each other. I brought my sculptures as decorative components and made the wine racks the centerpiece of my booth, although I hoped somebody would take an interest in a more expensive piece.

I worked the booth far more like a salesman than I usually do. The nature of the show suggested it; I was trying to remember more and more what Gene had told me: always to consider my audience. At times I felt silly; almost like somebody on an afternoon infomercial, but it paid off. I sold one, and then another. People complimented my other work, and though I tried I got no bites. It didn't matter to me, though. I had a mission to sustain myself and stared through denials or failed pitches.

The idea of keeping my dream afloat kept me moving with each sale, and by the end of the day, I felt alright. I was starting to pack up when an old woman came up to me.

"How're you today ma'am?"

She squinted her eyes and looked suspiciously around my booth. Her eyes darted from sculpture to sculpture. I was about to speak up when she walked past me up to one of my pinups. She squinted even harder and put her face a few inches from the wall.

"Why do you have pornography hanging at your booth?"

"Ma'am?"

"It's indecent!"

She flung her head towards me, the veins in her neck lifting from her skin. Her gaze was icy and made me throw my hands up.

"Oh, come on."

"Straight out of *Esquire* magazine!"

She jutted her cane out. I could tell I was making her angrier.

"It's not porn. It's supposed to be vintage and classy. Like— an old pinup drawing."

"That *was* the pornography of my day!"

She moved by me as fast as she could. She shook her head as she passed by me into the crowd.

"Just indecent."

I watched her disappear into the crowd and then I continued to pack my things up.

I-93 was backed up on the way home. I sat in traffic and stared at the waves of heat lifting between cars. I'd sold a few of the wine racks; nothing else. It would be enough money to keep me alive. I tried to process my conversation with the old woman. I hadn't thought of the pinups in that way. I knew she was old and of a different time. Pinups held a different connotation to her because of her experience. They weren't a nostalgic mystery of the past, they were an aspect of her life that used to be the present. I began to think again about the stool I built and what Gene told me at the gas station. "Audience," is what he talked about. That woman was not the correct audience for the pinups. I laughed to myself but there was truth in the experience. If I wanted to sell my work, why would I willingly narrow my audience? I loved the pinups I sculpted but I felt like I might be shooting myself in the foot. I needed to create something universal; something nobody could wave a cane at and something that everyone could relate to. It wasn't a revelation solely about sales, either. Over the years, I'd learned that one of the true joys of creating art is relating to somebody to some degree; finding common ground and using your work as a conduit. It's what made it worth it.

Once I got my bills and immediate finances under control, I went back to the garage to brainstorm something new. I wanted it to be relatable to everybody. Because of that, I knew I couldn't venture too far into any heady design work. I was learning it sometimes came off as pretentious, and many people didn't see the same beauty in it that I did. I knew it couldn't be polarizing in any way either, so pinups or anything remotely explicit was off the table. Yet, it still had to be striking. It had to be instantly moving to people if I wanted high hopes of making sales. Finally, I needed an attack plan for actually pulling a profit. The sculpture would have to be efficient in terms of resources.

The question of *what* tormented me for months. I was beginning to encounter one of the great compromises of being an artist. Thinking of my work with such an emphasis on generating sales, while at the same time trying to bloom into something unique made my head spin. They just nearly contradicted each other. At times, I'd think too hard and feel as if I were already selling out, sitting with a pen and paper trying to pander to people I didn't know.

On the other hand, if I caught myself too concerned with something like that, I'd grow angry with myself. I had my one year old son Parker in his crib next to me; his whole life in front of him. I wanted to give parker a wonderful life, and I wanted to be close to him when he got older. No level of artistic credibility could surpass that.

I burned through trade show after trade show and couldn't come up with anything that fit the bill. I continued trying to get a spot at a gallery as well, but nothing came from it. When I would return home, I'd find my son smiling and excited to see me. It was the only thing that brought light to things. I began to joke with myself that we were already a great team. I knew if I didn't have him, I probably wouldn't put my nose back to the grind wheel each day.

By day, I worked in the garage. The older I got, the more I was reminded that this was as physically difficult as it was mentally exhausting. My body began to hate me for what I did, no longer able to bounce back the way I once could. By the end of the day, I was sore and covered in metal shavings, soot, and sweat. Still, the weight of remaining stagnant pressed me. I'd stay up hours into the night working out ideas and blueprints. My refrigerator would be empty, save for a few Tupperware containers of leftover meals. I'd scarf down whatever I could and crack open a beer and scribble ideas, then toss the duds all about the floor. Before I knew it, I'd have the crumpled cans and crumpled papers all around me and my watch would read some god-awful hour of the early morning. Everything would be swept away into the trash and I'd wander away to bed, practically collapsing on to the mattress and often waking up in my work clothes.

I never saw much of anybody besides Parker. I became reclusive—trapped in my head. I drank pots and pots of coffee to keep myself upright and moving through the day. I kept a pot of it in my garage all the time. The lack of sleep and stress and hangovers killed my appetite. Sometimes I'd skip multiple meals, forgetting to eat something until I sat down in my kitchen to sketch. My clothes began to look baggy on me and my face looked gaunt. More than a few times I fell asleep on my garage floor or leaned over my workbench, exhausted and lightheaded in the lingering heat from the welder and plasma cutter.

    I wondered if people thought I was crazy when they saw me. I wondered if I thought I was crazy. Sometimes I thought about it; especially when the money ran out. What had I willingly walked into? I couldn't remember the last time I did anything but weld metal, sketch, or go to trade shows. Most times, I could barely keep my eyes open as I drove from state to state trying to make money. It didn't feel so good to pat it in my pocket anymore. I stopped enjoying driving from place to place because I was too exhausted to compose a stable thought or take anything in. If I did, it was something negative. One night I drove through the dark forested roads of upstate New York and watched the street signs warp in front of me. The wind howled into the cracks of my truck and I stared ahead thinking of the years as they flew by, trying to recall what drove me to do this. Nobody had warned me—or maybe they did, and I just blocked it out. I thought if I squinted my eyes, I could see the truth as to why people got jobs in offices or factories. It was not just fear that kept people from trying to do this, it was *common sense*. I was the one who moved with fear. I was so afraid of losing the fire I felt within me and now I feared I'd stomped it out. Only a few burning coals stuck around, and I desperately tried to keep them glowing.

    The only thing I could think to do to keep the fire going was to keep searching for the design that continued to elude me. I felt like

EXIT 48

I was chasing it in the dark, running towards the faint sound of its footsteps. I just barely kept up, and I chiseled through pads of paper searching for my way out.

It made me so frustrated one afternoon, I threw my notepad across the garage. I watched its pages flutter as it skipped across the concrete. They were pages filled with mediocre ideas. I sighed and walked out into my driveway, slamming the door behind me. The sun was out, I could hear kids playing down the street. I felt like going for a run. Running always cleared my head when I felt overwhelmed, ever since I first started doing it as a kid.

I took off from my driveway still in my shop clothes. I ran a large loop around the industrial park that surrounded my house, breathing in the hot heavy air and feeling the sun on the back of my neck. Eventually, I neared the farm and figured I'd pop in for a visit.

I jogged up to the bottling plant on the farm. Some of the workers were outside on a smoke break and I waved to them as I slowed my roll to a walk. I grabbed a water from one of the crates and cracked it open, asking them how they'd been. We talked for a while as they burned through their cigarettes and talked about my days on the farm. They told me about their lives since then and let me in on some new gossip. It made me miss working there with them. It made me miss a lot about the past. I drifted off and went for a walk around the farm. The fields were empty, aside from a couple of elderly cows grazing. I thought about when I was little—how big the farm seemed to me back then.

I walked through the swaying outgrown fields down to the tree line. As I squirmed my way through brush and thorns, I could see the brook glimmering between the leaves. I eventually walked out into a clearing under a cluster of massive pine trees, their needles cushioning the earth as my sneakers sunk into the ground beneath me. I laid on the forest floor under the trees and felt my breathing slow. Chipmunk Village hadn't changed one bit. Debris and decrepit forts from years ago still stood around me. The chipmunks still chased each other from tree to tree. It made me smile. I closed my eyes and listened to them scamper around, muffled by the flowing rush of the brook next to me.

I almost fell asleep laying there, when suddenly I heard something large shuffle when blue eyes emerged from the dark of the brush and stared at me. It was one of the farm dogs. He'd grown old over the years. His face was brushed with white whiskers around his eyes and mouth and he moved like an old man.

He dipped his head towards the ground and hobbled up to me. I lay back down, and he plopped himself by my side. I lay there with him for a while and scratched behind his ears as he huffed and rolled in the pine needles. Eventually, he shifted sideways and put his head in my lap. I smiled. I'd always loved dogs. There was something so heartwarming about them. I thought about how crazy a person would have to be to dislike them. I was convinced nobody truly disliked them; that they were loved to some extent by everyone.

The thought made me jump in the air. The farm dog leaped up too, jumping to his feet and moving back from me. His eyes grew wild and concerned, then shifted back to a lazy gaze as he laid on the ground again. I was already running, though. I was practically sprinting as I barreled out of the woods, headed uphill past the bottling plant and my grandparents' old house and the barn and tool shed and across the fields. I cut through the woods, panting now, and desperately headed towards my house and the notepad on the garage floor.

I poured my bottle of water on my face as I jogged up to my

driveway and burst through my garage door into the still heat and dark. I flicked on the light and watched the dim gold pour over the sheets of metal cast around the floor. I snatched my notepad up from the floor and began to draw a rough concept feverishly. I scribbled an ugly outline of a Labrador. It was a young Labrador, thin and proud with its chin raised towards the sky. The drawing was ugly, but I could see the image between the lines. This was it.

I spent the next few days hunched over the table, perfecting my design. Through pot after pot of coffee the dog began to take shape. It was from the perspective of a side profile-view, and I made sure not to overcomplicate anything. It was simple and elegant, and each curve deserved to be where it was. I planned to build the dog entirely out of COR-TEN as if it was covered in a smooth coat of fur. Structurally, I knew I'd make it similar to my wine racks: out of sheets of steel welded into a three-dimensional structure. I also made sure it didn't have a single straight angle on it. I couldn't afford a brake for my shop and it took an immense amount of time for me to make a flat angle compared to other people. Too often I saw somebody else's sculpture and knew it took them a quarter of the time it'd take me to do because of that one tool. Metal brakes couldn't do curves as I'd devised. If I was going to be forced to do more work than others it was going to be worth it. If anyone wanted to copy this design from me, they'd have to work just as hard for it.

The final touch came organically. I incorporated a simple cutout of a bone into the dog's torso. It just looked good, and I knew then it was done. I wasted no time bringing it to life. The first few attempts were disasters. The number of curves in the design made it more difficult to do than any I ever had before. Many points of contact needed to be welded and everything had to be shaped perfectly to not make the piece look comically bad. Other things I'd sculpted had a little more wiggle room and were more forgiving, but this design had to be perfect.

When I finally made the last weld, I stepped back and looked at the dog. It stood three feet tall and stood proud. For the first time in a year, I felt proud of something. I could feel a small amount of relief course through me. I practically hugged it.

The dog felt like a little beacon of hope in the dark of my garage. Still, it didn't come into this world without bringing risks with it. Creating it nearly cost me four hundred dollars, which rendered me unable to purchase supplies to build anything else than what I already had laying around. I looked around and realized I didn't have enough scrap to make anything else. For the first time in longer than I could remember, there wasn't anything else for me to do in the day. I left the dog standing in the middle of my garage and stumbled up my stairs, feeling the ache in the heels of my feet flicker up through my legs. That night, for the first time in a year I got a full night's sleep.

There was a string of festivals coming up and I decided I'd hit all of them. I wanted to sell this dog; even if I sold nothing else. As time came around, I drove out to each event and sold the items I built. I'd try and build what I could in between to keep the merchandise flowing. To my dismay the dog stood still, coming home in the bed of my truck after each festival or trade show. I began to get nervous and second think myself. It wasn't until the very last show I had booked that anyone took notice.

The event was The Paradise City Arts Festival in Pennsylvania. I'd driven all the I didn't have much to sell. There wasn't enough money coming in to keep up and I was starting to resent the dog for the financial hole it dug me into. A man approached me, and I could tell the dog caught his eye. He looked fifteen years or so older than me and I could tell his shoes weren't cheap.

"That's my newest design. Do you like it?"

"I've been looking for something just like this—for our summer home."

He ran his hand on the dog's head as if he were petting it.

"Is that rust?"

I explained to him the process of how I make them. He began to talk about his summer home and his job and possibly buying it as a Christmas gift for his wife so she could put it in her garden.

"How much are you selling it for?"

"That piece would be $650."

The man took a step back and laughed in a way that irritated me a little. I didn't see what was funny about what I said.

"Six fifty for a piece of lawn art? It's three feet tall."

For a minute I almost lost my top. I thought about the hours it took to build it, the months and months to think it up and design it. I knew I had to keep my composure.

"Well then give me a price you'd pay for it."

The man took a step back and rubbed his chin. I could tell he wanted it. Even people with a lot of money aren't quick to pay for something they think is "lawn art." It looked like two smaller versions of the man were debating inside his head.

"I'd give you four hundred for it."

I inhaled sharply and put my hand on the top of the table at my booth. I was about to say I couldn't do that and explain how I wouldn't make any profit, but the other side of me took command and told him it was a deal. I just wanted someone to buy it, so I knew there was a market for it somewhere out in the world. I didn't want to wait to make back the money it took to build it either, so I watched the man drive off to his summer home with my first three-foot dog sculpture for the price of raw materials.

Afterward, I sat at my booth sipping coffee. Now that I had time to cool off and think about it in an unbiased way the man was right, as blunt as he was. Who *would* pay six hundred bucks for lawn art? My profit margin wasn't greedy at all, but the price wasn't right. I thought about the first thing he countered when I told him the price: that it was only three feet tall. I started to get lost in my head thinking about it; how people are willing to pay more for it if it's simply larger. It was a weird way everybody thinks, but I couldn't deny I thought that way too. Then it occurred to me.

It took two sheets of metal, four feet by eight feet, to build the dog. Afterward, I remembered collecting the scrap and thinking of how it had all gone to waste. The fact the scrap was unusable made the dog cost as much as a potentially larger version. I could build a bigger dog for the same price.

I spent the next afternoon buying sheet metal and beginning to build a new dog. I told myself I wouldn't risk it until I had more money to play with, but I couldn't shake the idea of building a new one from my head. I settled on building one that was a foot and half taller than the previous one, bringing it in at being four and a half feet tall. A foot and a half may not seem like much on paper, but proportionately it makes a huge difference. I finished the dog the next night and looked at it. It was much taller than any real dog now and looked even larger in my cramped garage. It was almost too heavy to pick up. I cleaned up around my garage and noticed it was particularly hard to get around the sculpture. It couldn't stay inside if I were going to get anything done until the next trade show, so I dragged it out of my garage and down into my front lawn to test my lawn art theory.

I wiped the sweat from my forehead and stood out in the street facing the sculpture. If it was lawn art, then it was too big not to be the center of attention.

I left it out front to oxidize. The next morning as I worked in my garage, I heard a car's brakes squeak and come to a halt. There was a man in front of my house, his head sticking out the driver's side window and staring at the dog.

"I'm jus' lookin' at your statue. That's somethin' else."

I smiled at the man and told him thank you. We talked for a little bit about metalwork and he drove off. He said he might come back later and buy it, but I knew he most likely wouldn't.

What mattered to me is that the man felt the need to stop. If it got a random person to stop their car and stare at my front yard, it'd be bound to get people to stop at a trade show they brought money to. I began to feel excited again; like I was propelling forward towards something. I decided to use the money to build a second dog instead of more clocks and wine racks.

The dogs attracted some less exciting attention towards me as well. As I positioned the second one out on my front lawn and the two of them shifted from silver to orange, I got calls from family members and friends about it. Some thought it was great, but some called concerned for me. More than one person gave me a talk about throwing in the towel. They said the ship has sailed; that it was a good try but that it might be time to start thinking of some other way to make money, not building more oversized sculptures and digging myself in deeper.

I knew they weren't saying it out of any ill-intent. They all cared about me and probably thought I was going crazy. I looked run down and never spoke to any of them. I barely even left my garage and all of a sudden, I'd installed two metal dogs out of nowhere out in the front lawn. If they'd told me to call it quits before I built them, I would have probably listened, but now I had a lot of sculpture to move and I was filled with hope.

When the next show rolled around, I had two giant metal dogs almost as tall as me in the bed of the truck. They were a hassle at first but once I got them in the bed of my truck, I discovered they were less stressful to drive with. The two profile sides of the dog were completely flat and thus nested together well. I ratcheted them down, but I didn't even feel like I had to. I stacked my thinning odds and ends around them.

It was a Saturday. I booked a show for the following Sunday as well. I had the dogs priced at eight hundred dollars each. I couldn't believe how right the man that bought the first dog was. People were fascinated by them. They drifted over in groups and asked questions about them. There seemed to be something inherently intriguing about them now that they were a foot and a half taller. I talked to people through the whole first day about them until finally, someone bought one at the end of the day; an older couple out together for the afternoon. Luckily, they came in a pickup truck and I just had to drag it out into the parking lot and load it up, but the following day when I sold the second one early in the afternoon I walked into a predicament. The woman that bought it came to the trade show in a sedan. The dog didn't even come close to fitting in her car. I wasn't going to turn down a big sale for that, though. I figured I'd leave after I dropped it off and get an early start home.

I went home with $1600 in my pocket and knew I'd be having to drive my pieces to people's houses from now on.

EXIT 48

I used the money to make more dogs, and soon I had a small fleet of them that replaced the wine racks as my bread and butter design. They nested together in alternating directions in my truck as I drove from show to show each week. As time progressed, I sold one at every show I brought them too. Sometimes I'd even sell two. I could feel the confidence seeping back into my bones. Things were becoming more hectic and stressful but in a healthy sort of way. It was a type of stress that I welcomed, as it brought money with it. It wasn't the type of stress one has when they feel cornered and desperate. Similarly, the physical stress I put on myself began to change as well. I was doing much more physical labor than before, but I was also eating better and maintaining better habits. I worked in a little extra time to sleep since I didn't have to obsess over discovering something new.

Things were running more efficiently. I worked out a healthy routine in my life. I stood from the garage while I ate a sandwich and looked at the row of dogs outside. I turned back towards the inside of my shop. I had a calendar on the wall; a 2004 edition of some artists' work they gave me for free at a show. I couldn't believe the years that had passed. I was happy to be where I was financially, but in all reality, it was nowhere great. I just didn't feel on the verge of collapse every day. When it came down to it, I was still essentially working for less than minimum wage.

What's more, I had abandoned my dream of breaking into the world of high art. I'd put an immense amount of work into selling the four-foot-tall dogs and getting them to where they were self-sufficient in their return of revenue that I didn't have time to run around cornering gallery owners. As I stood and stared at the calendar, I began to feel the creeping feeling of immobility return back. I didn't want this to be the top of my climb. I wanted to be more.

I couldn't simply raise the prices of my work. Oftentimes I'd run into artists selling their work for obscene prices. I'd see them during loadout carrying those same pieces out to the car time and time again. I had a steady flow of sales and made a profit I thought was at least fair for myself. People were beginning to respect my transparency in regards to pricing. They liked that I could map out why the dog sculpture cost as much as it did; it helped assure them they weren't being hustled.

The internet was also drastically changing the world of art. People had reference prices now. You couldn't sell a sculpture in a remote part of Pennsylvania for whatever you wanted anymore. I was happy to leave the wine racks behind for that reason, among others. It was bad enough competing with other people at trade shows, never mind the entire world.

I spent the past few years trying to figure out a design I knew was worth pushing. I knew I'd found it, but now I was confronted with the challenge of carrying it forward to greater heights.

It sounded like a joke in my head at first, but the more I thought about it the more It sounded like a good idea until I found myself drawing the plans out. I would just do what I did last time to solve the problem I was in and build a bigger dog.

10

Once at a trade show in Connecticut, I met another sculptor at a concession stand. He was a short, stout man with a seventies' mustache who grumbled on about things. It was funny to listen to him talk. He had a sharp enough wit to get away with being so negative.

We started talking about art. I'd just begun to dig into the work of more contemporary sculptors, and I liked listening to people talk about it. The man seemed to like the newer stuff, but his work was as traditional as I ever saw. He cast things in bronze—small, desktop-sized pieces of an older way of making art. I thought it was neat.

His opinions on different artists made my head spin. I wondered how someone could have so many views and be so concerned. I was about to say my farewells when he nodded at something behind me. I turned around and saw two men bickering, their sculptures blocking the main artery of the show.

One of the men's sculptures was massive. It was made of wood; some type of pattern carved seemingly out of an entire tree. The other man had wire sculptures coated in bright enamel paints. I turned back to the man. He was groaning and shaking his head.

"If you ain't good you go big, and if you can't go big you dress it up in bright colors."

The memory made me laugh to myself while I watched the delivery truck pull up to my driveway. He'd probably have a heart attack if he could see the game plan I had now. I didn't know whether my art would be considered *good* but going big was the plan. The supplies to build this new dog cost me any comfort the four-foot dogs' relative success could've brought me.

I was nervous; especially because if nobody wanted it, I didn't know what I'd do with an eight-foot-tall, ten-foot-long metal dog. I had bolstered my confidence, though, and made a few breakthroughs that let me build the dog for cheaper than I was proportionality building them for prior.

At first, the way I had designed and built the dogs was simple. I simply drew out of a rough sketch, then designed it in CAD software and ran it through the CNC plasma cutter. Both side profiles of the dog were cut out whole from a single sheet of COR-TEN steel. From there, I cut out the strips that comprised the depth of the dogs, and then fought my way through bending the strips into shape and giving them clean welds.

If done right, the outcome was beautiful—but the process would leave me with large, awkwardly shaped chunks of scrap sheet metal. It didn't seem like a lot to me at first, but once I got into building them, I began to see piles and piles of it build up. At one point, there was enough square footage of scrap for me to have built *several* dogs out of it if it was uniform sheets.

I pondered how I could be more efficient with the building until the answer came to me at a software swap meet. I was attending software swap meets whenever I could. There wasn't any other way for me to figure out what I had to. What's more, I didn't have the money to buy software and at the swap meets I could trade my license keys for others.

I told somebody about the predicament, and they asked why I

didn't seam together the sculptures.

"What do you mean?"

"Make seams in the sculpture, cut them out in squared-off pieces."

The man explained to me how stamped metal machinery uses seams to minimize metal waste. He explained the process of doing it on the software I had, and I made mental notes as best I could. I hadn't looked into the software much; only enough to get by doing it the way I always had. Computers were all around difficult to operate at the time, and mine was nowhere near a premium setup of the day.

I made time to learn the ropes of the software a little more and worked out seams for the dog. I positioned them so that they wouldn't be intrusive to the overall design. Luckily, the oxidation would be on my side as well and fill over the seams. With this new design concept, I cut my cost down and barely wasted a scrap of metal. The dog would be cut out of several sheets of metal into squared off sections. Then I'd weld them up into the full profiles, then hand shape the connecting pieces.

I was in high spirits the day I got the files running through the CNC computer into the plasma cutter. One by one I cut each piece out and deburred it. When everything was cut and ready to go, the welding began. I sat at my bench with my tig welder connecting each piece, trying to keep everything smooth and clean.

The process poured one day into another, and another into the next. When the day came that I had assembled the first side of the dog I didn't know whether to be impressed with myself or horrified. The side of the dog lay on its side, stretching ten feet long across the garage. My garage was only twenty feet wide. When you account for the five feet of equipment that sat on either side there was no room to move back and forth.

I held off on welding the other side together first and began working on shaping the cuts of steel that would connect the two faces of the sculpture. I took meticulous care in shaping them along the curvature of the dog. This was the most meticulous aspect of the whole process and took weeks. Since there was no room to work, I was usually working on top of the dog itself as it lay flat.

Once the hand-shaped cuts were welded onto the first face I could weld the seams onto that. Each seam I welded made it more difficult to work on the piece. By the time it was almost finished, and I was doing sanding work I had to duck, jump, and climb around my garage. Nonetheless, seeing the dog come into existence was exhilarating. The sculpture's size was an annoyance and worry, but even more so, it was captivating and exciting. Something about the fact I might not be able to get it out of my garage made me excited for the future.

The day the sculpture was done happened very abruptly. I was finishing the sculpture with an orbital sander when I stepped back to take a sip of coffee. I turned and looked at the sculpture on the floor and realized it was done—right there and then. It had been weeks and weeks since I first started, and my eight-foot dog had finally come to life.

I had big plans for the dog. I wanted it to be my first public piece, no matter what. I learned by now that galleries were hopeless for me. I'd practically hit every gallery in New England and got denied by everyone. It didn't matter to me, though; I had bigger fish to fry. I wanted to give the dog away for free.

"For *free*?"

My mother looked at me in disbelief. I could see the worry

spreading over her face from under her sunhat. We were at the bottling plant on the farm.

"Yes, for free. I think it would be a good marketing move."

"Well if you say so."

I could tell she thought it was silly. I could also tell she was debating with herself whether she wanted to stop me. I thought it was a good idea though, and I tried not to change my mind. I figured if I offered it up for free, a local municipality was bound to take me up on the offer. My first target would be good old Haverhill itself. The idea of having one of my works displayed downtown made me feel proud, just like having pieces in the high school art shows did so many years ago. I mused over the idea of my old art teachers seeing my work displayed downtown and finally knowing I never gave up and I didn't sell out. I wanted them to know I was doing it and I was doing my best.

The same week I finished the dog, I took photos of it and stopped by Haverhill's city hall. When I stepped inside the building it felt ancient. The musty hallways were dimly lit and smelt like aging paper. I remember my parents telling me how they went to high school there before the one I went to was built. You could almost tell it used to be a high school just from being inside—like the memories of all the city's older residents left a permanent effect on the air.

I went from room to room asking different officials where to go. Every time they sent me to somebody that person would send me to somebody new. My eyes were beginning to glaze over. This was by far the least fun part of trying to be an artist. I finally stumbled upon someone that would let me sit down and talk in the parks and recreation office. He was an older man with a comb-over and wrinkled tie. Sweat shined across his forehead in the harsh white light. I hadn't noticed until now how hot the old building got. I picked at my shirt while the man scribbled something on a sticky note and lifted his glasses from the bridge of his nose. I seated myself in the old vinyl chair and introduced myself.

"Hello, my name is Dale Rogers."

"Bob."

I nodded and he looked back down and began scribbling. There were sticky notes all over his desk. It was an older desk made of sheet metal painted beige and chipping at the edges. It reminded me of the old desks my high school teachers sat at. I wondered if they were from the same place.

"I'm an artist. I've just built a sculpture. I want to gift it to the city."

The man didn't look up from his scribbling. He just sat there with his nose to the paperwork. I wondered if his hearing was bad.

"I have a sculpture I want—"

"I heard you the first time."

He put his pen down with a heavy *clang* against the hollow desk. His eyes scanned his workspace, squinting and vibrating in his head. He stuck the sticky note between two older faded ones and let out a sigh.

"You can fill out an application, but I can almost assure you it'll be denied."

I shifted in my seat. His eyes stared back at me in a haze through the must of the office. I felt insulted and put my hands up.

"Did you not hear me? I want to *gift it*—as in for *free*."

The man put his hands up the same way I did. I wondered if he was mocking me.

"Did you not hear *me*? You can fill out an application. Do you have the slightest idea what it takes to install a public sculpture?"

I sat in my seat and didn't say anything.

"Inspections, permits, multiple insurances that need to be filed—"

The man shook his head while he listed off the multiple expenses. He looked like he was going to go into a fit and I got the point. I picked up my folder full of photographs and pushed the seat in.

"I understand. Thank you."

I could hear the pen begin to scribble again as I pulled the door. I walked quickly through City Hall and trotted out into the parking lot and away from the stale air of the offices. Outside the weather was warm. I kicked an old glass bottle in the parking lot as I walked to my truck.

I hadn't been through downtown in a long time. I was starting to miss it; even the smell of the river, which most from out of town would grimace at, filled me with memories of my youth. These days I was so busy driving back and forth around the east coast I usually skipped out on driving through my city. I could smell food frying in the air and saw two kids on bikes slouched over their handlebars at the crosswalk. I eased into my breaks and let them cross. One of them yelled back to the other as they glided across the pavement. For a moment, it made me miss my old friends. I hadn't seen any of them since I was still riding my bike around town and getting into trouble. Some of them weren't even alive anymore.

I tapped my fingers on the steering wheel. I wanted so badly for them to let me put a sculpture in the city. It hurt to hit a brick wall more than usual, and I began to realize on my drive home that this feeling was different. There was something else I had invested in this dog that I had invested never before in a sculpture. It was more than a marketing decision, It crept up on me from my subconscious. One way or the other, my dreams for my art were always really dreams for myself. I dreamt of having my work in galleries so people could see my name on the white card pinned next to it. I dreamt of the money of being successful in the trade circuit. I didn't dream of any of that with this sculpture. For this sculpture, I wanted people to think of themselves instead of me. I wanted it to make them happy and for it to bring a little piece of happiness into their lives. Whether they knew who I was or not didn't matter; I just cared about whether they'd be able to sit and look at the sculpture. I wanted it more than I wanted anything, and I felt a wave of understanding come over me. *This* was the point; that's what it meant to be an artist to me.

I was disappointed the city denied me, but the revelation pumped adrenaline into my veins. I spent the next few weeks hitting every city hall I could think of. I started with spots I wrote in my notes as places I thought would be strategic; places that were social hubs and tourist traveled. I went to Newburyport, Portsmouth, Portland, Hampton, Topsfield, and Rye. When I got denied from them, I tried towns all around the Merrimack Valley: Lowell, Lawrence, Groveland, Andover, North Andover, Amesbury, Methuen, Chelmsford. No dice. I tried smaller rural towns like Boxford and Derry. I hit everything up the Merrimack River with a city hall, from Manchester, New Hampshire down to where it spilled into the Ocean in Newburyport. Everybody told me the same thing: that it would cost the city far too much and that they couldn't take sculptures.

At the end of my long search, I sat and stared at the dog in my garage. I felt the old anxiety of finances and survival begin to creep back into my brain. The afterglow was beginning to wear off and I could see now what I had done in the pursuit of my dream. A giant metal dog lay sleeping on its side in my garage, its legs spread out and kicking into my tools and workbenches. I tried to think of what I could do with it. I didn't even know if it was going to fit through my garage door.

Fortunately, it just barely did. I worked up a sweat pushing the beast of a puppy out my garage door into my driveway. Then I pushed it off to the side against the grass. It couldn't stay indoors. My money was beginning to run out and I had to build four and a half foot dogs to flip at shows if I wanted to eat.

My life was beginning to slip back into a state of madness. The dogs began to sell less at trade shows, and my joints and back hurt a little more each time I fought to pull them out of my truck in a trade show parking lot. I started to doubt the design as a golden ticket. I spent the nights again scribbling up new possible designs. I had an idea in the back of my head for a cardinal. I also began playing with the ideas of making the sculptures more three dimensional, composed of many small flat angles and polished surfaces. I wasn't quite sure how I'd pull it off yet though.

I fell into the vicious cycle of simultaneously trying to move forward and sustain myself for the next few months. The center mark of the decade was speeding towards me and I'd barely gained any ground. I sat up at night with a cup of coffee and a can of beer next to each other feeling my throat dry out. Sometimes I'd stand up from my seat and walk to the kitchen window. I'd wipe the dewy glass and stare at the blue outline of the eight-foot dog, lopsided and half laying in my driveway as the sun gave its first rays of light. I'd try to squint and see if I could find the seams along the dog's surface. The dog had oxidized nicely; clean and uniform. As I predicted, the rust filled in and sealed the seams somewhat like caulking. They were barely noticeable, but if you knew where to look you could find them. If I could, I knew it was time for sleep.

I hardly noticed the earth cool down around me. It wasn't until I noticed the dog covered in leaves that I realized autumn had rolled back around. When thanksgiving crept up on me, I was happy to head over to my parents' house. I'd begun to feel like a hermit again. Whenever I fell into the rut of trying to find my way as an artist, I stopped talking to the people I cared about most. I hoped the holidays would let me forget about my worries and enjoy time with my family. I hoped nobody would want to talk about sculpting metal.

Thanksgiving on a farm in New England is everything a person would expect it to be. It was almost postcard-like, with all of my weathered and aging family members huddled around a table laughing and talking about old times. I practically fainted over the food. I missed home-cooking on the farm and was reminded of it every time we all got together to eat for the holidays.

Thanksgiving that year was particularly special. My family welcomed my second son, Dale, into the family. We called him Tripp, and he had the biggest smile in the world. It made me happy to watch Parker, still so young, already looking out for Tripp and watching out for him. I knew he was going to grow up to be a great big brother.

At some point amidst the commotion my cousin found me. I could tell by his face he was in the mood to egg somebody on.

"Hey, what's with the big dog sleeping in your driveway?"

I laughed and shook my head.

"Nobody wants it. I tried to give it to every city on this side of the state. *For free.*"

"For free, huh—"

He leaned against the back of one of the dining room chairs and rubbed his chin. His eyes trailed off whimsically towards the ceiling like he was lost in thought.

"Well—"

He pointed his finger at me and leaned in. His voice lowered and became raspy as if he was about to expel the words of a prophet.

"You could always prop it up on the highway with a sign that says 'free.'"

"He broke out into a fit of laughter, slapping his knee and pushing me. I shook my head and laughed under my breath.

"You'll figure it out."

He walked away still laughing at himself and began to yell something to a crowd of relatives. I rolled my eyes and laughed, picking up my plate and walking to the trash can. I mocked him under my breath as I dumped the Styrofoam plate into the trash bag.

"You could always prop it up on the highway with a sign that says 'free.'"

I paused. The plate hung off the tips of my fingers, the plastic utensils sliding off and plummeting into the bottom of the bag. I remembered when I was little; the day my father got angry with us for wandering out by the highway. Our farmland stretched up to practically the pavement of I-495 south. At one particular point, there was only about twenty feet of grass between our property and the interstate. The more I thought about it, the more my cousin's idea didn't seem half that bad, save for the "free sign." The piece of land I had in mind was right in front of the off-ramp for Exit 48, and it was visible from both sides of the highway. I grabbed two Moxies from the fridge and wandered through the halls of my parents' house. My brother was in the living room watching football. I tossed him the soda and let myself fall into the couch. I cracked my can open.

"Are you busy next weekend?"

"Me? I got no plans. None that I know of."

He shrugged and sipped the fizz from the top of the can.

"I need help with something."

"Sure thing. You robbing a bank?"

We both laughed. I took a sip and sighed.

"It'll probably be just as much a pain in the ass. I want to move the big dog onto the side of 495."

"Why?"

I could see my brother's face twist while his eyes stayed glued to the television. He must've thought I'd gone crazy if he hadn't already before.

"Well for one it's killing about half the grass in my yard."

We both laughed and sipped our Moxies. I kicked my feet onto the footrest.

"No, I just figure it might be a good way for people to get a look at my art."

My brother nodded and smiled.

"Makes sense to me. Good advertising. I'm in. just give me a call once I get out of work next Friday."

When I left my parents' house, I patted my cousin on the back.

"Sometimes I think you're a genius."

"Wish I could say the same about you, kid."

He gave out a final whooping laugh while I smiled and shook my head. The next morning, I woke up and spent the day figuring out how I'd move the dog onto the highway. The more I crossed off options, the clearer it became I would have to fit it in the bed of my

EXIT 48

truck. As the days came closer to the following weekend, I started to have other worries. In all reality, I had no idea what the legal details of putting a giant sculpture on the side of the highway were, whether it was my family's property or not.

When the day to install the dog rolled around, I borrowed a trailer from the farm and slid the dog onto it using plywood scraps to ramp it. I picked my brother up, and we drove to the Exit 48 off-ramp. We managed to wrestle it out of the trailer, although it almost tipped off the side a few times. We brought eight-foot landscape timbers to secure the dog with when it was installed. After some debate on its final position, we finally settled on one and stood by the truck. I tried not to show how ecstatic I was; I didn't want to continue to look like the craziest person in the world. I was excited though. I thought it looked magnificent on the highway and I thought of all the people passing by and seeing it. I didn't want to leave. I wanted to stand there and look at it for the rest of the day, but my brother was already headed for the truck and I could tell he was ready to call it a day.

"You wanna get something to eat?"

I nodded at my brother as I climbed into the driver's seat. I sat there for a second again staring at the sculpture. I hadn't been in a car with my brother for some time. Sitting there with him reminded me of when we were younger. I thought about sitting in my father's truck with our faces pressed to the window waiting to see if we could catch a glimpse of the monkey in the cage on the side of the road. I hoped in the back of my head my sculpture would become something like that for kids on their way to wherever they were headed. I wanted them to sit and wait by the back windows of cars to see the eight-foot dog on the side of the highway.

We had lunch together at Ari's pizza. We used to go there when we were kids sometimes after school. I sat in the little restaurant with him and ate a chicken finger sub.

"You alright?"

I nodded and looked down at my plate. My mouth was full of food, but I gave him the thumbs up. He nodded back and took a bite of his food.

"So, what's your endgame with this?"

"No idea."

He shrugged and put his sub down.

"Well—you think you're on the right track?"

"I have to be."

"You got that right."

After we finished eating, I dropped my brother off and headed home. The coming weeks turned into months. The whole time I had this feeling like I was waiting for a package to come in the mail. I don't know what exactly I was waiting for, but I was waiting for something. Nothing crazy came of the dog on the highway, though, and I continued with working into the night and dragging myself through trade shows to pay the bills.

My family was very enthusiastic about the dog on the highway. Since it was on their property, they felt even more invested in it—like they were a part of it now. My mother called me sometimes and told me she saw a friend at the grocery store who asked about it. Other times my brother said guys we knew in high school were talking about it at the bars. I never really got asked about it personally. Still, it sent a beam of motivation into my head every time one of my family members told me they heard chatter about it.

My psyche had hit the ground running, but as the months

trudged on and New England froze over my good spirits began to deplete. Many bad habits of mine continued to get worse and my lifestyle felt like it was killing me. Like everyone, my wallet held my emotional state by the throat. My welder broke and I had to buy a new one, which sent my financial situation into do or die. It felt like the weight of the world was pressing down on me. . I walked through life only half awake and the dog on the highway was seeming like a dud. I felt as if I sent out a distress flare for help and I was too far out for anybody to see.

    I sat one night watching television instead of brainstorming designs. It was a game show where the contestants were competing for twenty grand. I could remember being younger and thinking twenty grand was so much. Hell, I still thought it was a lot, but I knew now how fast that money disappeared; especially in this business. I was trying to fight off the thought I'd been having. Somebody had brought up getting certified as a welder. I knew what that meant. The only reason a person needed a certificate is to get a welding job somewhere. The worst part of it was I didn't completely shut the idea down. A stable income, a regular schedule; it didn't sound half bad. Outside, I could hear the rain coming down hard. It coated my living room in a wash of soft noise, like static over a radio. One of the hardest parts of being an artist is how many opportunities one is presented with during their career where giving up would be the easiest solution. Continuing is always the path with the most thorns.

    I stood up and hung my head. I felt like the room was spinning. I walked over to my bedroom and threw myself onto the mattress. I tried to think of the times when I was younger, hanging out with friends. They were simpler times and helped me fall asleep. The rain was beginning to send me into a slow descent into dreams. I was beginning to feel the last fleck of my consciousness slip when I heard a loud banging come from downstairs.

My eyes shot open, but I lay still, trying to decide if I were hallucinating or not. When the banging happened again, I hobbled downstairs towards the door. I paused for a moment, worried at what I'd find waiting for me outside. At this point, I'd believe anything. I peeked through the curtain. Of course—just my luck. I opened the doorway and a Massachusetts State Police Officer stared at me in the rain.

11

The morning after somebody tried to steal my sculpture, I dragged myself out of bed and called my brother and he agreed to help me out. When I arrived at his house he was out front sipping his coffee. I explained the whole story in depth to him as we drove to the Exit 48 off-ramp. We drew close on the highway and I could see my sculpture laying on the grass like it was asleep. It looked as if somebody had slammed into it with a car. I saw now that the whole run of the fence had warped when it crushed the ten-foot section. My brother leaned forward in his seat and turned the radio down.

"At least they didn't get away with it."

The officer had guessed it was teenagers. I couldn't figure out why anybody would want to steal it. I couldn't get my work into a gallery and I couldn't get a city to take it for free, but people were driving in the middle of the night to steal it off the side of the road. I parked the truck in the grass, and we got out and walked up to the crime scene.

My brother Harold asked "what the hell do you think they were thinking?"   He stood with his hands on his hips looking at the dog tangled in fence wire. The ground around us was kicked up and torn from the officer and I moving it the night before.

"Guess we should get the trailer from the farm."

I walked over and sat on the dog as it lay in the grass.

"Alright, I'll call and—"

"I just remembered Uncle Richard's helping somebody down the street with it."

I exhaled out my nose and stood up. I felt my joints creak in my legs and remembered dragging the dog through the rain the night before. I didn't want to leave it the way it was. The last thing I needed was this. I was already surprised I didn't catch any negative attention for installing it months ago, never mind leaving it in the haphazard state it was.

My brother walked over and touched one of the landscape timbers jutting up into the air. He squinted and then turned his gaze towards my pickup running behind us.

"What if we just put it in the truck?"

"Yeah right."

"Hold on."

He jogged over to my truck and climbed into the bed. He knelt and I could hear him fumbling through the tool bags I kept scattered over the bed floor. He stood back up with an old hacksaw flashing in the sun. When he walked back my way, he began cutting one of the timbers right where it met the dog's feet.

"I don't think that thing will fit in the bed of a truck."

"Sure it will. Look—"

The piece of timber splintered and toppled over to the ground with a resounding *thud*. He crossed over to the other side and began sawing the other piece.

"The only thing keeping it from fitting are these timbers at the feet. If we cut it down and stand it up it'll fit."

"It's ten feet long."

The saw ground through the middle of the pine. He stood

back and then pulled on it until it split at the cut and fell apart.

"And it's also eight feet tall."

He tapped the side of his head with his fingers and placed the hacksaw in my hands.

"Cut the other two sides. I'm gonna make room in the truck."

I cut the rest of the timbers. We piled the scraps by the dilapidated fence, and both grabbed a leg of the dog. I dug my feet into the mud and pulled. It felt even heavier than the night before. We made our way across the grass until the dog was leaning against the side of the truck. We pivoted it halfway onto the tailgate, headfirst as if it were a real dog jumping up onto a countertop. I stood in the bed and pulled the dog while my brother pushed it up and over. I pushed the dog upright and we ran a ratchet strap over its back.

When it was over, I wiped the sweat from my face and jumped over the side of the truck. My brother was drinking a bottle of water and walking backward with his eyes on the dog. When he got back fifteen feet or so he began to fold over himself laughing.

"That's just ridiculous. Your truck looks like a golf cart!"

I shook my head and laughed. I reached my hand out for the bottle of water and turned around towards the truck. It did look ridiculous. Even more so, it looked terrifying. My brother was right regarding the head and tail being tall enough to gap the front cab and tailgate. The head of the dog sat above the front seats and the tail extended several feet out behind the back of the truck. It looked like it was going to bottom out over the back tires.

"Let's get out of here before we have to explain ourselves to anybody."

My brother followed me into the truck, and we took off down the off-ramp. I winced every time we took a turn. If the dog rolled overboard, I had no idea what would happen. I might even get arrested. I didn't care though. The past few days had felt like one long nightmare and I just wanted to get home.

Cars beeped their horns and joggers twisted their heads backward when we passed by. I could hear the feet of the dog jump every time we hit a pothole or bump. When I turned, its feet tipped to one corner and fell back down. Eventually, I got the hang of it. It wasn't all so bad, besides the way it looked. When I dropped my brother off, he continued to laugh in his doorway as he watched me drive away.

I left it in my truck when I got home. I felt like I would fall asleep standing up and the thought of getting it out on my own sounded horrible. As the week droned on, I forgot I'd even left it there. I was stressed and trying to finish up a couple of sculptures in time for the Paradise City Art Festival that would be happening that weekend. It was in Northampton , Massachusetts and I was excited to gain some local traction.

When the night before rolled around, I stood staring at the dog in my truck. I was trying to figure out how I would unload it when it occurred to me: I could just bring it to the show. It was right in Massachusetts, after all. I figured if I could drive it five minutes down the street there was a chance, I could drive it a couple of hours to Northampton. I threw a couple of extra tiedowns crossed its back just to be safe.

When I left for the show my truck was filled to the brim. I stuffed sculptures anywhere I could, and I barely had room to move in the driver's seat. I drove steady in the slow lane the whole way there. Peoples' heads twisted as they passed me. It made me smile. I figured maybe they'd have a story to tell later in the day. Some people didn't react very happily. I got a slurry of beeps and curses thrown at me, but that was alright. I also got mean-eyed by police cruisers along the highway but luckily none of them felt like pulling me over.

When I arrived at the Paradise City Arts Festival, I got out of my truck and introduced myself to the owners, Jeff and Linda Post. They were a lively couple beaming with energy and enthusiasm. They seemed to care about the artists and their art at the show, which isn't necessarily common in the business. They pointed me to where the sculpture pieces would be exhibited.

The show was located on an old fairground, not unlike the fairgrounds I once attended in Topsfield. Some structures and barns were being repurposed to house exhibits and booths. Some of them spilled out into the dirt lot that connected each building. The area where sculpture work was being set up was called "the sculpture garden," and sat along a gravel path on the outskirts of the event. When I pulled my truck up, I realized I was going to have an issue. The sculpture garden was a pathway of small exhibitions woven into different patches of flowers and shrubs. None of the other sculptures took up more space than the average person, and they were pretty close to one another. I wasn't going to be able to fit a ten-foot-long dog by a long shot.

I decided I'd go find Jeff or Linda and explain my situation to them. I was nervous about coming off as a bother. It couldn't be easy coordinating such a large event and I didn't want to damage any possible ties with new people in the business because I brought a massive sculpture without giving any notice.

I sped through the crowds of artists and craftspeople loading in at the center of the show. Finally, I found Jeff talking to a man at a table. The table was a massive piece of live-edge timber. Around it sat various cupboards, dressers, and tables. They were some of the most beautiful pieces of furniture I'd ever seen.

"Hey Dale! This is Ken Salem. He's a furniture maker."

I shook his hand and told him I loved his work. He told me that each piece was made from reclaimed hardwood and I was amazed. I told him I'd dabbled in furniture making with my early work, but that I had sculpted it from metal. He began to explain the stories behind some of the pieces; where the wood came from, what it used to be. I got so sucked into conversations between the two of them I almost forgot about the dog. I jumped when I looked at my watch.

"I'm sorry to be a bother, but I don't think one of my sculptures is going to fit in the sculpture garden."

"What are the dimensions?"

"Ten feet, nose to tail."

I held my breath. I hated to ask favors; especially of people I barely knew. I'd learned enough from early on in life that people liked you best if they didn't have to put any work into being acquainted with you.

"You're right. That definitely won't fit there. But you know, I bet you could move it here—right by Ken's set up, outside the main entrance to the show."

Ken nodded at me. I felt immediate relief and thanked them.

I ran to my truck and pulled up to where I'd be loading the dog off. I pulled some plywood and pine boards I'd brought along and made a ramp off the tailgate of my truck. I inched the dog down the ramp, being careful not to let it slip and catch momentum. It took most of my load-in time to get the dog several feet through the dirt and propped up. Afterward, I scrambled to set up everything else in the sculpture garden as the first patrons began to wander onto the property.

EXIT 48

I sat most of the day without making a sale. I half expected not to when I got there. There was a vast array of great artists there. As I surveyed all of the artists around me, I began to feel intimidated and inspired at the same time. It excited me to realize I walked myself into the upper echelon of trade shows. These people were heavy hitters; an entirely different realm than the markets I frequented with Gene when I first started trying to sell my work.

One particular sculptor that grabbed my attention was Whitmore Boogaert. Like me, he also used mixes of different types of metal. His work included color, though—which I thought was a great touch. Some type of vibrant, powder coat was added to small accents of his pieces. Others were coated entirely in color. Another metal sculptor that impressed me was an artist named Zach Weinberg. His work was in a booth indoors that I found while wandering around. His booth was decorated with various pieces of furniture he built, but what caught my eye most were several mounted metal pieces that had a stained glass look to them. I wondered what type of technique he was using to finish the surface with such interesting, fractal patterns of color.

It wasn't until the latter half of the day when I was strolling around that I noticed somebody looking at the eight by ten-foot dog. I walked over and introduced myself to them. We talked for a good while and when the question of price arose, I shot my shot.

"I'm looking to get $9500 for it."

The man nodded and rubbed his chin.

"I just don't know how I'd get it back to my house."

"I'll deliver it."

I tried to say it with confidence. I thought about the effort it took my brother and me to load it into a truck, and the effort it took myself on my own to move it several feet off my truck.

"Free of charge?"

"Yup. Free of charge."

The excitement started to swell in my chest. This dog costs me so much more time and money to make than anything before, but $9,500 was almost nine times as much as I'd made on my biggest sale prior.

"Could you do cheaper? Say, seven thousand?"

I shook my head at the man. I knew enough from trade shows at this point that people shoot low for the hell of it.

"If we seal the deal here and now, I'd sell you it for eight."

The man tapped his foot and continued to rub his chin. I could tell he liked the dog. I'd noticed that some people become painfully attached to artwork when they see it. It was captivating to watch a person become attached to a piece of work in real-time, and it filled me with pride when it was one of my own.

"Okay—eight grand works. When can you deliver it?"

"Do you live in Massachusetts?"

"Yes, a couple of towns over."

I shook the man's hand.

"Give me a day in between. I'll be there the morning after tomorrow."

When the check was signed, I felt weak in the knees. It didn't hit me until the man had left that I had just made an eight-thousand-dollar deal. I patted the dog along its side and smiled.

When I got home that night there was a voicemail on my answering machine. I sat and listened in the dark to the voice come through the thin speakers. It was somebody from the *Eagle-Tribune*; they were notifying me they did a bit on the dog's attempted theft. It would be in the next issue.

I was awestruck that they would. I wasn't even sure whether anybody noticed my sculpture while it was there. It propelled the dream state the whole following the day. It only wore off the day after when I realized I had to move the dog five hundred feet into its new owner's gated yard.

I had to think quickly. I looked around my garage at what I had. Plywood would be helpful, no matter how I did it. I grabbed the largest sheet of plywood I had and tossed it in my truck. Next, I gathered up some pieces of old six-inch PVC pipe I had laying around. I cut the pipes up into shorter lengths and tossed them in the truck.

When I got there the man looked excited. He greeted me and we exchanged words as I ramped the dog off my pickup as I had for the show. Once he went inside, I began the long journey across his yard with the dog. I dragged the dog on top of the plywood and then shimmed it onto the first pipe. Once it was on the pipe, I gave it a nudge and it rolled onto the next. When I got to the end of the row of pipes, I picked up a few from the back and moved them to the front. After that, I'd slowly push the dog forward and repeat the process.

Doing this inch by inch took over five hours. With installation included, it ate up the whole day. I leaned against it once it was installed, exhausted and relieved it was finally done. I vowed I'd figure out another way to move them. If I wanted to get to the point I was aiming for with my work, I couldn't be spending an entire day moving one sculpture five hundred feet through a yard.

I looked at the dog one more time before I left. I suddenly felt melancholy; I'd grown attached to the dog on the highway. We'd been through a lot at this point together. Nonetheless, I had eight thousand dollars more than I had before—something that seemed unfathomable from a single sale until just yesterday. The notion filled me with excitement, and I felt like I had my mobility back.

When I got back to Haverhill, I picked the paper up at a gas station near my house. I flipped through it until I came across my debut article. It was brief, but it was there in ink and I couldn't believe it. They referred to me as a local artist. It talked about the mysterious vandals who tried to steal an even more mysterious piece of art; a sculpture of a dog that nobody knew anything about on the highway. The end of the article noted that the dog had since disappeared and that the editor was unaware of what exactly happened to it since its attempted theft.

As the week progressed, something strange began to happen. It started with phone calls from relatives. Then it was phone calls from friends, and then strangers. My inbox on my email flooded with names I knew and names I'd never seen. They were all different, but they all wanted to know about the dog on the highway. They called concerned about what happened to it and whether I'd be installing it again. Many of them asked what it was even for in the first place. They wanted to know why it was there, who I was; what the purpose of it or meaning was.

I didn't know what to tell them. I was too dumbfounded with each new call or email to hold up a conversation. I didn't even know most of the people on the other line. I'd thought for so long that my sculpture was ignored and now I was being asked whether I was going to put it back up. I wanted to. That's all I could tell them, and I had no idea what I would do next. The only thing I was sure of was that I no longer owned my eight-foot dog. My other issue was the possibility of people stealing it again. I didn't want to relive that experience and I didn't want to lose a chunk of the money I just made from an easily avoidable mistake.

It also just felt retroactive to put another eight-foot dog up. I wanted to move forward, and stagnation was the enemy. Something was occurring that felt urgent; like a golden key was floating by me I may never see again. The solution to all the issues was simple, and it was something I'd been thinking about since I got the eight grand in my pocket; to up the ante and build a bigger dog.

Dale just after finishing his first 10ft Dog build

Installing the 16ft Exit 48 Dog in 2006

The Big Dog Show heading to one of it's first exhibitions

The original hoist system used to unload the Big Dogs

Students attend a field trip to the Big Dog Show in Haverhill, MA

The Big Dogs on full display in Beverly, MA

The Big Dog Show in Bonita Springs, TX

Dale's Crew after loading a trailer full of 8ft Dogs
(Left to right) Dave Matteson, Andy Talbot, Dale, and Evan Talbot

Dale at his Manhattan Big Dog Gala

Celebrations following the Big Dog Show in Charlestown Navy Shipyard

Dale's crew building the new fleet of dogs for the Phoenix Big Dog Show

Howl-O-Ween Dog Parade in Margret T. Hance Park - Phoenix, AZ

On the road to the Phoenix, AZ Big Dog Show

Dogs on display in Margret T. Hance Park - Phoenix, AZ

10ft Big American Dog at Haverhill High School's A-Wing.

12

Around the time I'd put up the first dog on the highway, people all around the world were tuning in to see the launch of *The Gates,* a massive public art exhibit created by Christo Yavacheff and Jeanne-Claude. *The Gates* consisted of 7,503 steel and vinyl "gates" draped with saffron-colored nylon that spanned across various sections of Central Park in New York City. The exhibit covered twenty-three square miles and used 5,390 tons of steel and had been in the works since 1979. I was amazed by the massive scale of the movement and the endurance and motivation that must've been required to pull it off. The exhibit ran for 16 days in February, 2005 and then ended. When it was over, the news kept talking about it long after. There was something about *The Gates* that impacted me on a deeper level, but I couldn't wrap my head around what the actual point of the exhibit even was.

Months later I'd begun building the new dog for the highway. I'd decided on making the dog sixteen feet tall by twenty-six feet wide, which was double the size of the last one. Embarking into this territory came with a new challenge: the dog would be wider than my entire garage. What's more, I didn't have anything that could transport a sixteen by twenty six-foot piece of art. I racked my brain for a long time trying to figure out what I could do when it occurred to me that connecting the dog's seams was a relatively simple process.

It didn't require any tools that couldn't be moved in my truck, and I could quickly show my brother how to help.

Once I worked out a basic assembly plan, I felt eager to begin. However, before I fell off the deep end I knew if I would keep going bigger, I needed something to move the pieces of the sculpture in. Even unassembled, the pieces wouldn't all fit in the bed of my truck. I landed on buying an old utility trailer in the newspaper classifieds. I could tow it with my truck, and it doubled my carrying space.

I had my transport situation squared away and began sourcing material and designing the new dog. Every dog I'd made prior looked the same, and this one would follow suit. What truly made it different was the amount of work I put into designing the seams. I worked around the clock to ensure that this dog would be the most cost-effective and elegantly designed yet. It would be composed of six separate pieces, which proved challenging to design but would pay off immensely when it came time to move it. I trudged day in and out through the whole design process and months began to feel like years. I continued to receive scattered emails and phone calls inquiring about the dog on the highway and it was making me impatient. I wanted to show the world, but I knew my restraint would pay off.

When I had finally figured out a design that hid the seams and looked perfect, I was reeling with excitement, but as I began the actual build I was struck with waves of fear and anxiety. I had three children now, and a cool eight thousand dollars can solve a lot of dilemmas that come with starting a family. As they grew older, I felt an increasing pressure to provide and knew that my decisions carried weight like they never had before. It's one thing to worry about your own suffering, but when the wellbeing of the people you love are in the balance it becomes unabashedly real.

I spent weeks shaping and welding each piece until I was finally left with six puzzle pieces of the sixteen-foot dog. Aside from the actual amount of metal I had to work with, the sixteen-foot dog was actually much more comfortable to build than the eight-foot. The eight-foot had just barely fit in my shop and I had to climb over and around it constantly, often working for extended periods in awkward and uncomfortable positions. However, when I'd finished the welding it was a bit strange not being able to step back and look at my creation. There wasn't the same type of instant gratification. The anticipation itched at me and I quickly set up a day to install the dog with my brother. When the morning came around that we'd be assembling it, I loaded all of the pieces onto my utility trailer. I tossed the materials and tools I'd need in my truck and drove to pick up my brother.

When we arrived at the Exit 48 off-ramp, I began to set up. I pulled bags of concrete out of my pickup bed and lugged them over to where the old dog used to be. I'd never built a sculpture so giant and had no idea about the logistics of whether it'd stay upright or not. I knew only that it would take out a whole lot more fence if it were to fall or somehow be toppled over. I decided that I'd pour a concrete base for it just in case.

As we mixed and poured the base, I heard a car ease off the road into the grass. Through the windshield, I could see my farther's face smiling. He'd brought my mother and my kids with him to the build site. In my mother's arms was the newest addition to my family; my newborn son Jude. Parker and Tripp held my father's hands as my mother walked up to meet us carrying my new son Jude.

Piece by piece, everybody helped wherever they could as I connected each metal seam of the dog. The day burned away, and everyone stuck around to watch it come to life. My mother brought sandwiches and we ate before adding the last pieces. I was standing next to my brother when he turned to me.

"How're you going to get this thing upright?"

I chewed my sandwich slowly and scanned my brain. I didn't have a definite way to get it standing on its concrete base. I'd managed to finesse my way into moving everything else I ever built on the fly, but this was a different animal. There was no chance of it budging from the lot of us trying to lift it. The bigger my sculptures got, the more the logistical issues like this reared their heads. As soon as I felt like I had everything under control, something would emerge out of plain sight and stop me in my tracks.

"Your father said he had an idea."

I turned to my mother. She shrugged at me and pointed out towards the fields. I could see the shrinking silhouette of my father walking towards somewhere out in the distance.

I looked at my brother and he shrugged too. He had finished his sandwich and wiped his hands on his jeans.

"Might as well put the last pieces together and worry about it later."

I nodded and we got to work. One by one, I pulled the last pieces of metal from the bed of the trailer, and my brother and I connected them. As the last piece went on, I felt a rush of excitement as my children laughed and pointed at the shape of the dog finally materialized. My mother cheered as my brother and I stepped back to get a look at what we've been building all day.

I stared at the dog in the grass. My cheeks began to hurt, and I realized I'd been smiling from ear to ear the whole time I was looking at it. My brother patted me on the back.

"Now we just—"

"Look!"

I followed my mother's gaze out into the road and saw the faded yellow of an excavator passing the corner. Through the haze of exhaust rumbling up from its tracks, I saw my father hanging off the side of it waving.

I knew immediately where it came from. The field we were on shared a property line with Haverhill's resource recovery facility, the Covanta Plant. Many people in the area simply know them as the smokestack with a big, illuminated star visible from the interstate into Haverhill, but my father knew some of the workers well.

When they drew close, I ran up to the excavator and shouted to the man in the driver's seat.

"Thank you so much for doing this. I was in a pinch."

"No problem. All the guys missed seeing the eight-foot dog on their way to work."

I smiled and nodded at the man. It may have seemed small to him, but it meant a lot to me. Sometimes it feels even more precious to know that your art is a small joy in someone's day rather than something immense and profound. People have always told me it is life-changing to see the Sistine Chapel or the Pyramids in Egypt. I'm sure they're right, and the people who brought those things into the world deserve the immortality their work has granted them, but I am not so sure that the only purpose of art is to create a single moment of awe. The food a person eats every day is just as important as the meals they've eaten at five-star restaurants, and if they couldn't eat the food they ate every day I'd reckon it'd affect them more than if they couldn't eat lobster or a nice cut of steak.

It was at first strange to me that people only cared about the dog once I took it down, but I was learning more and more every day the power of missing something once it's gone. As the man in the excavator moved its arm under the dog, I scanned the members of my family standing around and smiling and realized how much I've missed them. I lived so close to my entire family but was almost reclusive about my work as an artist. It involved almost no one else but me and was somewhat of a lonely life traveling the trade circuit. I was beginning to realize that my art itself reflected that. I wanted my life as an artist to always be like this; to be by the side of the people I cared about. I wanted to find a way to bring the art to my family and to bring them to the art. I never applied direct meaning to my work, but I saw now that it was a visual culmination of where I come from; *who* I come from.

 I turned to the highway. I could see the peaking tops of mills and factories over the trees. Haverhill was one of the many New England towns devastated by the collapse of the industrial era. Every person in Haverhill lived in the shadow of a lost time; a time when things were reportedly easier. The shockwave of America's golden age fizzling out hit the farms just as hard, and I often felt for members of my own family as they faced new struggles to keep the farm active in one way or the other. I had a more acute empathy for them now, as I toiled through the years as an artist watching my efforts collapse over and over again. Yet, when I made the occasional trip downtown, I'd often see little budding seeds of hope, like a new restaurant or flowers, hung on the streetlights. It made me feel the same as seeing my brother get a new piece of equipment for the water bottling company, and it made me feel how I felt watching the new dog be titled up onto its concrete base. I imagined what I felt was something all Americans felt on their ways to work when they saw something positive and promising, no matter how little. I knew then I'd name my design *The American Dog*.

In the middle of my daydream, I heard a flurry of car horns piercing the air. I jumped and looked around. My brother was laughing at me while I walked up to him.

"Why are they beeping their horns? Do you think they're gonna call the cops?"

My brother laughed and pushed my shoulder.

"No, you goof. They're happy it's back up!"

I could see the lowering sunlight shining through the center bone cutout out of the dog as it finally stood proud and tall. A car horn rang across the highway, but I didn't turn around. I just kept staring at the sculpture with my family and the worker from Covanta. I thanked him as much as I could and shook his hand as he headed back to the plant.

I went home and slept that night tired from the labor and eased from the peace of mind. The coming months were some of the best I'd had since I decided to be an artist. My new trailer and construction methods eased some of my original issues, and recognition of the dog began to spread like fire. People I'd never met recognized me now at trade shows, and my work began selling more often for better prices. Things were becoming seemingly as stable as the lifestyle would permit, as I was still required to continually travel to sell my work. The traveling in some ways was becoming more difficult the more well regarded I became, as I began to expand outward across the east coast. I could no longer make it home in a single night and spent many nights alone in cheap motels or sleeping across the backbench of my truck.

My constant traveling about the east coast, loading in and out, and mingling with customers and fellow artists were broken up by random spans of boredom and waiting around. Sometimes trade shows would be dead, or I'd be so wound up from the stress and excitement of the day and unable to fall asleep in my truck or whichever motel I was camping out at. To pass the time, I listened to audiobooks on my Mp3 player. I never truly recovered from my poorly addressed learning disabilities, but through the years of emails and documents, I had to sharpen up a bit. I still read at far too slow a pace to chew through novels but yearned to be caught up and on the same page as everyone else.

One night, I laid across the backbench of my truck outside a Walmart. I rubbed the chamfered edge of my Mp3 player and fixed the headphones in my ears. The thin beams of passing car headlights grazed the window and I stared at my reflection as it flickered. I was listening to *The Raven by Edgar Allan Poe.* Most of what I listened to were classics. There were so many I had yet to discover that everybody seemed to know like the back of their hand. I'd download a few audibles of different works I never read in college or high school and would go at my own pace. Sometimes I didn't even pay attention; it just felt right to listen.

I tried my best to use my lack of reading skills to motivate me; to use it as a reason to prove everybody wrong about the kid on the short bus. Sometimes it was difficult to think that way; almost exhausting. Deep down I wanted to be as good as everyone else at reading and writing and I wanted them to know it. Some of the people close to me had tried to cheer me up about it throughout my life by saying I had "creative intelligence," but still, I wondered why I couldn't have the same as them. I felt bound to my work at this point; like if I couldn't create sculptures, I couldn't exist at all.

I began to think about how it is strange that different people are born with different ways of expressing themselves. Some people have a natural inclination towards creating visual things, some through music, and some through writing words on a page. Most often it seems like whatever they're good at pushes them away from being good at the other two. For a moment, I wished I could write instead of creating sculptures. It seemed unfathomable to create something like *The Raven*; I wouldn't know where to begin. I wanted the world to see I could do it, though. I wanted to be held to the esteem of great writers and people who read great writers. It was something unattainable, and that was half of why I wanted it so bad. I shook my head at myself and rolled over. I concentrated hard and tried to tune into Poe, but my mind blurted an idea out at itself. I could incorporate the writing of others into my sculptures.

    I wanted to somehow carve the words into the steel that my sculptures were created out of but doing so would be far too time-consuming. Even if I managed to do it, I could never pull a profit and I'd run the risk of ruining expensive material from a botched letter. When I returned home later that week, I did some digging around for a person or company that could help me get a poem carved out on one of my sculptures.

    I ended up finding a company called Salem Metal Fabricators. They had a laser cutter in their shop and would be able to route out the small and intricate typefaces I planned to use. After I got the quote, the numbers began to run in my head, and I realized that I'd been losing money all along by cutting roughs on my CNC plasma cutter at the shop. They often had to be touched up and the time it took to do so, as well as run the machine itself could be spent doing other things. From then on, I began relaying all my designs to them to cut the individual shapes of my sculptures. After that, I welded them together and connected the seams. They were precise and elegant and allowed me to dedicate more time to new designs.

I had a friend I often talked to at the trade shows. His name was Steven Potts and we'd become close from constantly running into each other. He was a fellow sculptor and made small, intricate vessels from turning exotic woods. They were hypnotizing to look at; almost alien like. I'd sit and watch as people were drawn towards them.

I was at a show set up next to him when I saw him sell one of his pieces for a sum well into the double digits. The woman wrote a check on the spot as he wrapped it carefully for her.

I walked over to his booth to congratulate him. His face was full of color as he neatly packed the check away.

"Not a bad payout, huh?"

He nodded and said with a grin.

"It's definitely going to pay some bills."

I agreed to that and looked at his pieces. They were well beyond the skill of most things I ran into on the trade show circuit.

"What are we doing, Steve?"

"Huh?"

He was carefully placing another piece on display.

"I mean—what's the bigger picture? Look at this stuff you make. It deserves to be in a museum. There has to be a way to break through the ceiling we're under."

He chuckled, wiping the remaining flecks of dust from his sculpture with the bottom of his shirt.

"Well, if you figure out a way to do that you better come back and tell me. Let me tell you this, though—"

He pointed his finger at me with a serious demeanor.

"An artist that takes his eyes off the money is playing a dangerous game. You've got to know *exactly* when to pivot—I mean *exactly*. If you miss your shot, you might lose everything on both ends."

I nodded and crossed my arms. Ever since I built the first dog on the highway, I'd felt a burning in me to move forward. Steven was right, though. There seemed to be a trap every single one of us at these trade events fell into and now we were pinned down. Any error when we tried to make our escape and we'd be done for. I couldn't help it, though. I couldn't stand my own daydreams. *The Gates* was still getting coverage over a year later and it flashed through the backdrop of my life. I thought about it regularly now and began to love everything about the exhibit. The fact that I didn't get it now inspired me, as I began to understand more and more a deeper level of public art, which paradoxically was that grand exhibitions of art didn't have to be profound or pretentious. Art wasn't about enlightening anybody for me; it never was. I didn't think *The Gates* had a point I had to understand at all. I thought it was just something brought into the world to make people's lives a little better one way or the other, and that's all I wanted too.

The more I thought about it, the more I wanted to do something like *The Gates*. I wanted it to be over the top and in everyone's face—not confined to the booth of a trade show. At trade shows, I daydreamt about having my own exhibition until my dream morphed into a monstrous obsession. The momentum I'd been gaining as an artist was like gasoline on a flame. I devised an exhibit that would consist of 100 eight-foot dogs positioned throughout the Boston Common, each one nestled in different shallow hillsides and sidewalks spreading out into Tremont, Park, Beacon, Charles, and Boylston Street. Frog Pond, which sits in the center of The Common, would have several dogs positioned around it as if they were playing by the water. I envisioned people walking between the dogs, either for leisure or on their busy way from the subway to work. I imagined street performers gathering crowds around my sculptures to perform extraordinary feats and children running around my sculptures at Frog Pond in the summer heat. I could see perfectly in my head what it would look like if I were to be standing on the steps of the golden-domed statehouse, staring outward at the multitude of eight-foot dogs scattered about the grass and streets.

I began talking about it to people and they'd give me looks like I was nuts. I had nowhere near the amount of money it would cost to fund the exhibition, but that didn't stop me. One day I hatched the idea to pre-sell the dogs before the exhibition to fund it. The idea filled me with so much excitement that I drew up basic plans and began booking appointments. To my dismay, each appointment proved that the process of doing so would require an immense amount of planning and resources I didn't have. I was being given the runaround by different officials and could feel myself becoming fatigued. Each one told me I would have to first pay for professional consultations that would provide me with presentable documentation on how I would move the sculptures and their temporary and permanent effects on the park and city. They also told me it would be impossible without having a corporate sponsorship and partnership with a non-profit, even if I could somehow gather the funds myself.

Eventually, I got the message they were sending my way. I was discouraged, but not enough to stop scheming. I drove home that night and flicked through the channels. *Rocky* was on. I'd loved the movie ever since I was a kid, but it took up until then to realize why. He was cornered by life and cornered by himself. The only thing that kept him going was that he was too stupid to stay down; too thick-skulled to know when it was time to lay down and die. I knew that was how I needed to be; it was my only way forward and the only way out. If Boston wasn't going to let me exhibit, I would make sure my art circled them like a hawk. My sculptures would still touch a hundred plots of ground, they'd just be mobile. The idea was this, if I broke the exhibition into five different cities all with separate dates, I'd only have to build twenty dogs to get the same amount of placement. They wouldn't be permanent, so I'd avoid a lot of the barriers I hit before. If anybody thought I knew how to take the hint I should quit, they were wrong.

13

I was headed to Naples, Florida from Fort Lauderdale. The heat cooked me through the windshield, and I swatted at gnats while I tried to read the dilapidated signs along Interstate I-75. The road was nicknamed Alligator Alley, as it passed through the everglades and had remained relatively remote since it was first built. My truck was running low on gas and I knew I'd be passing one of the only stations around the halfway point.

When I pulled off to the gas station, I ran the pump and leaned against the side of my truck. A cool breeze ran over my face and I felt my eyes flutter from fatigue. The Florida heat was dense and wet and felt as if I could ply it with my hands. I watched a patch of palm trees struggle to wave in the wind against the backdrop of flat concrete and vibrant, blue southern sky. I'd been spending more and more time along this highway. Naples had become one of my lifelines as an artist. The extravagant oceanfront mansions, courtyards and shopping centers painted in soft pastels housed a population of some of the wealthiest individuals in the United States. Many of them were collectors and patrons of the arts, and I'd built up several relationships with enthusiasts in the area. The city was also a tourism gold mine and many people traveled there with the specific intention of going on a shopping spree. It was too important of a city not to brave the heat and highways.

I heard the pump click behind me. I squinted and read the pay screen; one hundred and fifty dollars to fill my truck. That was the most I'd ever paid for a tank of gas in my life. I shook my head and pressed my forehead into the aluminum of my truck until it burned my skin.

I'd heard the word *recession* be thrown around a lot in the months prior and was truly beginning to understand its meaning. It truly started affecting my life months earlier during the 2008 *Crafts at Lyndhurst* festival in New York. I sat at my booth sipping a coffee and listening to *The Great Gatsby* in one ear on my Mp3 player. It was a sadder book than I'd ever realized; how no matter how hard Jay Gatsby tried, he never became the thing he wanted to be—and all simply because he wasn't born that way. I looked around at the festival's patrons, draped in hand-tailored overcoats, and toting designer handbags. Sometimes as I watched the wealthier folks at trade shows I felt like I was sitting in Gatsby's mansion trying to peddle sculptures. I felt no resentment for them; in fact, I'd become close with many of them and they were good people. It wasn't my place to judge them and they were only benefiting me. They could be spending their money on things much worse, and I was just happy that a few would buy a sculpture and help me live my dream. Still, I couldn't help but feel absurd being caught in the middle of it all.

I swirled the bottom of my coffee. It had become lukewarm sitting in my hands, and I decided I was going to get another. I hoisted myself up from the arms of my seat and noticed something strange. It was hard to pinpoint exactly what, but something was off; like the door had been kicked open and a flood of cold wind had rattled the crowd. Some whispered to each other with beaded eyes darting back and forth about the room. Some stared like statues at their phones and some screamed into them.

I leaned into the booth next door and motioned Steve Potts to come over to me.

"Hey man, you notice something weird going on?"

"You didn't hear?"

I shrugged my shoulders at him and tossed my coffee cup into a trashcan.

"The market just dove. Took the biggest dive since the Great Depression. Half these people just lost their fortunes."

I raised my eyebrows at him. It was a lot to register. I couldn't think at the moment how it would trickle down and affect the entire country. I thought about my old friend Gene and hoped he was alright.

"Well before anything, I need another coffee."

I walked through the crowd avoiding eye contact with people. I began to think about my friends and family back home. How would this affect us? I wondered if the country was going to fall into a state of collapse; some post-apocalyptic state like I'd seen in movies growing up.

When I got to the food tent, I filled my cup with coffee and sipped it to myself. I started to feel more and more nervous the more I thought about what was happening. What's more, some guy was staring at me while I tried to enjoy my coffee. I finally turned my head and looked at him.

"This suit—"

The man leaned in, his stool practically tipping over.

"This suit cost four grand. Now I'm worried about buying a beer."

He turned back to the bar and crashed his elbows onto the table. I watched his head drape against a rack of candy bars. When I returned to my booth, Steve yelled over to me.

"Hey, Dale,"

I walked over to him, and he dropped his voice to a whisper.

"I'd say it might be time to take a chance on something new, considering we could be screwed either way."

I agreed.

By now, the sixteen-foot dog had been standing at Exit 48 for a couple of years. The months leading up to the recession had been good to me. I spent each week with my pedal to the floor, headed to different cities on the east coast. In many ways it made me feel like I was on an endless bike ride home. The physical and immediate stress kept my mind clear and straight. I loved the moments in between the chaos where I could sit in the bed of my truck and take in the world around me.

I had met a plethora of artists from all over the country and the world. As I befriended each and saw the different corners of the coastline, inspiration gripped me over and over again. I designed heaps of new sculptures. Many of them were in the same vein and style as *The American Dog*. Some were abstract and ventured into new territories, but I remembered not to forget the sentiment I found with the dog. In all of its simplicity, there was something about The American Dog that spoke to people like none of my sculptures before.

Nonetheless, I still tried out new things. One specific style I began to experiment with is multi-faceted sculptures. These sculptures contained many small faces welded together at different angles to create a three-dimensional structure. It was very challenging in every way. Designing them on software and then executing them in real life required close attention to every angle of every facet, as they could very easily become warped and lopsided if not meticulously done.

I always felt like I didn't even have a second to breathe, but it felt good for my greatest problem to be time. Being unable to create as many sculptures as I wanted to was much better than having a garage full of ones I couldn't sell. The fear of failure and going broke began to subside, but as I began to settle into greater comforts, I felt a shadow looming overhead. There was a feeling as if everything was going too well in everybody's life. The country had been in a confusing conflict for years and advances in technology and culture shook up nearly every professional vocation. Yet, things remained upwardly mobile and people seemed to be living better than ever before. Old friends I'd run into had told me about the loans they'd taken out for homes and cars and boats and it all felt wrong. I knew something was bound to break as I traveled to each trade show and reaped the benefits of people's increasing willingness to part with a few bucks.

I shook it off and lived in the moment as everybody else did. I'd taken advantage of the surpluses in cash to slowly upgrade my shop. With Salem Metal Fabricators handling the initial cutting of sheets of metal, my plasma cutter was sold off. Old tools were replaced with new tools; pieces of equipment I definitely shouldn't have been using were cycled out and replaced with something more robust and industrial. I also had my eyes on a new trailer for my exhibition that was slowly cooking to a boil.

Like everybody else, it shook my life up when the market crashed. People became less able to spend money on the less "essential," joys of life, like artisan and craft goods. The actual cost of being an artist became more expensive. I spent ridiculous amounts to move my pieces across the country and paid what would've once been considered premiums for steel and other building materials. Still, I felt grateful for my position when I saw other people's lives. I was my own boss and couldn't be laid off. As long as I could flip one more sculpture, I was still afloat. I still made enough sales to keep my head above water, even if it wasn't as great as before.

All things pass, and I knew that eventually, the economic nightmare would subside. It drove me all the more to pursue the exhibition. I knew it was much better to begin planning an exhibition during a recession than for the market to tank in the dead middle of it. It made me feel less bad about splitting my time thinner at trade shows to focus on planning, and I was praying that I'd hit the timing just right so that the nation would be in a state of euphoria after surviving a recession. If we didn't recover from it, my exhibition wouldn't matter so much anyway.

Ever since I'd been denied from exhibiting a hundred dogs in Boston, I'd spent years undergoing the process of planning my touring exhibition. I didn't have anywhere near the finances back when I decided, and I spent my time putting a little bit of money aside from each sale to bolster the amount of money I'd have to play with. I eventually began the tedious process of contacting each city and convincing them to let me exhibit my art for a day. It was difficult and often a winding loop of speaking with multiple officials, but I kept reminding myself that *The Gates* took decades to accomplish and I was making good time in that regard. I thought about *The Gates* a lot in my daily life now to keep me going. Many people I knew were opposed to the exhibition and tried to talk me out of it. They were convinced it'd be a financial nightmare; especially during such trying times. The worst part was I couldn't refute them; I had no idea how it would turn out, but I couldn't get it out of my head. The recession showed me all the more that the lifestyle I was living was volatile anyways.

Each dog was as tedious to build as the first eight-footer I put on the highway. I found myself climbing on top of the pieces, weaving under and over the legs and tail to connect seams. The fact I had to build twenty of them made it feel more like a job at an assembly line than anything. My nerves ran hot after the first few dogs. Sometimes I would break out into a fit and yell at the dog I was working on. I'd pause and look up at the insulation on the ceiling and shake my head. Maybe I was crazy.

My garage was too tiny to do more than one piece at a time, so they came together one by one and I rolled them out into my front lawn to get them out of the way. Through the months the army of dogs grew. I hadn't noticed how strange it looked until I was already halfway through building them. I stepped outside to check for a place to put the tenth dog and paused for a moment. The other nine dogs looked outward to the street in a neat row, filed like marathoners along a starting line. It sent a jolt of excitement through me.

Around the halfway mark, I also realized that there'd come a point where I simply couldn't keep moving forward without help. I was losing money between trying to complete the exhibition pieces and trying to manage my income from trade shows. Every moment spent on one of the dogs was a moment pulled away from making something I intended to profit off of.

I thought for a long time if I could risk hiring employees. I thought about who I should hire; what they should do. The first thing I settled on covering was somebody to handle the logistics of things. My shop was scattered with receipts and scribbled addresses, payment records, phone numbers, and event dates. I could barely find time to work on my sculptures between trade shows, never mind keep books and coordinate deliveries.

I ended up finding a woman named Allisa Rudden that would help me. I hired her right before the recession hit. She was managing accounts for multiple other clients and I heard about her through a friend. We settled on having her work one day a week for me to manage money coming in and out. Eventually, I tried to explain The Big Dog Show to her. She had asked about the row of them in my yard.

"I'm going to tour New England with twenty of them."

She stuck her head out the garage door and then looked back at me.

"Aren't they all the same?"

"Yes, that's the point!"

She squinted her eyes and nodded slowly.

"Just wait. It's hard to explain but it'll make sense when you see it."

She smiled politely and went to work organizing my mess of finances. Eventually, as she became accustomed to working with me once a week and I think I porved that I was keeping the ball rolling with my artwork. I asked her to work more days of the week when I began to hit brick walls with the big dog show. She was apprehensive at first, but I eventually convinced her to help me sort out the show. She also helped me manage other logistics such as delivery dates, promotion, and communication back and forth with potential clients and organizers.

Around this time, I also began teaching a young kid, Andy, the basics of welding and working with metal. He worked on the farm for a few years and his mother knew a few family members of mine. He loved art himself, and his mother told me he was meticulous about his own art and work at the farm. He sounded like a great fit.

EXIT 48

As the months drew closer, we all began to feel like a team. I liked having people in the shop around me and I liked that I could share the excitement with someone. The first city to answer us back was our own. I knew Haverhill would be the easiest to get on board, but it was no less shocking when the first stone was finally cast. It was going to happen, so long as we could pull it off.

I'd spent months strategically planning which cities to shoot for. I made sure that every city I'd be hitting could be reached within a single day, to keep the large financial burden as low as possible. At the same time, I wanted to space them far enough apart from each other that I would have an even spread of interest for as long and far as possible.

From a publicity standpoint, Portsmouth was the prize of the bunch. It was a small, near-ancient town on the ocean a little north of the New Hampshire and Massachusetts border. As far as New England towns go, it was a tourist powerhouse. Many people from the easternmost New England states spent their summers there lounging in bars and perusing the different seaside shops that come and go. For how quaint and traditional looking of a town it was, it was also particularly well known for its happenings in the music and the arts, and many of the city's residents were artists themselves.

Similar to Portsmouth, Newburyport would also pack a punch in terms of publicity and location. Newburyport was a town similar to Portsmouth, but much closer to some of the most popular beaches in New Hampshire and Massachusetts. People often spent the day at the beach and then headed to Newburyport to enjoy the downtown area and its food, bars, walkways, and public events.

Other towns on the prospective list included Lowell, North Andover and Andover. They were all right in the Merrimack Valley and each had their advantage. Moving further into the North Shore area, I focused on Beverly, Massachusetts, and its college atmosphere. Finally, I wanted to make it a three-state exhibition and hit a city or two in Maine, so I decided to contact Kittery and Ogunquit and see what sticked.

My confidence in the show was slightly crippled when I received swift rejections from Andover and North Andover. They were the cities I cared for least, but I'd anticipated they'd be easiest to win over out of the bunch. I felt like there was a constant pit in my stomach as I waited for answers from the rest of the cities. I'd already begun building dogs and dumping large sums of money into preparing for the exhibition and frankly had no idea what I'd do if they turned me down.

I tried to think a lot about the little things that would make or break the exhibition. I knew enough by now from trade shows that it was always a match that lit the whole house ablaze. An exhibition would be much less forgiving.

I took the plunge on a larger trailer. There was no way around it, and although I knew I'd eventually need it regardless, it hurt to watch the money disappear. Nonetheless, my new trailer could carry four times as many dogs as my old utility trailer.

Next, I thought about how I'd manage to transport and move twenty dogs into position in a single day. I ended up welding custom pushcarts specifically designed for the dogs. I equipped them with off-road tires to account for different terrains I'd be moving them across. It still wasn't easy to move them, but it made moving them possible. Next was figuring out how I was going to get them off the trailer. I was staring at it in my driveway, the dogs baking in the summer heat behind it. I pictured something like a pulley in my head.

"Good news!"

Allisa car was scaling my driveway, her head hanging out the window. My mind froze up immediately and I forgot why I was standing and staring at my trailer.

"Portsmouth and Newburyport are both on board!"

I didn't believe her at first. For all the time I thought about the exhibition, it never seemed completely tangible. It was almost as if a part of me was expecting for it never to happen at all—and to some degree took comfort in that dismal thought. Every defining moment of a person's life requires courage in one way or the other. My old self didn't want to believe her. Believing her would drag it into existence. I'd long put that version of myself in the passenger seat though, and I practically jumped in the air when Allisa's words registered in my head. There was no turning back now.

In the coming months, the other cities followed suit. Having Portsmouth and Newburyport in the bag proved to give me significant leverage in converting other cities. I'd broken the old catch twenty-two of needing someone to agree before anyone would at all.

The days dwindled like a chisel on marble. We ran an advertising campaign across New England, mailing out flyers and brochures anywhere we could. I put posters up around downtown and asked friends and family to spread the word. We'd worked out an official schedule. Starting August 5th, 2009 I'd move week to week between six New England towns exhibiting twenty *American Dog* sculptures. From there, we were working on securing later dates outside New England.

An immense amount of planning happened before the exhibition dates. Multiple events were planned out and secured for the time spent in each city. Supply lists and time frames were written, thrown away, and rewritten. No matter the amount I tried to plan everything out, I felt nowhere near ready when the day of reckoning rolled around. When the calendar read August 4th, I paced and yelled like my hair was on fire. In twenty-four hours, I'd be embarking on something I'd spent years anticipating. I couldn't tell if I was excited or sick to my stomach; so many paychecks and hours of work, inside the shop and out, were riding on this.

    We loaded the dogs onto anything we had that could move them. My old utility trailer ended up carrying four of them, lined up head one facing the opposite direction of the other and overlapping the baseplates at its feet. My new trailer held the remaining sixteen. Once the dogs were loaded in, I began to feel nerves run up my spine. The axles of the trailer were much farther back than I'd noticed before. I looked back at my truck in the driveway. It was over a decade old at this point and was practically screaming out for the abuse to stop. I'd taken it across the east coast over and over again, each time filling its bed with tools and sculptures and often towing a trailer filled with even more. The placement of the trailer's axles left a tremendous amount of unsupported weight between my truck and any support the trailer would offer. My truck was never designed for the limits I'd pushed it to in the first place, and now I'd be attempting to pull sixteen times the weight I usually subjected it to with little help from the trailer.

    It would have to do. It was easy to not think about it since I had plenty of other things to panic over. Suddenly, the past decade of my life felt like a blur. So much had happened, and I felt like I'd just barely managed to keep a grip on the world around me. Every gallery that ever denied me seemed to wash away and seemed without purpose to any bigger picture. I'd be bringing my dogs out into the world

EXIT 48

whether I liked it or not. It terrified me. I kept reminding myself it was what I always wanted. I asked for it, over and over again. No turning back now; the world would have its chance to take a look at the last two decades of my life and tell me what it thinks— starting with the place I grew up, bright and early.

14

    I've traveled the road from my house to the Bradford Common my whole life. Countless times I've turned onto Route 125 and traveled the winding stretch of road spotted with Industrial Buildings, Dunkin Donuts, and Gas Stations until coming up to the local businesses such as Academy Lanes and Ari's Pizza. It was spots like them that defined my youth, wasting free afternoons away over French fries and a soda. Beyond that, the old colonial homes of Haverhill's past still stand tall and teem with inhabitants outside in their wilted lawns on hot afternoons. The ancient homes are intertwined with budding nail salons and shops, along with the aging brick-laden remains of what was once the renowned Bradford College.

    Finally, the Bradford Common sits facing the Basiliere Bridge, which bleeds into mainland Haverhill. The Bradford Common is a small, grassy piece of land canopied by trees. Several benches and a beautiful white Gazebo rest inside the park. It is surrounded by road; one of which serves as a connecting offshoot to the large, colonial-era church that towers in the park's backdrop. The church is immensely tall for one of its style. The steeple reaches up above its large arched doors like a needle puncturing the sky above it. It's an immaculate white but shows little signs of chipping and wear as every building in New England does with each coming winter.

    I sat for a moment in my truck parked on that street thinking about each of these things. Something about the drive there, two trailers filled with twenty dogs in tow, felt foreign to any time I've driven it before.

I took a deep breath and let my nerves settle a bit. My watch read eight AM. Dew speckled the greenery and sidewalk and I could hear sparrows chirping up in the belltower above me. I was happy to be early and had prayed the whole two-mile stretch nothing catastrophic would happen between my truck and my trailers. When I stepped out and saw the bow at the hitch of my truck, I felt lucky to be alive. I'd have to figure something out before the exhibition moved on to Portsmouth.

In preparation for the exhibition, I'd invented a device to help me unload the dogs from the trailer. It consisted of several I-beams, nylon straps, and a chain hoist. It was one of the most integral tools for the whole operation. I'd create a frame from beams above the trailer by shoring them up with ratchet straps. I'd connect a chain hoist to an I-beam overhead supported by the frame to run it on a makeshift "track." Then, I would strap one nylon strap around either end of the internal bone cutout on a dog, clip them together, and lift it into the air via the hoist. I could then run it along the upper beam until it was off the trailer. It was rickety and unconventional, but it worked.

The first dog seemed as if it took all day. I had them pressed up against each other right up to the edge of the trailer. I had to balance on what little space I had and fight with the sculptures to get the strap of the chain hoist around the first dog. I could feel the stress riding up on me but if I moved too quickly, I'd send the dogs toppling on top of me off the edge of the trailer.

Once I got the first dog secured, I hoisted it the few inches off the ground it needed to be and backed it off the trailer's edge. From there, I carefully lowered it down onto the ground. It was nine AM by the time it touched the concrete. When I heard the steel feet clang against the ground, I sighed and jumped down off the trailer. I sat and leaned my back against my truck's fender. The thought of moving nineteen more for multiple weeks seemed scary to me, but I knew the rest would be easier than the first. I pulled myself up to look for a bottle of water and noticed something strange. People had begun to gather around the trailer. A woman and her teenage daughter had walked over to see what was happening. They circled the sculpture curiously.

"Did you make the dog on the highway?"

The mother was craning her head and looking at the trailer. She walked with her arms crossed and began looking at the contraption I built to get them down.

"Yeah, that's my dog."

She laughed and smiled.

"One of them is going in The Common?"

"Yes. Well—all of them are for a little bit. It's an exhibition."

"Oh! What is the exhibition called?"

I jumped up into the trailer and grabbed the hoist strap.

"We're calling it *The Big Dog Show*."

She told me it was a fitting name. As I fed the straps through the bone cut out of the second dog, I heard her calling her daughter over from talking to a friend. I looked back and the woman was still looking at me.

"My name is Mary, by the way. This is my daughter, Rebecca."

"I'm Dale. It's nice to meet both of you."

I paused for a moment. I wanted to talk to Mary longer, but she was already walking away. I looked up at the dogs still on my trailer and felt a jolt of urgency bring me back to my work.

By the time the first few were off the trailer, I couldn't stand it anymore. I wanted to see them set up around the park. I unloaded one of the carts I'd built and slid it under the belly of one of the dogs. I wheeled the cart through the common and looked around. I tried to think like a dog; where I'd want to be on a day like this. I set it over by one of the park benches where people were beginning to enjoy their day.

The most tasking aspect of setting up each dog was moving and installing their baseplates. The base plates were five feet by twenty inches long and made of quarter-inch steel. They were necessary to keep the dogs stable. The only issue with them was that the stability they provided came from the fact they were a hundred pounds each. I'd rack two at a time on a dolly and wheel them around the park, dropping them off and dragging them into a position to mount the dogs.

By eleven I had eight dogs in position, and by three o'clock I had set up sixteen of them. People began wandering around the park with their necks craned. I began to have to answer questions while I set up. Most of the time it was, "Why?" Although they didn't understand it, they still spoke to me about it in a curious way. This was a new perspective on my work that I was receiving from people. Most often if they didn't understand it, they viewed it in a negative light.

The street surrounding all sides of The Common provided excellent exposure. I hadn't realized it until the last few dogs were bolted into the ground, but just as many people in cars were responding to the dogs as in the park. They must've recognized the design from the one on the highway, as they would beep their horns or wave as they passed by.

All of the dogs were up by five PM. I sat sprawled across a park bench exhausted. I knew I could only lay and close my eyes for a second; I wanted to engage with interested pedestrians as much as possible. I went up and spoke to many people and everybody seemed to only have good things to say. I felt a beam of pride glowing in my chest.

My family stopped by that night. I saw friends I'd talked to days ago and friends I hadn't talked to in years. Nothing felt more right than catching up with them and being in the presence of something I spent years culminating.

When I got home that night, I could barely keep my eyes open. I had loaded all my tools and supplies in my truck and left the dogs in their temporary home for the week. The next few days were a dream. People seemed genuinely interested in my work, and even better it seemed to bring them genuine and simple happiness. I thought the exhibition looked great under the trees of The Common. My sculptures almost looked like real dogs enjoying their day in the park. Their larger than life appearance gave off the impression that a passerby was an observer in the life of the dogs. I couldn't have been happier.

Still, a pressing problem troubled me. Between the dogs' weight and the size of my truck, putting them back on the trailer scared me. I couldn't imagine it'd make it to Portsmouth without something giving out. It was still dark on Saturday morning when I began jacking up the trailer in my front yard. After I had the trailer suspended, I loaded a fresh disk into my angle grinder. The axles sat too far back on the trailer and didn't offer enough support, since the majority of the dogs sat between it and the hitch of the truck. After a lot of quick thinking, I decided the most logical move would be to move the axles forward, balancing out the trailer's weight better.

The silhouettes of my newest and oldest sculptures loomed around my yard. It was strange how many of them sat around me now. Sometimes it felt like it was just yesterday I was trying to slap together a wine rack at the farm. Sometimes it felt like centuries ago; especially when I thought about the big dog show. I wondered what my past self would think of me if he could see me gearing up to cut through the axles of a trailer so I could lug twenty metal dogs across New England. I'd tell him he didn't know the half of it.

I looked at my equipment strewn next to me. I didn't know much about vehicles and trailers, but the swap seemed simple enough. The trailer didn't have much going on underneath: a couple of axles, springs, rear brakes, and two big support beams that ran down the middle.

I tore into the steel with the angle grinder. The stones in the ground dug into my back as I burned through discs and the orange sparks bounced around the early morning. I shifted positions over and over trying to find a way to work. It took me until eight-thirty to finally free the axles from the trailer. I crawled out from underneath covered in grass stains and metal shavings. I felt like going back to bed, but I had to be at The Common in an hour.

I worked Sunday night into Monday morning to weld the axle further up the trailer. In the back of my mind, I began to think about Wednesday. I didn't know how we'd load all twenty dogs in one night and make it up to Portsmouth. I'd underestimated the time it took to set up and break down.

The trailer didn't look pretty, but it seemed sturdy enough. I was already running late but wanted to see how it held up before I took it back to The Common. I hitched it up to my truck and took it for a spin around the neighborhood, trying to listen closely for anything going wrong. It drove just as smooth as before and took turns just fine. After my test drive, I drove it up the driveway.

It helped me relax for the rest of the day. I sat watching people enjoy themselves in the park. It was slower than the weekend. At one point two siblings crossed by with their parents in tow. It was a brother and sister; the sister pushed her brother down in front of me and he fell into the grass.

"I'm the king of the dogs!"

Her brother was recovering from the attack while she jumped up and down and proclaimed a dominion over the dogs. I couldn't help but smile and laugh. It made me happy to see kids incorporating the dogs into their imaginations and games. I thought about my brother and me and when we were little; about all the landmarks around the farm and city that became part of our imaginary world. It's the best chapter of life until a person has their own children and watches them live through it too.

I spent the rest of the day laughing at dogs that came by on their leashes. They'd walk up perplexed by the sculptures and I'd imagine in my head they were impressed by the metal figures that looked like them. As the crowds fizzled out to lone dog walkers, I came to grips with reality and decided I'd pack up Tuesday instead of Wednesday. We advertised all along the show would be in town until Wednesday, but I wasn't sure anybody would miss it much anyway. Even if they did, there was simply no way we could pull off Portsmouth on time if we kept the dogs up to the last moment.

Consequently, the next day became the last day of the first stop for the Big Dog Show. I brought my father to spend the day with me.

"I have to cut the Haverhill dates short. I can't pack up and set up in Portsmouth in one day."

"Well, that's understandable."

My father was walking next to me and stopping to look at each dog. He took his time looking at each one, even if they were all the same.

"I just have been running into so many issues already—five minutes away from home."

He shrugged and tapped one of the baseplates of the sculptures with his foot.

"Big projects mean big problems."

It was a good way to think about it. Later that day, I explained to him the situation with the axle. I told him I already took the trailer driving and that it didn't give us trouble on the way there. I could tell he was apprehensive. It didn't seem urgent enough to change his mood, so I figured it shouldn't change mine either.

The next day my father came to spend the day while we packed up. To help me pack up I'd enlisted my helper, Andy. His help made things move along faster and I was happy to have a little extra time. Nevertheless, it still took much longer to load everything up than we anticipated while planning the exhibition. I was happier leaving a day early than setting up a day late.

When everything was loaded up, my father hitched the small trailer to his truck, and I hitched the larger to mine. I drove slowly down Route 125 with him trailing behind me. Everything was moving, which was a good start—but something felt wrong. The trailer felt like it weighed ten times more than it did before.

"Something's no good."

I tried to call my father to ask him what the trailer looked like from behind, but he didn't pick up. I kept trying to peer through my mirrors and keep an eye on everything. It was hard to see through the dogs blocking the back window. When the road opened up into a long stretch, I gave my truck a little more gas and let it accelerate. Suddenly I felt something pull me towards the center lane from behind. I swung my head around and saw tire smoke kicking up into my back window. I could see the shape of the trailer veering through the smoke, veering and making a horrible noise. The sound of the dogs rattling punched the glass, and my steering wheel began to kick back at me as I pounded the breaks hard. My tires skipped and sent an old cup of coffee flying across the passenger seat. I swung the truck into the grass and prayed while the trailer slugged behind.

    I grabbed a flashlight out of my center console and got out of the truck. As I approached the trailer, I started coughing. The air was hot and smelt like burnt rubber. I got on my back and slid under the trailer's bed, shining the light above me and under it. A support beam under the trailer was pressing down on the tires. The weight of the dogs had sent it downward, and I hadn't accounted for the space it needed to flex and move with the suspension. It was essentially acting as a massive emergency break. I had no shot of making it home, never mind Portsmouth tomorrow.

    I jumped up into the trailer and began lifting the hundred-pound baseplates one by one. I tossed each one into the bed of my truck and sprinted on after the next. Sweat began to pool down my face in the heat and I could feel my body straining. I fell to my knees in the mud and shined the light under the trailer at the support beam. It was still pressing against the tires; moving the baseplates hadn't done a thing.

    I through the flashlight against the pavement and ran my hands through my hair. My father pulled his truck off the road behind me and stood nearby with his hands at his hips. He looked enveloped in thought, his foot tapping in the grass on the side of the road.

"How long did it take you to weld that thing up?"

"Eight—nine hours."

He let out a sigh and shifted his stance.

"No, no, that won't do. We'll be halfway to jail by then."

I picked up the cracked flashlight and crawled back under the trailer. I peered around for a solution. There was nothing I could do that wouldn't take an entire day besides one thing.

"I could cut pieces of the support beam out."

"Something tells me it's there for a reason."

My father sighed and looked at me while I crawled out from under the trailer.

"But I suppose that's the best bet."

I told my father I had an oxy-acetylene torch in my garage. He took his truck to drop off the smaller trailer and to dig around for it. It was a portable kit I bought a while back and barely used. I thanked God now I did and prayed there was gas in the tanks.

I sat on top of one of the wheel wells and looked out at the passing cars. I couldn't keep my foot from tapping and felt sick to my stomach. Having to wait made me feel worse; I wished I could keep busy to offset the intrusive thoughts about the show in its entirety. I'd destroyed one of the most expensive assets of The Big Dog Show before it even left town. What's more, I needed to get everything moved to Portsmouth tomorr morning. My old utility trailer barely worked and I'd yet to figure out a good way to move the dogs long distances on it. I could feel the expounding weight of problem after problem already sitting on my chest like a ton of bricks. I wondered if it would get easier. I was beginning to see that progression didn't equate to relief, and more often than not just brought more stress and challenges.

I saw my dad's truck swing around the tree line and pull onto the grass. My father got out with the torch and the two corresponding tanks. I immediately got to work torching a section of the metal beam. Black smoke filled the underside of the trailer and caught the wind, traveling up in a flume over the road.

"Somebody's gonna think we're burning alive."

My father paced back and forth behind me. I could hear him digging through my truck. My body began to sink into the mud beneath me and the smoke and torches heat stung my skin. I saw my father's legs walk towards the trailer, a padded blanket dangling by his feet. He began to wave the blanket wildly and the smoke dispersed in little turbulences around the trailer.

The beam was beginning to get hot. I dumped a gallon of water from my truck on the trailer's wooden bed and splashed it underneath. Steam danced up with the smoke. I kept cutting away at the beam until it got so hot, I was worried it'd melt through the tires it was pressing against. I pulled my truck forward and the front of the beam fell into the grass. I rolled back underneath and hit the next spot at the back end of the trailer. Water pooled in a crevice in the ground and I felt my clothes become heavy. My father shielded the sparks and flames from onlookers in traffic and I prayed neither of us would get clipped by a car. I didn't know whether there'd be enough gas for my torch. If the torch gave out then and there on the last part of the supports, I'd probably curl up and die right on the side of the road. I just made it; the second section of metal gave way and the trailer squealed and lurched forward.

I laid in the puddle and closed my eyes. I could hear molten debris simmering out around me. When I managed to get myself to

EXIT 48

stand up, I packed everything as quickly as I could and left before my bad luck got worse. I met up with my father at the farm to thank him. When I pulled in, he was stepping out of the door of his truck slowly, laughing to himself. We talked for a while about life and our family. He could tell I wasn't feeling too hot and told me a few stories about the farm. Before he went inside, he turned to me and put his hand on the side of his truck.

"Big projects mean big problems."

He began to walk slowly towards his front door, his hand pointed in the air with his back to me now.

"But the show must go on."

I smiled and shifted my truck into drive. When I left, I could see him in my rearview still waving. He was right; it had to still go on. I was happy he told me that because I wasn't sure I would've told myself.

The next day came quicker than I would've liked, but I was excited and as ready as I could muster up the strength to be. My son Parker would be coming for the ride and Andy would be moving the smaller trailer. I tossed my bicycle between the dogs on the trailer.

"You ready?"

Parker nodded, his helmet already strapped to his head. I unclipped it from under his chin.

"You don't need that quite yet."

I rubbed the top of his head and threw the helmet in. Andy was at the bottom of the driveway. I gave him the thumbs up and he started his truck we'd borrowed from the farm. I started mine and we were off.

We took I-495 up to the city limits. I towed the big trailer behind me and listened to the steel feet of the dogs shake the trailer's wood bed. I'd decided to test my luck taking it on the highway with one less support beam underneath. It seemed to be working fine; much better than before I cut them out. It was a relief to me in the intense summer heat of the morning. My truck was filled with hot air locked behind the windows. The sound of the dogs rattling became a homogenous drone and I tried to keep my eyelids from fluttering. I hadn't slept all night; my nerves were frayed from loading up the dogs the day before and the previous trailer mishap, but my body was screaming at me to go to sleep. My back ached and I couldn't decide if it was from being on the ground too much or being on my feet.

I focused hard on the road in front of me to keep my eyes open. I tried to lock in on the utility trailer that Andy was towing a little ways ahead. Suddenly I noticed a problem. My utility trailer sat relatively low to the ground. Consequently, they have to be hitched up to a truck at an angle. The slope and increased speed of the highway was dragging the dogs backward towards the edge of the trailer, their hind legs nearly touching the whirring concrete below.

"Dammit."

Parker looked at me confused. I rolled my window down and sped up to Andy. I leaned half my body out of the truck and fought against the vacuum of wind.

"Pull over! Pull over at the next exit!"

I waved my arms at him like a madman. He turned his head back at me and then took a glance at the dogs. I saw his eyes bug out of his head for a moment as he read my lips and nodded.

Luckily, there was a rest stop right on Haverhill's border. I pulled up behind the utility trailer and got out. I began to think about the show. We were working on such a tight schedule that even a small mistake would affect setup. Andy got out of his truck and came around the back of the trailer. He tried to push the dogs forward as I walked up to him.

"I'm gonna need help moving them."

"We can't do it like that. We don't have time."

He held his watch up to his face and tried to read it in the glare. He exhaled heavily and picked at his shirt. The heat was rising from the parking lot and the air smelt like tar. I tried to think through it—tried to pluck a direction out of the current of wind brushing out from the highway.

"Bump them with the truck."

Andy and I both turned around. Parker was standing behind us pointing at the fender of my truck.

"*What* them?"

"Bump them!"

Parker might've been on to something. I looked at my truck. It was a truck that spent its life in New England and had suffered years of winter salt and pothole littered Massachusetts streets. There was no point in trying to save a little paint on the bumper.

"He's right. Good thinking, buddy."

I fist-bumped Parker and then threw my keys to Andy.

"Bump them forward. Don't slam into them or anything. Just give them a little tap."

He looked apprehensive and began moving cautiously backward towards my truck. It seemed like he was waiting for a punchline.

"Parker and I will stay here on lookout duty."

He got into my truck and eased it forward. I waved him in while scanning the street for any curious highway patrol. I had no idea whether there were laws about moving things back and forth in the way we were, and it'd throw the day into havoc if I had to answer questions. The truck got up an inch or so from the dogs and Andy hesitated.

"Keep going—slow and steady."

It lurched forward and the bumper made contact with the back heels of the dogs. I waved and nodded to keep him from stopping. Eventually, the dogs moved forward all together up towards the front of the trailer. I gave him the thumbs up and he jumped out of the car.

"We haven't even made it out of town yet. They're gonna slide back down again." I nodded and rubbed my chin. There seemed like there had to be a better way of going about this, but I knew there wasn't. We'd have to keep stopping and inch our way up to Portsmouth.

"We'll just have to keep doing this until we make it."

Andy walked around the front of the truck to the driver's door whistling.

"Well, there's a big parking lot by the liquor outlet in Hampton—and a few gas stations in between."

"You're right. Just stay in the right lane in case we lose one."

His face went white for a moment. I felt mine do the same as I backed up to my driver's door and pictured one of the sculptures skipping across I-95 at sixty miles an hour.

We made it work the rest of the way there, stopping every ten of the forty or so minutes it took to get to Portsmouth. By the time we'd nudged the dogs back forward for the third time, I could smell the ripe water of New England salt marshes. It's not a particularly good smell, but it's a smell that has brought a smile to my face since I was little. I imagine all New Englanders share that sentiment. The beaches of Salisbury, Hampton, Rye, and upward are encompassed

EXIT 48

by miles of these salt marshes. The spoiled smell is a greeting to many from the area; a promise of an anticipated day by the frigid Atlantic eating fried dough or walking along a jetty. The smell only becomes better as one drives closer towards the ocean. It becomes muddled in the exhaust of motorcycles and battered classic cars; the smell of food cooking and cigars and sunscreen. It never failed to calm me down or pick me up from whatever worry I had.

Once we got off the interstate onto Route 1, the dogs stopped shifting around so much. We cruised into the heart of Portsmouth, weaving through the century-old streets between passing pedestrians and bicyclists, past the old brick buildings and emerging sleek shop fronts. People from many surrounding towns came to Portsmouth to spend days and nights lounging. It was a social hub for New Hampshire towns like Rochester, Dover, Exeter, Newington, and Rye. It was a short way from the Maine border as well so plenty of people came down from Kittery, Eliot, and York. Consequently, the city was filled with life throughout the day and night. When I passed the streets filled with people, I was a little sore that the exhibition wouldn't be downtown, but when we arrived at the sight, I saw that we couldn't have been offered better. The exhibition was going to be on a little island off the city's south side called Pierce Island.

The island was filled with rolling meadows, salt marshes, and rocky cliffs. The scenery was breathtaking and as I jumped out and began undoing the first straps, I became filled with excitement. There was a public pool on the island, and I knew it'd help pull people to the exhibition. For that reason, I was thankful for the oppressive heat that would be around all week, but it was horrible to work in. I thought the ocean would make the island cooler, but the sun didn't care. As we hoisted the first dogs down, I began to feel my skin bake and burn. The heat pulled energy from us at a much faster rate than the shaded lawn of the Bradford Common. We came up with little innovations to offset our slower pace. We perfected the easiest ways to push the dogs on their carts and discovered that the hundred-pound base plates could be stacked inside the bone cutout on the dog when it was rolled on its side.

 The hills of the park made it difficult to position the dogs. The Bradford Common had been relatively flat, but this park's beauty laid in its hills and slopes. Because of these hills, there was much less real estate to pick from in regards to placing the dogs, but ultimately we came up with a great arrangement.

 The last issue at hand came once again from the heat. The dogs were *hot*; at times too hot to touch. They were so hot that I was concerned they'd burn the grass beneath them and possibly even start a fire. I cut and placed wood blocks under every sculpture in the park to bear the brunt of the heat and help give the grass some air to breathe.

 I was elated with the finished product. I sped around the park observing the placement of each dog. The blue of the ocean against their russet color was gorgeous. As I looked at each one, I wanted to keep staring and then maybe fall asleep in the grass, but I knew it wasn't over.

 We spent the last couple of hours of sunlight breaking down and organizing all the equipment we used to secure and move the dogs into place. I'd underestimated how long this part would take, and it made setting the dogs up feel like a bit of a false victory. Still, we scraped away at all the little tasks that needed to be checked off the list. When the final ratchet strap was rolled up and tossed in the utility trailer, I wiped my hands on my jeans and fell in the grass with

EXIT 48

a bottle of water. I cracked the lid and gulped while Andy walked over to meet me.

"What next?"

"Now we rest."

I tossed the bottle to Andy. He let out a sigh of relief and took a sip. Both of us were covered in dirt and sweat but I didn't take notice. The weight of worry was lifting, and I wouldn't have to think about moving metal sculptures or defective trailers for another week. I pulled a twenty from my wallet and leaned forward with it outstretched.

"I'm gonna stuff my face with food. You should too. Good work today."

He thanked me but tried to deny the bill. I waved him off and told him I'd see him tomorrow. He took the second truck back to Haverhill. Parker stood behind me by the trailer.

"What do you say? You hungry?"

He nodded and I pulled my bike from off the trailer

"Well then let's go find something to eat!"

We rode the bike downtown. I'd fashioned a bike seat my kids could sit on while I pedaled. It positioned Parker between me and the handlebars and allowed him to see everything front and center as we rode through the busy streets. The air was beginning to cool and the sun was hanging by a thread in the sky, coming down and fraying the tops of tree lines and buildings. All of the chairs in restaurant patios were being brought in for the night by bussers, and one by one the bars began to glow with the warm light of people meeting to talk with one another and catch up. The breeze felt good on my face after rushing to move the dogs all day, and even though I'd been up for two days I'd never felt better.

We both got burritos from a restaurant called Poco's Bow Street Cantina and ate at a bench on the sidewalk. People around us laughed with each other and told loud stories. Some walked alone with a dog or just by themselves and did what I imagine we were doing; observing all of the life a little city has to offer. Parker pointed different things out about different people, and I listened intently. I was always amazed at what children saw when they looked at things—as if the older a person gets the more a veil covers their sight to the world around them. After we ate, we biked down to the water and watched the boats move in the dark. I'd point out at the lights far off in the distance and tell him they were boats or homes littered along the very edge of the land. He'd talk about sharks or whales or starfish and tell me what he'd learned at school. I began to ramble, telling him about the city. I told him how it was the third oldest city in the whole country, and how a long time ago it was one of the shining hubs of America with boats full of fishermen and passengers and goods coming in and out all day long. It made me think about Haverhill and all the other cities in the Merrimack Valley. I heard people often talk about the lost age of industry in New England, but that was the same industry that wiped out all of these fishing towns. I imagined an old fisherman or merchant from Gloucester, Portsmouth, or Ipswich talking about the bygone glory days of being a sailor. Still, the city in front of me was beautiful and teeming with life and it made me realize that no matter what, people find a way to thrive against any opposition.

I lifted the bike from the sand and Parker stared at me.

"Were there Pirates?"

"Of course." I shrugged.

"Who knows. Maybe some of those boats out there *are* pirates."

His eyes grew wide as he looked out at the flickering lights off-shore. We sat for a while talking about pirates with peg legs and hooks for hands and then headed back to the island. All of the dogs were still where I'd left them earlier, waiting to meet the world tomorrow when the sun climbed back up into the sky. I yawned and looked at my watch; it was late.

"Should we camp out in the park tonight? What do you think?"

I watched his eyes light up with joy. He jumped up with excitement and began talking at a mile a minute.

"Where?"

"Well, I figure we've got a perfectly good pickup-truck sitting in front of us."

"Do we have blankets?"

"I have some from when I sleep ouafter trade shows."

"Are we going to have a campfire?"

"Well—"

I let the bike down in the grass and then walked over to the truck. I opened the back-passenger door and rummaged through some things scattered under the seat. I pulled out an old camp stove I used a few times camping out in Walmart parking lots.

"It's not a *real* campfire, but we're travelers. We have to make do with what we got!"

He laughed and lit up with a smile. I pulled the blankets from the truck and made a makeshift tent in the truck bed, then used the rest for us to sleep on. We biked over to a convenience store, bought a big bag of marshmallows, and then sat next to the truck roasting them over the camp stove. I let Parker tell ghost stories until I couldn't sit upright any longer. He must've been fighting to stay awake too because he passed out before I did. As I lay in the bed of the truck letting myself fall asleep, I felt within one of the happiest moments of my entire life. I didn't regret a single thing I did to get myself here. All those years of self-doubt and being ashamed of my passion seemed ridiculous. What else could bring me here? My pursuit of art had created a memory with my son I'd never forget, and there was nothing in the world worth more than that.

15

"Ow. what the—"

Parker ran down the aisle laughing. I tried to cut him off at the next aisle, but he was too smart; he'd evaded me completely. I thought he was nervous and wanted to hold my hand, but he'd gotten me with a hand buzzer.

"I'll remember that."

I laughed to myself and picked up a bag of rancid flavored jellybeans. We were inside Macro Polo, a gift shop in downtown Portsmouth. The shop specialized in prank and gag gifts and its eccentric shelves and baskets were filled with everything from false teeth to fake dog poop. Parker was in heaven. I caught a glimpse of him jumping from one aisle to the next wearing a pair of glasses with slinky eyeballs.

"Alright bud, I've gotta get back to the dogs."

Parker emerged cupping a rubber dog poop in his hands.

"What do you need that thing for?"

"Prank grandma."

I laughed and shook my head. I walked over to the barrel of dog poop and tossed him another one.

"Now that's as good a reason as I've ever heard."

We walked back to the park together. Our time in Portsmouth was coming to a close and I was feeling a little sentimental. The city had been good to us. As I'd hoped, the nearby public pool helped make the dogs a hang out spot. Their positioning outside downtown worked in my favor in the way that it turned them into an attraction of sorts. In Bradford, they were right out by an intersection, which offered its benefits. The drawback of the Bradford common was that nobody had to go find the dogs; they were right there as they drove by. Portsmouth brought people who specifically showed up to see the dogs.

My two younger sons, Tripp and Jude, had come up a few days of the week with their babysitter Tina. We all spent the afternoons together goofing off. They were very little, and the majority of the exhibition would be too wearing on them, but whenever we could make it work, we'd spend the day and have fun.

All week, I talked with strangers until my voice became raspy. I loved it. It was different from trade shows. At trade shows, I often felt like I could talk to a thousand people in one day and not learn anything about any of them. Most of my interactions were only five to ten minutes as the moving hoards of patrons dragged them away like a riptide. That was the other thing about trade shows; everybody was a patron. It didn't dilute the connections I made with anybody, but there was a constant awareness of the looming wall between the buyer and the seller. That's why I went to them, after all; to make money.

I was often on edge at trade shows, sipping a beer or mixed drink to dull my nerves out. There was something about them that rattled a person's brain in their head; the constant five-minute conversations, the chaotic setup and load out, the sense of competition to simply sustain a livelihood. It felt completely different from the exhibition. The setup and breaking down was more stressful than any trade show

EXIT 48

I'd attended, but in between was plain old fun. In Portsmouth, I spoke to many people for over an hour, learning about their lives and explaining to them what mine was all about. I had time to explain myself to people and it didn't make me feel so crazy.

What's more, the distance between the buyer and seller had vanished. I wasn't concerned with anybody buying my work; I just wanted them to enjoy the moment. I felt like they could sense that too, and it made conversations and interactions feel genuine. I didn't feel the pressure of winning over a sale or coming home empty-handed, and my health benefited from it.

At one point in the week, a couple walked up to me. They had been walking around looking at the dogs and talking amongst themselves.

"Are you the artist?"

I was eating a sandwich. I scrambled for a place to put it down.

"Yes, yes. My apologies for—"

"We love your work."

"Thank you, that means more than you think."

I'd settled on keeping the sandwich in my hand. I wiped my free hand on my shirt and shook both of theirs.

"I still remember when the first one on the highway went up! On Exit 48, right?"

I smiled and nodded at them. I loved it when people brought up the dog on the highway. It made me feel like the headache was worth something.

"Thank you. It's right outside the town I'm from."

"Oh! We know. We're from Haverhill too.

The husband fixed his sunglasses and smiled at me. I prayed I hadn't met them before and that I wasn't being rude by introducing myself. Haverhill is a strange sized city where you feel like there are thousands of people around you that you've only met once.

"You know, the first stop on this whole exhibition was just in Haverhill."

The wife nodded.

"That's why we came here! We planned on going on Wednesday, but The Bradford Common was empty."

I apologized to the woman as sincerely as I could and tried to explain the nature of the mishap. Neither of them seemed to mind at all and we transitioned into a conversation about life as an artist. I told them how this was my first exhibition ever and it seemed to make them excited to be a part of it. I wanted to kick myself over packing up early but knew it was the only way. I'd never even expected anyone to notice I was gone, never mind drive out of town to catch the next location. It was a bit hard to wallow in regret over it for that reason. I felt much more elated over the fact that people cared enough to make an effort to come out.

The day we packed up; I thanked the city for giving me such a wonderful week. Everything went smoothly but I couldn't shake the feeling I was forgetting something. I was settling into the seat of my truck to make the drive to Maine when I saw Andy get out and wave at me. He was standing by the utility trailer. I knew immediately and got back on my feet.

"I can't believe I—"

"Yeah. I forgot too."

The trailer was just as we'd driven it a week ago; tilting backward and undoubtedly going to cause the dogs to slide off once we hit the highway.

"Let's go figure something out."

EXIT 48

We unhitched his truck and drove it to a trailer supply store in Portsmouth. After wandering around for a while, I found a hitch that would sit lower to the ground than the current one. Andy waited for me with the truck running. When I jumped back in, we both eyed the new contraption.

"Will it work?"

"It should. But your guess is as good as mine."

He shrugged and started to pull out of the parking lot. The utility trailer was old as hell itself and It definitely wouldn't be a perfect fit by any means. When we got back to the park, we rigged up the new hitch and tested it out. It looked a little funny and I tried to think of anything catastrophic that could happen. My primary goal had become to avoid having to cut another axle on the side of the highway.

"Won't the dogs still slide?"

"Not as much—hopefully."

The trailer was still at a slant, but it was far less drastic than before. We took it on the highway to Ogunquit, Maine without any mishaps or life-threatening scenarios. The hitch seemed to do the trick. I was filled with relief, and that night I slept like a baby; far better than the night before the Portsmouth setup. In the morning, I made a coffee and took my time, enjoying the densely wooded roads of Maine. As I drove into the beautiful little town of Ogunquit, I began to see the Ocean. The Ocean in Maine looks different than it does in Massachusetts or New Hampshire. It's strange how close Maine is to the rest of New England and how quickly the terrain changes. I could see the moss crested slopes of black stone cut against the water, stalling the land's rich vegetation in its slow creep closer and closer to the shoreline. The beaches of Maine continue in this fashion up the northeastern coast, growing in magnitude the further up one goes until the rocky shores grow to vast, looming cliffs in the Acadia Region.

    Ogunquit is what I imagine somebody from outside envisions all of the ocean towns to be in New England. The town is defined by its wooded terrain that opens up into a quiet postcard of lighthouses, painted bridges, and wood-shingled homes. It is a wealthy community, and the homes that are not salt-stained relics are most often massive and elaborate, each most likely commissioned and designed to be unique symbols of power and wealth against a grassy ocean bluff. Many of the homes along the ocean towns between Salisbury and Portland attract people from all over, driving through ascending hilltops with their mouths agape at the ornate mansions hidden quietly away from the bustle of the mill towns and Boston.

    The strip along the main beach is an exception to the serenity. It's filled with locals and tourists alike, traversing the narrow pathways between lobster shacks and gift shops. I hoped The Big Dog Show would be plopped right in the center of it all, as people would quite literally have no choice but to pass by. However, the exhibition would be held in a small park a little ways away from the heart of town. The town had told me they'd operate the trolley that passes by the park, which I was grateful for. I hoped it'd help pull some people away from the main drag.

    Compared to the past two locations, setup went well. I finally felt like I was settling into a groove. There weren't many surprises, which was great. We just went about our routine and placed the dogs beneath the canopy of trees that shaded the park.

    I knew very early on that Ogunquit was going to be far slower than Portsmouth or Haverhill. I spent most of the day sitting around in a lawn chair I'd brought. The heat ran me down; even from under the treetops and even just sitting around. Few people came by to see The Big Dog Show. Some of the days I could count on my hands how many showed up. The trolley helped a little, but not much. Now and then a couple or family would get off the trolley car and wander around the park. I'd talk to them for a long while and learn their names but ultimately, they'd be off to the next attraction the beach town had to offer.

I started having my kids come each day for the rest of the week. We explored the town and ate seafood and lounged on the beach. I didn't bother staying at the park full time; the dogs could talk for themselves if they had to. We got ice cream often and looked for sea creatures in the vast jetties along the ocean.

Towards the end of the week, I felt like we had run out of things to do. I tapped my foot anxiously. I hated sitting around in an empty park. My kids were growing restless too and we were all getting tired from sitting in the heat. I wanted to move and clear my head.

"Are you guys hungry?"

All of my kids nodded. There was a market somewhere on the main strip that I had passed a few times. I decided I'd go down and grab some lunch meat and toppings.

"I'll be back, and we'll make sandwiches. Stay with Tina."

I walked downtown. It was hot; I was already beginning to sweat through my shirt. The sun lit the pastels and weather-worn browns of the various shops and houses. The air sweeping in from the ocean stung my nose and face and I held my hand over my eyes and squinted to look for the storefront sign. Traffic was heavy, the cars inching painfully slow in the heat. I could feel the heat steaming off the cars' sides as I scanned both sides of the narrow street. Before my eyes landed on the market, they caught a little blue sign that read *Abacus*. I shrugged; it looked interesting enough and I wanted to get out of the heat.

When I walked in, I was greeted with an immense array of art. It was a gallery tucked away unbeknownst to me. I wandered through its halls and looked at all the different mediums that were displayed. It was almost overwhelming. There were so many ideas nestled together in the narrow halls of the gallery. I found a room with large three-dimensional sculptures and got excited. I forgot how much I loved browsing other people's work; I'd been in full Dog Show mode the past few weeks. I suddenly remembered I wanted to be displayed in galleries. I thought one of my pieces might fit in great amongst the other works and wanted to ask about having a piece displayed. I bit my tongue and left.

"*Abacus. Abacus.*"

I repeated the name of the gallery over and over on the walk back. I didn't want to forget it. I pulled out my phone to make a recording of it and noticed I had a voicemail from our first day in Ogunquit.

I listened to it and winced. Somebody had left me a very angry message about leaving the Portsmouth location early. They said they had driven forty-five minutes just to see the dogs and couldn't believe we packed up and left before the flyer's date.

I hung up the answering machine and quietly walked home. It made me happy that someone would drive all that way to see my work, but that's also what made it sting more. I didn't set out to disappoint anybody; especially not the people that would travel all that way to give my art a chance. I felt silly now that I barely had any visitors at our current location. I wished I could somehow make it up to them,

EXIT 48

but I knew from working the trade circuit that the ship had sailed.

That night I brought the kids out to the beach. I sat on top of the sea wall and watched the inky waves crash against the shoreline. When the waves receded, they pulled a piece of the beach in with them, little by little. Parker, Tripp, and Jude had flashlights they'd brought with them. Parker and Tripp pretended their flashlights were lightsabers while Jude scanned the sand a few feet from me for treasure.

"Find anything?"

Jude looked up and shined the light at my face. I squinted my eyes and tilted it away from my face. He let the beam of light back into the sand and I could only see the soft silhouette of his face.

"Nothin' yet."

The tide came in quick and strong. We left the beach as the water began to creep up and touch the seawall.

The rest of our time in Maine slipped by. Before I knew it, we were packing everything back up. For the first time, it felt boring—almost numb. It gnawed away at me during break down. Ogunquit felt different than the others and the dogs felt a little more heavy than usual.

16

Newburyport sat at the very joining point of the Merrimack and the Atlantic Ocean. I knew the place well; it sat a short drive from Salisbury Beach. Salisbury Beach was a place I loved like an old photograph. It was unchanging for as long as I could remember. I could still play the same arcade games with the same slice of Tripoli's pizza I'd eaten as a kid. I loved Newburyport for the opposite reason. It had blossomed since my youth into a prim oceanside town, full of gourmet restaurants and locally-owned storefronts. Driving from Salisbury the town lay just beyond a rural stretch of Route 1A and over a bridge above the Merrimack. The dense cobblestone streets are somewhat of a surprise as the corner is taken and the landscape shifts to uniform greenery, docks, restaurants, and a boardwalk that follows the edge of the city.

We set up a couple of days prior on the boardwalk. It was the beating pulse of the city, often decorated with street performers or live music. When festivals took place vendors and food carts would spill out from the downtown streets into the lawns surrounding the boardwalk. I could see boats floating lazily towards the ocean from where I was, their fiberglass hulls lurking between the beams of streetlights that carried into the open water.

I was exhausted and struggled to keep my eyes open under the sound of roaming crowds of people. For a moment I let them close, leaning my upper body over the railing of the boardwalk.

The exhibition was positioned at the very end of the boardwalk. It was a small lot connected to an old Antique Mall. We'd vied for the location because it sat behind a local maritime museum, but it seemed to not make much of a difference in traffic. The area we were granted was very small and we ended up cramming the dogs pretty close together. It looked a lot different from the other spots we'd set up and I wasn't sure I liked it.

I sat for the first day mostly on my own. It felt a whole lot like Ogunquit, wrangling stragglers from the main part of downtown far and few between. I spent most of the day doing nothing. As the sky grew dark and the bars lit up, I was gearing up to go home when I noticed a group of twenty-somethings circling the dogs. I could smell the alcohol on them as I walked up to say hello. They were all very amused by the dogs, circling them and joking amongst each other.

"I feel like I'm in a maze."

One of the kids zigzagged between the dogs with his hands stretched out. I was a little worried he was going to crash into one. I went back to packing and gathering a few things to leave when more people stumbled upon the exhibition. The crowd continued to grow and linger and chat amongst each other. Eventually, I became too involved in greeting people to remember that I was leaving. I talked to people into the night. Each wave became deeper and deeper into their drinks until eventually, I had people trying to climb the dogs and shouting, old and young alike. I hadn't anticipated the influx of beachgoers that would show up to wander the streets from surrounding towns like Salisbury, Hampton, Seabrook, and Rye. They'd come all at once and before I knew it, I was packing my things past midnight.

The pattern continued throughout the week. I found myself ensnared in a scenario where I felt obligated to head the exhibition in the day but found the most attention at night. The drive past the beaches in the morning was long and congested and I had to be up early to make it for any daylight. I began to lose more and more sleep trying to be there for the nightlife. Eventually, I let loose and began to take part, hitting bars and restaurants with friends and family when they came to visit. There was a bar called The Thirsty Whale I frequented throughout my time in Newburyport. It was owned by my old friend Stephen Jewett and served great food and drinks. It was hard not to indulge a little while we caught up.

In the end, it only added to the struggle to keep going during the daytime as my stomach turned over in the intense heat. As my brother went off with my family, I leaned my back against the boardwalk railing and looked out into the pockets of people congregated between the maze of sculptures. The Christmas lights hung year-round on top of the consignment shop painting them all gold as they chattered and snuck nips out of wallet pockets and purses. I wanted to talk to them; I wanted to tell them who I was and why I was doing all of this. The days spent in empty parks left a nervous impulse in me to take advantage of any attention I could get, but my legs felt like they'd crumble if I walked across the parking lot. I hung my head and closed my eyes. It couldn't be worth much to go talk to them, anyway. All the people I spoke to through the last few days were aloof—barely present. It mostly felt like I was talking to crowds of brick walls as they swayed and hooked into different conversations mid-sentence. Sometimes they'd even walk away while I was talking, enthralled by a goofy stunt one of their friends were doing.

I began to feel barely present. I thought about the nature of what

EXIT 48

we were all doing. Every day most of the world spent its time doing something it didn't want to, all of its inhabitants chipping away at a stack of papers or job sites until they could punch out at dinner time. Then they'd spend the few hours they had left trying to make up for a lifetime. If they had children, they might sit around with them and listen to what they did at school or soccer practice, nodding intently and trying to make the minutes count. If they didn't, they were here, out in the streets jumping from spot to spot aimlessly with friends or the person they loved. I kept trying to figure out whether they were trying to remember or forget something—feel something or dull themselves out. Tomorrow for them would be monotonous. Maybe they would feel sick to their stomachs or wake up feeling better than usual, but the predictability was guaranteed. It was the predictability that bound everybody to things they didn't want to do. It was better than being entirely unsure of each coming day because I saw now that it was exhausting. Maybe between their trip from one bar to the next each night, they'd run into something like me.

The majority of humanity seemed absurd, but not any more absurd than I seemed to myself. I felt like the exhibit rather than my sculptures; like a primate at the zoo banging my fist against the bulletproof glass. They circled me and inquired, not because they were impressed, but because they wanted something to amuse them along their predictable stroll into the future. *'Look at the artist!'* they would say to themselves. They'd wonder why I keep up with it each day. They wonder why I don't settle down into something assuring and comfortable and instead play the part of the rodeo carnival clown. I remembered being young and watching a clown climb a grease pole at the Topsfield Fair, my cousins and brother and I enthralled by the stakes. I could now see the crowd he saw as I climbed the span of my dream inch by inch, everybody hoping I make it but just as entertained if I let go and fall back to the earth.

We'd managed to secure a meet and greet at a gallery in Newburyport during the exhibition's planning stages. I was jumping up and down when it happened. I wanted to rub it in the face of every gallery that turned me down through the years. Now on Friday morning I washed down a handful of Tylenol with my coffee and looked at myself in the rearview mirror of my truck. I looked miserable. Dark rings formed around my eyes and my whole face sagged with fatigue. I fixed my hair, slapped myself a few times, and trudged into Chameleon Gallery.

Inside, the space was small and filled with paintings and small crafts created by locals. In many ways a quintessential Newburyport shop, painted with soft beige colorings reminiscent of ocean towns and preserving much of the architecture from a different era years ago. The owners, Chris and Lucinda, greeted me with enthusiasm and settled me in.

"It's so exciting for a local to be doing such a large-scale exhibition."

I sat down at the table adjourned with information booklets and photos of my sculptures. I tried to perk up through the daze I was looking at them in.

"Thank you—and thank you for doing this. This is all amazing."

"Just let us know if you need anything."

They walked away up to the register and began organizing. I eased into the fold-out chair at the desk and sighed. I was so grateful they were willing to help me and I hoped they could see it through my exhaustion. I hung around for the day speaking to patrons that found their way inside. I tried to keep myself awake by tapping my legs and when somebody came in, I put the best act on I could. Many of them were very interested in my work and lit off little sparks within me. Still, I felt as if none of the sparks could ignite a fire in me as they did weeks prior. The interactions were blending into each other and I began to wonder if people were just being polite. I no longer felt a rush of excitement when somebody showed interest; just gratitude they were willing to. Some of them seemed like they were expecting me to say more than I did. They wanted to hear the passion and the story before I sold them on the art, and my enthusiasm was in low supply. I didn't know what to tell them; they were my sculptures, and they were all I had to show.

    I stayed there until nine PM, thanked Chris and Lucinda, and then walked over to The Grog. The Grog had always been my favorite spot in Newburyport. It was opened up in 1969 and never bothered to change with the times. Low hanging lights hung all across the bar and dining area and gave off an intense golden glow. The hardwood of the bar and tables was deep amber, complemented by red vinyl cushions and stools. I always liked to sit back and scan the walls, looking at the mementos the owners accumulated and hung up through the years.

    I ordered a drink at the bar and listened to a young group of kids laugh and bang their fists on the countertop. Behind me, older folks finished dinner and left cash tips on the tables. The streets outside were busy; the busiest they'd be all week. I left Andy to brave the crowd that was inevitably all over the dogs right now enjoying their night. People would pile into the pub every few minutes and be crammed somewhere with big smiles on their faces. I figured that the place must make a killing being in a wealthier area where people love to eat and drink. Whoever owned it was certainly comfortable now, but it must've not always been like that. Somebody once told me Newburyport was a rough spot through the seventies. I was too young to notice or remember if my parents had brought me. It was hard to believe now that it was ever anything less than what it currently was, with its spotless brick streets, parks, and boardwalk. All of the homes were coated in fresh paint, completely refurbished and preserved as they were built long ago. The restaurants and shops were all somewhat upscale, and a plethora of cuisines and goods from different cultures had made their way into the brick buildings the city had remodeled and refurbished. It was utopic to some degree; everybody seemed quite comfortable. Yet, The Grog must've opened and stayed opened through the darkest time for the city. I imagine it was difficult then to stay afloat, as all the cities along the Merrimack gasped for breath in New England's new post-industrial era. In the end, the owners had to have felt like it was worth it. The city blossomed around them and their years of struggling came to a close.

    I swirled the bottom of my drink in my cup. When would I reach that day? I tried to think of what I originally wanted out of this exhibition. I couldn't recall it. It was some far-off dream that the world around me would bloom and lift my art far above where I was now. I had hoped that I made it out of the hard times and my saving grace was an exhibition away. I began to think of all the bars and restaurants like The Grog that must've existed at the beginning of the seventies, all gone to history and victims of happenstance. I was beginning to wonder if I was like them. Maybe I wasn't holding out through the hard times for the good times; maybe I was telling the same bad joke to myself over and over again. I felt guilty when people were more excited about the exhibition than I was now. It was like I was selling them something bound to break.

I put my elbows up on the table and sighed. It was getting late. I rummaged through my pocket for some cash and loose change to pay my tab and left it on the table. I was about to get up and leave when I stopped and picked up one of the quarters I left.

"Heads I keep going, tails I don't."

I flicked the coin into the air and watched it flash in the hanging lights. I was about to catch it when my phone began to vibrate on the countertop. The quarter bounced off the bar and rolled under the stools. I picked up my phone; it was Allissa.

"Hey. Good news and not so good news."

"Good news first."

I crouched down and began to look for the quarter.

"New York is confirmed."

I gasped. I couldn't tell if it was out of horror or amazement or both. When we were planning the exhibition, we stumbled upon an event hosted by The Northshore Animal League in Manhattan. It would be a massive fundraiser event with all kinds of big fish floating around. Proceeds would benefit animal shelters across the east coast. I told Allissa to reach out for the hell of it and expected so little out of it that I forgot I ever even did.

"Bad news is they want you to meet them on Long Island to discuss logistics."

I sighed while I moved my hand around under a stool.

"That's great to hear. Let's talk about it in better detail tomorrow. Thank you."

I hung the phone up and moved my hand under another stool. I felt the quarter and paused. I carefully slid it out to where I could see it and pouted.

"Heads it is."

I put the quarter on the table with the rest of the cash and left The Grog. When I got back to the dogs, Andy was talking to a group of people. There was a small crowd weaving in between the dogs like currents through a rocky brook. I braced myself and took them on for the rest of the night.

We packed up at the end of our stay in Newburyport and drove the dogs down to Beverly, Massachusetts. It would be Beverly, then Lowell, and our New England exhibition would be over. We were at a gas station when I noticed Andy in a daze.

"You good?"

He snapped out of it and wiped the sweat off his face.

"Yeah—yeah I'm alright. I feel like I haven't slept in a week."

"That's because we haven't."

We both laughed against the trailer. I could tell we were both trying to laugh the hurt away. We both looked like we'd seen the devil. We must have collectively lost twenty pounds during the whole exhibition. We dropped the dogs off at the Beverly Common and headed straight home. I collapsed into my bed that night and fell asleep as soon as I hit the mattress. Somehow, things had turned out so hectic that I was getting *the most* sleep in between move and setup days. When I drove back to the Beverly Common the next day a kid was setting up PA speakers and running wires. I was confused and a little annoyed, so I walked up to figure out what was going on.

"Hey man, there's an exhibition being installed here. What's with the speakers?"

I followed him while he ran a cable to a power amplifier and plugged it into the back. He turned around and looked at me through his sunglasses.

"Town is having them set up. I believe they're for your exhibition. And the parade."

"Parade?"

He nodded and walked with a lackadaisical swerve to his step. He reached into a duffel bag and pulled out another coil of cabling.

"Yessir. They're making a community event out of the exhibition."

I jerked my head back. I didn't know they were making such a big deal out of it. When Andy arrived, we got to work setting them up. The Beverly Common was a spacious collection of fielded areas connected by pavement walkways. We put some extra work in and managed to get the dogs spread out all over the park. It gave it a drastically different feeling than Newburyport, with each dog nearly isolated from the next.

I hadn't shaken the feeling that latched to me in Ogunquit. It was like a parasite sucking the passion for my art out of me. Even so, in the next few days I couldn't help but have a smile on my face. The town had coordinated corporate sponsors for each dog and donated the money to organizations in need. Different kindergarten and elementary schools had crafted collars for the dogs, each one unique from the next and made by different hands. Local pet shops and groomers set up tents giving free haircuts to dogs. It was amazing and humbling to watch a community come together and turn an art exhibition into something much greater than that. It became something else entirely, and I felt as if the dogs were simply an addition at that point. It didn't bother me; especially not now. My children came up many of the days and played around the park. I hung around and talked to different members of the community.

I tried to stay alert and awake. Students from the Montserrat College of Art came by to ask questions and I didn't want to appear worn down, but there wasn't enough time to get any sleep. I looked over at Parker, Tripp, and Jude playing with a few new friends they'd made. I tried to focus on them and preserve the memory in my head. It's the only thing that was guaranteed at this point. My bank account was drained from this exhibition and I wouldn't recover for years by the looks of it. I'd be hitting trade shows more than ever if I even kept up with the art. My heart felt a little heavy as I watched little kids play around the sculptures. Even if I wanted to keep going, there may not be a possible way to do it.

"Are we gonna do this forever?"

I looked down. My son Tripp had strayed off from playing with the other kids and was staring up at me. I rubbed the top of his head. I didn't know what to say.

17

I've always felt like life is strange in the way that no matter how much I've planned each step towards the goals I wanted to achieve, I still never felt like I'd been a step ahead. By the time I sat in Lowell's Kerouac park for the last stop on my art exhibition, I was staring into the last dwindling months of another decade. The question of what it meant to be an artist became more confusing to me by the day. I felt as if I should've been premised somehow. It would've been nice if somebody gave me a textbook or pamphlet on becoming an artist. I thought of the days visiting Gene in New York and spending time with kids from art schools. They seemed so confident and poised; as if somebody had sprawled the golden game plan out in front of them and there'd be nothing to worry about. My reality was something different. So much of my career as an artist was a tangled web of fate of thinking on my feet. Maybe it was happenstance or maybe it was something burning deep in the pit of my heart, but I often thought about how fragile the strains of my web were. Years ago, I drew pictures with pencils on the desks of classrooms. Then, in the dawning years of my adulthood becoming an artist felt like something unattainable. I'd daydream about it unbeknownst to people around me and keep it bottled in; even bottled away from myself. Now it was happening but was unlike anything I anticipated. I wondered if the kid I was back then would still daydream if he knew the backstage work of being a sculptor—if he knew about the endless hours on the road, the time spent breaking your back for an empty park; the denials, the fatigue and isolation and perpetual worry over going broke.

Back then, the web of my life was small and manageable. Now it appeared in front of me as a twisting mess, each strain untraceable to the point at which it began or connected to another.

Sometimes I felt like my feet began running somewhere before my mind or heart knew where we were headed. There was rarely time to catch up, never mind think or sort things out. My money had almost run dry. My equipment was run down, and my body was even worse. Moving the dogs over and over had taken years off my life. My whole body ached without end. Each day it felt harder to roll out of bed and lift each piece of equipment or sculpture against the clock. It became increasingly apparent I was getting older. I shook at the idea of getting hurt. Things had to be done quickly and with little time to think. A dog could easily fall on top of me or I could get cut by a bandsaw or angle grinder at the shop. Even if I tore something lifting a baseplate, the outcome could be devastating. There was no worker's comp or paid leave to fall back on; I'd be out in the cold. The thought of being unable to support my children was devastating. I carried it each day with me at the forefront of my mind. Their lives were just fine now, but I had built nothing for the future. It was all just in the moment; just enough to keep going.

I couldn't tell if anything I'd done in the past months had gotten me closer to where I wanted to be. I didn't even know where that was. There was no way to gauge success or failure, I just knew I didn't feel the way I thought I would. I knew from the start that the exhibition wouldn't become a world affair, but I was driven each day by some small hope it would send a shockwave far beyond the coastal cities of

EXIT 48

New England. I hoped maybe I would even just grip some precious gem of insight by the end, but I still stood in the dark with just little reflections of light to guide me. If this was how it would be forever; alone in the dark with only inklings of light to guide me, my body and bank account barely able to press on, I simply couldn't do it.

I sipped from a foam cup of coffee. The air was humid and warm, but the heat of summer had slowly regressed as New England rolled into the first days of September.

"Everything is good to go."

I tipped my cup to Andy and we hopped in the truck carrying the smaller trailer. We still had to drop four dogs off at the University of Massachusetts, Lowell.

Like most large cities in Massachusetts, the end of the industrial era spelled hard times in Lowell. A city that once had the largest industrial complex in the entire country had disintegrated into an area that struggled to keep its head afloat. The mills all still stood, abandoned by the people who promised prosperity to anyone willing to work. In the background of this decline, the acts of genocide committed by the Khmer Rouge in Cambodia led many Cambodians to seek refuge in Lowell. The city also gained a large influx of people from Latin America. Both groups brought new diversity and life to the city, and in the coming years, a new glimmer of hope emerged. Massachusetts was quick to jump on the tech boom in the late eighties, and the emergence of new tech startups in the state brought jobs. It became known as the "Massachusetts Miracle," as post-industrial cities found new life in the markets of the future.

The boom in jobs never brought the same prosperity to Lowell that it once had, but it was enough to keep it afloat. The city scraped up the money to restore and preserve the old mills, and where other mills across Massachusetts have crumbled into hollow tombs the ones in Lowell still stand in their original condition. It is a testament to the strength of the city.

I looked out at the city as I drove. Generations of different cultures and businesses sat on top of and within each other. So much of the area's success had come from repurposing; what once was a laundromat was now a restaurant; a department store was now a young art gallery taking its first steps. Between the new still sat the old. There were bars around the city like the Worthen House, which sat right where it did since the mid-1800s. Between the redbrick rows of buildings and cobblestone alleyways were several boxcar diners that had existed for generations, such as The Club Diner and The Owl Diner. They reminded me of my mornings at The Agawam with my grandfather.

Once, we dropped the dogs off at UML, I went straight back to the main exhibit. I didn't have time to explore. I wanted to be on-site for anyone, even if the exhibition never saw the light of day again. All I needed was a miracle. It didn't need to propel me into stardom; it just needed to be enough to keep me going. It just had to be like the miracle Lowell and other towns around the area were given; just enough. I thought that maybe then I could keep doing this, but I wasn't going to hold my breath.

The days spent at the Lowell exhibition were somewhat laid back. It was easier to get to than other locations. I spent most mornings eating at Arthur's Paradise Diner, which sat in a little boxcar across the park. On one of the days, the Cultural Organization of Lowell had been kind enough to lend me a hand and put together a meet and greet. I fought through the fatigue to talk to people. Regardless of how run down I was it was humbling that people wanted to hear about my work. I spent the day talking to many prospective young artists from The Merrimack Valley and gave them whatever wisdom I'd gained through the last decade. It put a smile on my face to see the younger ones excited to chase a dream and reminded me of my first days chasing mine.

On the final day of packing up, I sat drinking my final cup of coffee at the Paradise Diner. Allisa was texting me whatever information she could get a hold of about the New York situation. The thought of doing another show made me want to throw up into my coffee cup. I didn't think my body could take it; I'd probably drop dead in the middle of setting up. I typed out a text asking her to inquire about canceling the whole thing. I read it over and over inside the diner, gritting my teeth. I was already of thousands of dollars in the hole from the locations I'd already done. I was back to scraping by, and the thought of even spending the money to just drive out for the meeting at Long Island pained me.

The gig was the best I'd ever landed. It would be in the heart of Wall Street and I would be in an exclusive position for exhibiting my work. The event would be huge, with high profile guests like Martha Stewart, Beth Ostrosky Stern, and her husband Howard Stern in attendance. A little over a month ago, if I saw myself typing a text to cancel our appearance I would have screamed and lunged for the phone. I was just so out of steam—so beaten down from the physical and mental exhaustion of independently running an expedition. I was beginning to have worries about how I'd fill my fridge and it was bringing back memories of just beginning as an artist.

I had my thumb on the "send" button but couldn't stop thinking of the Beverly show. It was my favorite stop of the entire exhibition. Beverly was a small town, but the way they had rallied and turned the exhibition into something for the entire city had amazed me. It showed me that art could bring a community together. I wanted something like that again; something bigger than the art itself. I knew the New York show's purpose was to benefit the Northshore Animal League. The Northshore Animal League had been around since 1944 and I'd done my homework on them. They were the largest no-kill shelter in the world and saved tens of thousands of animals a year. The idea of my art somehow benefiting a greater cause made me feel proud and like I was doing something worthwhile. Plus, I just plain loved dogs. People must've at least known that by now since I dragged twenty metal shrines to them around New England.

I shook my head. There was no way backward. I'd dug myself too deep and even if I wanted to, I doubted I'd be able to climb my way out of this life I'd set in motion. Not today, at least—inside a diner in Lowell while my exhibition is on public display. I deleted the draft of my text and left the diner to load up the sculptures.

We loaded up slower than usual. There was nowhere to be this time but home. The whole thing felt a bit morose. I'd spent two years on this feat, and it had ended as abruptly as the flickering showers in late summer. I felt like I was just getting started and at the same time, I felt like I couldn't move another inch forward. The evening was beginning to get cold, as they begin to do in September. For the first time on the exhibition, the sweat on my back felt cold in the breeze between the mills.

I walked slowly between loading each dog onto the trailer. I wanted to take it all in and get some type of resolution. I wanted the violins to cue in and feel the happy ending, but what it felt like most was the day after Christmas. It was time to clean up and drag the tree out to the curb. Soon, the dogs would finally be home—and I had no idea what I was going to do with them.

When I returned home, I flicked the light on in my garage. Everything sat as it did yesterday, with cables tangled and tools scattered about. I sat in the middle of the garage floor and held my head in my hands. I fell asleep like that, until early in the morning when the birds began to sing outside the garage door. I hobbled upstairs and gave myself the morning to sleep in.

When I woke up, I shuffled around my house staring at everything I owned. The dogs gave it all to me, and they could take it all away. I walked to the window and stared at the dogs still on the trailer. For a moment, I felt an urge to hitch the trailer and drive, but there were no more stops on The Big Dog Show for now.

I walked back down to the garage and began organizing. Andy was standing outside, and I let him in.

"I don't think there's any work to do today—unless you wanna unload those dogs with me right now."

"What about the backorders?"

"Backorders?"

He stepped back with a weird look on his face. I hadn't realized I yelled; I was still half asleep.

"We had a few orders we got before the show but couldn't finish."

Andy laughed awkwardly. He must've been trying to figure out if I was pretending not to remember or actually didn't, but I really did forget. Upon remembering a feeling of dread filled my body. I'd forgotten all about the back ordered sculptures until now. It would be right back to the grindstone with no time to breathe.

"Backorders. You're right. Let's get to it."

We got to work on the new sculptures. As we began to piece

them together through the day, I began to feel a sense of relief coming over me. These orders would keep me afloat a bit longer. It wouldn't give me much money in the grand scheme of things, but it would keep us going.

As we continued to work, The New York question kept eating at me. I needed a second opinion. I flipped my welding hood and wiped the sweat from my forehead.

"So— New York."

The sparks flew up from the sculpture he was working on. He finished his weld and looked up at me.

"Yeah. You're headed to Long Island to figure out the details, right?"

I shifted in my seat.

"Well—I'm wondering if we should even do it."

"What do you mean? This show is huge."

I looked down at the half-finished sculpture of a cardinal at my feet. I couldn't tell if I wanted someone to talk me out of it or talk me into it. I flipped my welding hood back down. I didn't say anything back.

If I had wanted somebody to try and talk to me out of it, I got my wish in the coming weeks. It seemed like everyone I casually brought it up to thought I was nuts. I'd spent a heap of my cash on the exhibition; everybody knew that. Friends and family looked at me now the same way they did when I told them about the exhibition in the first place. It was a look that drove me mad. I wanted to shake them and tell them I'm not crazy. I wanted to tell them this is what it takes to make it. That's what I'd been telling myself all along and I hoped to god it was true. I'd set out on The Big Dog Show to prove everybody wrong; to wipe the look they gave me off their faces.

EXIT 48

It seemed in their minds all it did was fortify their old beliefs about me.

It's strange. When I first began showing people my art in high school, I was fueled by praise. I used it as a social currency; as a way to convince people I was worthwhile. It was something tangible I could hold up in the air and say, "I did this!" Most others couldn't and because of that, I felt unique and of value. Now, I found that opposition drove me more than anything else. I wanted to prove people wrong when they doubted me, not prove them right when they praised me. I suppose in a way, it's all the same thing.

When October arrived, I made provisions and set out for Long Island. The folks at Northshore Animal League wanted to see my art in person before the event, so I strapped one of the exhibition dogs down on the bed of my pickup. I hopped in my truck and flew like the wind down I-495, past Lowell towards Marlborough, Massachusetts. From there I hopped different interstates down through Worcester into Connecticut, past Hartford and towards New York.

Driving along the Long Island Sound was a headache with the dog. I didn't even want to think about what it would be like lugging the whole exhibition into Manhattan.

When I pulled into the Northshore Animal League's headquarters, I was a little taken aback. It was an entire compound. It looked like a college campus more than anything, with fresh lawns and modern furnishings and designs about the area. I didn't know what to expect initially. I knew they had to be running a large operation to be putting on an event like one I was invited to, but I hadn't ever seen anything close to their compound in regards to animal leagues and shelters.

I found the entrance to the building I was supposed to meet

them in and was greeted by two women in business attire. They looked serious and important but had smiles on their faces.

"Nice to meet you in person Mr. Rogers."

I shook both of their hands. We walked around the main building and then took a tour of the rest of the facility. It was massive; unlike anything I'd seen before. In a way it was intimidating. I felt like I was in over my head at points, as the two women explained the tasks the organization takes on and the scope of the event my art would be featured in.

"This is one of our sanctuary houses for cats."

"That? That's an actual house!"

One of the women laughed as we walked by. It was a legitimate house bought by the organization on the outskirts of its property and it was just for fostering cats, never mind the rest of the animals that fall into their lap.

"This whole place is very impressive. It feels amazing to be a part of what you're all doing."

"Thank you!"

We made our way back to the main building. My truck sat close by and they wanted to catch a glimpse at the dog I'd brought.

"We'd had great success in the past few years. Our locations are spreading out across the United States and ultimately, we hope to rebrand as North Shore Animal League *America*. We'd like to become the premier organization in the United States."

I looked over at the main building. Cars were filling the lot, and I could see people bustling about inside.

"I'd say you're definitely on your way—more than any animal shelter I've ever visited."

As we walked and talked the dog came into sight on top of my poor old truck. Its head stood proud hovering above the roof of the front cab; its tail jutting over and behind the tailgate. I remembered how my brother and I laughed the first time we strapped a dog up into the truck bed; how it made the truck look like a little clown car. I imagined the two women were trying to hold their laughter back.

"Well, people will definitely take notice if you can get it inside the building!"

I laughed and nodded. The women circled the sculpture and looked at it from head to tail.

"These will be great. We've been looking for the right thing to bring flair to the fundraiser and I'm happy they chose you. How many of these comprise the entire exhibition?"

"Twenty, but I'll be bringing sixteen down for this event."

I wanted to bring all twenty, but I knew we'd be a train wreck if we had to lug two full trailers through New York with two trucks. I could fit sixteen on the larger trailer; I knew that well by now. That would be enough trouble moving down to make someone want to pull their hair out anyways.

"And how much of your staff will need passes?"

I laughed and they both gave me a perplexed look. I realized I wasn't helping myself and rubbed the back of my neck.

"Well—I have one helper. He'll need to be there. Otherwise, my brother helps out sometimes. If possible, my parents would love to get out of the house too."

She nodded.

"Done deal. Just make sure you let everybody know its black tie."

She smiled and the two women began to walk. One of them motioned me to follow. I thought about Andy and I dressed up at the event. It looked funny in my head; we were usually in work gear at exhibitions and unkempt from running around all day.

"Come on. We'll catch a train into Manhattan so you can see the event space."

I winced a little and hobbled on after them. I was beginning to wonder when I'd feel fully recovered from the New England locations. My body felt like it had a permanent ache and I'd been stuck in a weird fog from the sporadic sleep schedule I'd been on. As we boarded a subway into the heart of Manhattan, I slouched into the hard acrylic seat and watched the humming lights of the tunnel flash by my face. It felt strange to be back in New York; like some flash of electricity ignited from under all the static in my head. The emotions I felt years ago exploring the city with Gene flooded back into me as I saw the oceans of faces and lights. Massive fluorescent advertisements waved to me like they once did; the smell of food carts mingled with the stale air of subway terminals. As we emerged from underneath the concrete world, I felt the coolness of October penetrate the heat and smog of bustling Manhattan, blowing through boutiques and yellow taxis and bicycle spokes. There was a band playing somewhere. I could hear the music drifting from a loft where people were eating and conversing over cocktails.

"It's coming up a little ways ahead."

I nodded and tried to look casual. I wanted to run off and explore like old times and hoped I didn't look too giddy. I felt like I should push my eyes back into my head. Coming back to the big city after a long time away in some ways feels like visiting a fair or festival. There is so much happening all at once and everything is immense. The droves of people are immense—the buildings, the billboards, the sounds. As we traversed into the financial district and wall street, the city's colors evened out into a serious, busy bustle of white and black suits with leather briefcases. People spoke tentatively on cell phones and Bluetooth headsets. They pulled their sleeves up and gazed into expensive watches. Some tapped their feet at crosswalks and pouted.

The buildings became serious and braggadocious alike. Even the sternness of the financial district filled me with excitement. I wanted to be a part of what they were a part of and I wanted to be a part of what the people in residential areas were a part of and I wanted to be a part of what the tourists were a part of. It was all alluring to me.

I shook myself out of the trance and saw the sign for the event space up ahead. It stood in the street ancient and expensive looking with stacked roman pillars and ivory-colored brick. I followed after and climbed the stone staircase up into the doorway. We were greeted by a man that looked to be a manager or event organizer.

"Welcome to Cipriani."

I waited for the two representatives from the shelter to shake his hand.

"Good to see both of you again. And you—you must be the featured artist for the event."

"Yes— Dale Rogers. Nice to meet you."

He smiled and motioned us in. We walked through an echoing hallway while he rattled off facts and locations around the building. We were brought to a doorway that opened up into a massive ballroom adjourned with a painted dome ceiling. Stage lights and a massive glass chandelier hung overhead, with a pillared stage and curtains in the far corner. The entire room was lit with a golden hue that danced off the intricate molding on the walls. It felt straight out of the age of flapper girls and top hats.

"Over there will be our designated area for photos with our celebrity guests. If you look further down, you'll see the stage where the awards will take place. We'll also be accommodating multiple television screens mounted where you see brackets on the walls."

The man went on about the logistics of the event, the history of the building, and food and drinks that would be catered. Now and then the women from the Animal League would interject with important questions that seemed catered towards me. I tried to stay focused and make mental notes, but something was distracting me from the conversation. I tried to wait to ask but I couldn't think about anything else.

"Where's your loading dock?"

"Loading dock?"

I paused for a moment and felt my heart sink.

"You must have an area to load things into the building. How do the catering companies get everything inside during events?"

The man chuckled and nodded. I saw a look of pity fall over his face as he realized what I was fretting over.

"Typically, everything comes right in through the door you just came in through."

I exhaled and nodded. Out the corner of my eye, I saw one of the women from the Animal League looking at me. I could feel the worry radiating from her.

"Why? That's not going to be an issue, is it?"

I looked at her and paused for a moment. There were a couple of answers I could give her, and I didn't feel like any of them would lead to a resolution. I smiled.

"No, no. Not at all. We'll make it work just fine."

The worry lifted from her face and she nodded. I spent the rest of the afternoon discussing logistics with them and learning about the event. I knew enough before I went out to meet them, but it was good to get an entire synopsis of what it was and what it would be like.

The event was officially called the Dogcatemy Celebrity Gala. It was the Northshore Animal League's premier event of the year and featured an award ceremony that involved judges voting for different videos that celebrities at the event had made with their pets. The event would be a massive fundraiser and attract the donations of the elite class in New York, bringing a heap of aid to multiple efforts the organization coordinates to help neglected, abused and abandoned animals around the globe.

My dog sculptures would be set up similar to how they were at any other show, spread out and placed via my discretion in a pleasant and nonobstructive way. I asked if I could sell my sculptures at the event on the account that I'd be ultimately losing money to drive out and be there. The Animal League agreed that it'd be alright as long as a portion of the proceeds benefits the fundraiser. I was more than happy to agree.

When we left the building, I turned around and looked at the doorway. It was standard-sized; about six and a half feet tall. I shook my head to myself.

"Not a chance."

"Come again?"

I swung around. One of the Animal League women had stopped too and was looking at me.

"Oh—nothing. I'm sorry. I was talking to myself."

She gave a polite look and kept walking. We took the subways back and officialized things. By the time everything was said and done, I was sitting in my truck in traffic, the dog still strapped down and hovering over my head. We'd wrapped the day up at the tail end of rush hour and I was feeling waves of contrasting emotions as I hung my arm out the open window and smelt the exhaust fumes. I'd felt silly now for being apprehensive about doing the New York Show. Just talking about it made me realize it was unlike anything I'd ever done and a different caliber of opportunity entirely. I was also overjoyed that I'd landed an opportunity that was good for myself while being for an immense cause. Plus, just being in New York had reignited a small flame in my heart. It reminded me of the feeling that started it all.

However, I knew well enough that sometimes once in a lifetime opportunities turned out to be just that and nothing further. Aside from the everyday logistical anxieties, I was utterly at a loss for how I was even going to get the dogs through the front door. If I couldn't do it then I had the feeling they'd just tell me there was nothing anybody could do. Then I'd have the new reputation as the artist who couldn't get any of his work through the front door.

I sat wincing at the idea of the embarrassment. That would truly be the end. I sat thinking about the issue when someone's voice interrupted my stream of thought.

"HEY— HEY!"

I could see an eighteen-wheeler in my peripheral. I exhaled and got ready for a yelling match. A leaned my head out my window and pivoted my head to make eye contact with the man shouting from the cab of the giant truck.

"I've seen that before! Is that the one from Haverhill? The one on 495? The Southbound side?"

The man waved a cigarette at my sculpture and embers danced around the windshield of his truck. I immediately started laughing and slapped my steering wheel. All of my preprepared road rage dissipated into a laughing fit and I had to compose myself. I leaned my head back out the window.

"No, it's not. But *this one* is *that one's* cousin. I've got a few of them."

The man took a drag of his cigarette and put his thumbs up.

"Good stuff, man. Good stuff. I knew it right when I saw it."

I smiled and waved to him. The traffic finally broke as the city melted into a tree line and then the tree line turned to dark shapes in the night. I drove home laughing now and then at the exchange with the trucker. He may have swayed my opinion on things just enough in one direction from the other.

I called Andy to come over the next morning.

"So—the dogs aren't going to fit through the doorway? But you said yes?"

I nodded. He stared at me for a second with his eyebrow cocked. He opened his mouth like he was about to say something and slouched leaning against one of the dogs.

"I'm not sure what we're going to do."

I started laughing at the absurdity of the problem. Andy started laughing too. Eventually, we both laughed so hard I was leaning against the wall of my house trying to breathe.

"You know—"

Andy stood up as the laughter was subsiding. He was trying to speak between gasps of air.

"Might as well just build a whole new set that's a little shorter."

I chuckled and then stopped and looked at him.

"That idea ain't half bad."

I ran into the garage and he followed after. I found my notepad on the workbench and began scribbling rough figures. I knew how much the twenty, eight-foot dogs had cost to build and tried to estimate off the cuff what sixteen would cost that were just short enough to make it through the door but still large and in charge; six feet. I hadn't built six-foot dogs yet, but I had a pretty good idea how much it'd cost after a few minutes of laying my thoughts out.

"Okay, okay."

Andy tuned in and peered over at the notepad.

"So, I figure we have a little bit of change from those backorders we just secured the money on. If we combine that with the funds left in my account, we'd be able to do it."

Andy sighed and shook his head.

"Sounds risky."

"You're telling me. This is the last of my cash."

Andy walked back and forth for a moment and rubbed his forehead. He started to clear off the area in the center of the garage where we worked.

"Well, I guess if it does you in then I need to find a new job. But—"

He picked up his welding hood and shook the stray metal debris off its face.

"If you shut things down now, I need to find a new job. So, I say do it."

I patted him on the back and headed for the staircase to my living room. I had a few calls to make to get the ball rolling. I turned and looked at Andy. He was still holding the welding hood.

"That was just the pep talk I needed."

18

The kids were asleep. I dug through my duffel bag in the living room trying to think of anything I could have forgotten. A beam of light shined in my eyes through the window. Andy and my brother were both in the front yard, the sound of their chatter coming through the wall. They double checked everything we packed a few hours ago during the daytime. I looked over towards the kitchen at the clock on the stove; it read half past midnight. If we left any later, it'd be impossible to set the dogs up in Manhattan.

I grabbed my bag and headed outside. I always felt better in the morning—or middle of the night for that matter, once I stepped outside.

"Everything looks good to go."

"Great. Let's get a move on."

I started the truck up and began to maneuver the trailer into the street. Maple leaves blew across the road in the glow of oncoming headlights. I hit the brakes, and the car flew by us. My brother flew forward in his seat and the seatbelt caught him.

"Damn it. I just sent half a text message. I can't remember if I had my suit ironed."

I was half-listening to him. I was about to hit the gas and finally get us straightened out in the road when his words finally bounced around in my head.

"Your suit?"

"Yeah for the—"

"My suit!"

I slammed my truck into park, and he flew forward again. I ran up the driveway and through the door. I scrambled around my living room and bedroom grumbling until I found my suit hanging from a doorknob in the bathroom. I got back to the truck and tossed it in the back seat next to Andy.

When we were finally on the highway, I started to feel better. We passed the sixteen-foot dog sitting on Exit 48 and I gave it a little salute. Suddenly, I felt wide awake, the adrenaline overtaking the fatigue from lack of sleep. We all chattered back and forth about the ensuing excitement. More than ever before, it felt like we were in the big leagues. In a day's worth of time, we'd be rubbing elbows with celebrities.

The highway was empty until we hit New York, save for a few people heading home from a night out, or a police cruiser prowling. I watched the blur of pavement pass in the headlights. Andy and my brother eventually fell asleep and caught some rest before the big event. The dogs rattled in the trailer behind me, the sound echoing through the cab of the truck like a droning hum. I started to yawn so I dug an apple out of my pocket and bit into it.

My parents took the kids apple picking a few days back and we had a stockpile at the house. I wanted to go more than anything, but the weeks leading up to the event were insanity. We went forward with building sixteen new dogs just for New York. They were all six feet tall, so hopefully they'd fit through the six and a half foot doorway without any issues. I ordered the metal the day we hatched the idea and drained the last of my cash. We spent weeks in the shop making them.

One by one, the new dogs came together. This was my first time making a limited-edition variant of the *American Dog* Sculpture. We engraved the North Shore animal league's name into each of the sixteen in the exhibition. If they were going to be specially made for this event, I wanted them to be tied to it forever. At some point, we received a notification from the North Shore Animal League that they wanted to pay us to build miniature versions of the dog that would act as table ordinances. I naturally said yes, but I didn't have enough money to make one for each of the fifty tables at the event. I'd already spent more than I intended building cat sculptures to sit on top of several of the dogs. The Northshore Animal League was very adamant about helping all types of pets and I thought they'd appreciate a few cats hopping along with the exhibition.

The table ordinances would be simple to make; I just needed to find the money between building sixteen of the six-foot dogs and four cats. A few days after we agreed to build them, Andy and I were cleaning up the garage before we closed up for the night. I watched him stack pieces of scrap in the corner of the room. A whole section of the scrap pile was cutouts in the shape of a bone from all of the dogs built between the New England exhibition and the new six-foot exhibition.

"Hold on a minute."

I grabbed a tape measure from the workbench and held it up to one of the cutouts. I smiled.

"Built all these sculptures just to make money off the scrap leftover, huh?"

"What?"

Andy was headed to pick up the rest of the scrap.

"We're going to have to put the main attraction on hold for a while. I'll see you here tomorrow."

The next day we got to work making fifty miniature dogs from the bone cutouts. We scaled them correctly so that we could make several of them from a single cutout. We had fifty miniatures, sixteen special edition dogs, and four cats loaded on the trailer when all was said and done.

It all amounted to tens of thousands of dollars in art and by the end of it, I barely had enough money to fill my truck's tank. We stopped at a gas station on the New York Border. Both of the guys were awake now. I was looking back at them a bit nervous while I swiped my card. I hoped I wouldn't have to end up asking for a loan from my brother or employee; luckily my card went through.

I left the pump on and went inside the gashouse to buy an energy drink. There was an old man at the counter, and I said hello.

"What's with the dogs on that trailer?"

I fumbled through my wallet for a few dollar bills. He stared out at the trailer tentatively.

"Sculptures. A whole lot of sculptures for an event in New York."

"You the delivery boy?"

He squinted and glanced at me. The energy drink wasn't scanning in the register.

"I'm an artist. But I'm also delivering them. So yes—I guess"

I handed him the bills and he began to thumb through the register for change. He didn't say anything while he did it; he just slouched and sighed and dropped the coins in my hand. I nodded and waved to him while I headed for the door.

"You don't look like no artist."

I nodded with my back turned and walked out towards the

EXIT 48

truck. I suppose I probably didn't, and I suppose people didn't expect that most artists have to do their own work. I know I didn't expect it at one point. I was well aware now! It was a whole lot more lifting and driving than it was creating actual art. I looked down at my clothes while I walked. I was in an old Carhartt and work boots. For a moment I was annoyed with the man, but I probably would've guessed I was a truck driver too.

I downed the energy drink and headed into New York City. As the winding forested highways turned into concrete outskirts, I felt the adrenaline come back into my veins. Things were heating up. The traffic was beginning to swell, and I had Andy on the lookout helping me maneuver the trailer through the congesting roadways. I could see the first rays of the sun creeping up between the growing city skyline. The air was turning blueish and I was beginning to see the outline of the world around me.

The closer we got to Wall Street the slower we went. It was making my hands shake. I felt myself reeling with anticipation like I was at my first trade show.

"Where are we gonna park?"

"No idea."

I could feel beads of sweat forming at my hairline. Outside, people moved quickly in cars, breaking often and speeding back up. All around me, taxis and commuters swerved around the behemoth trailer I was attempting to get through the tight corners of the city. I heard horns from every direction, most of them directed at me. I prayed I wouldn't miss a turn. One hop into the wrong lane would set us back an hour.

We finally made it to Cipriani at 6:30 in the morning and

hopped out in a scramble.

"You parked in a no-parking zone!"

"Where else are we gonna park?"

My brother threw his hands up.

"We're gonna get fined!"

"Travel expenses!"

My brother shook his head and waited for me to drag down the beams for the chain hoist. People in cars yelled and honked their horns.

I jumped off the trailer and tried pulling the front door of the building. Andy and my brother yelled to each other behind me over the blare of traffic growing. The building hadn't even opened yet.

"What's wrong?"

I ran back to the trailer and started placing the miniatures onto the sidewalk.

"Nobody's here yet."

"What are we gonna do with the dogs?"

I looked around. It was a congested area. There'd be people hurrying by soon and flooding the sidewalks.

"We'll have to leave them out front. We can't sit around with the trailer."

My brother poked his head into the conversation and nodded.

"We should get this thing off the street anyways."

The six-foot dogs were a bit lighter than the eight footers so we could make good time if we kept the energy up. The city was opening up, though, and the roads were filling with cars, trucks, bicycles and taxis.

"Screw the hoist. Let's just pick them up."

I climbed up with Andy and started pulling the dogs from their back legs. We lined each of the dogs and the four cats up on the sidewalk. When the sculptures were dragged out onto the sidewalk, we pulled our bags and suits from the truck and handed my credit card to Andy.

"Find a place to park this thing. Spend what you gotta."

He nodded and hopped in the driver's seat. He looked around nervously for a minute and booked it down wall street waving at cars as they honked. I looked over at my brother on the sidewalk. He looked restless.

"What now?"

"I guess we wait."

I walked over to the steps between the massive pillars of the building and sat down. I could see a hazy morning smog now that the sun began to shed light on the city. I smelt food somewhere—maybe miles away. I hadn't eaten since yesterday afternoon and was starving.

We sat until the first employee came into sight. He had a key and looked a little startled when we shuffled up to him.

"Can I help you?"

My brother and I looked at each other. We were already covered in sweat and panting.

"We're here for the Gala tonight. This is my exhibition."

I pointed to the row of dogs and cats on the sidewalk.

"Oh! Of course. Just let me unlock the door."

He unlocked the door and left it propped open. Once he went inside, I turned to my brother.

"Do I look like an artist?"

He shrugged.

"You're asking the wrong person. I don't know any other artists."

I held my chin and nodded.

"We don't look so bad, do we?"

He tilted his head and squinted one eye.

"We won't once we get some suits on. Come on."

He jogged over to the head of one of the dogs and got his shoulders under it. I dipped my shoulder under its tail.

"Okay. Time to get these things inside."

He nodded and we started down the line. We couldn't use a cart; the doorway and halls were too narrow. Everything had to be moved by hand. I was glad I got to visit the event space beforehand. I kept a mental note in my head of the layout and had many of the positions I'd place the dogs planned.

Inside was quiet and filled with nervous energy. Employees and management began to show up quickly and then were dashing back and forth to set everything up. I tried to lay low until the dogs were where they had to be. I had too many things on my mind and too much to worry about. My brother and I moved each one methodically into place. Once they were set up, we placed the four cats on top of four of the dogs. Andy returned holding my credit card and an armful of the miniature dogs.

"Just place one on each table."

I took my card and a few of the dogs and started putting them on top of the tables as I walked by. We raced back and forth placing them until there was a little army of miniatures positioned in between the six-foot giants.

We got most of the dogs inside the main event area with a few outliers positioned around the halls and separate rooms. When it was all said and done, I leaned up against the wall outside with Andy and my brother. We all looked out of place. All of the staff were already dressed in formal attire. I looked down at my cell phone; it was noon.

EXIT 48

The city was becoming hot in the way that only a metropolis can in November. The heat bounced off the aluminum of passing cars and windows and sunk deep into the concrete, radiating upward and hitting the bottoms of our faces. I could still smell food somewhere far away.

"Lunchtime?"

"Sounds good to me."

We walked down the street scanning the area. Everything around us was posh and upscale. We finally found a cafe a little way down and bought sandwiches. Our bags were strewn around the table while we sipped hot coffee and ate. I could see suited lawyers and stockbrokers around us talking on earpieces.

"I figure we go to the hotel after this."

Andy and I nodded at my brother. The city was exhausting; especially during the day and especially while trying to transport a trailer's worth of sculptures. It felt good to fill my stomach with food and I could feel myself dozing off.

"I wanna see the *Charging Bull* before I head home"

"Charging Bull?"

I nodded and swallowed a bite of food.

"Yeah. You know—that bronze sculpture of a bull in that park. I never ended up around these parts when I'd go to New York with Gene, so I've never seen it in person.

My brother crumpled his sandwich wrapper in his hands and tossed it in a nearby barrel.

"Better drink another coffee then. It's gonna be a long night."

I laughed and nodded. I'd always been interested in the *Charging Bull;* not so much for what it stands for or what the artist intended, but rather the way he went about installing it. He paid out of pocket to create and install the sculpture. He installed it illegally—right outside the stock exchange with a truck. It got taken away and reinstalled down the street when the public spoke out against its removal. I always admired the guts and determination it took to do something like that. I was continually finding myself more intrigued by stories like *Charging Bull* as much as stories of installations like *The Gates*. He wanted to do something, so he did it, and ultimately his piece of "guerilla art," bloomed into a tourist attraction and beloved icon in the eyes of the same people that tried to tear it down years ago. I daydreamed a lot about pulling stunts like that, and in a lot of ways, I felt like I could relate to what the artist must have been feeling.

After we ate, we walked back to our hotel rooms. The Dog-Catemy Awards was in a couple of hours and we all wanted to try and nap beforehand. I laid on the hotel mattress and listened to an audiobook with my eyes closed. I couldn't stop fidgeting; there was too much excitement, regardless of how run down I was. I closed my eyes and listened to the narrator until I began to feel myself drift off.

Before I knew it, I heard banging on the door. I sprang up from the bed and looked around. I'd fallen asleep and the sky outside was black. My hotel room had flooded with darkness. The banging came again from the doorway. I could see a sliver of yellow light creeping from the bottom of the door, a shadow behind it flickering.

"C'mon, Get up!

My brother's voice was muffled from the hallway. I glanced around the room and scrambled for my phone to check the time. I was going to be late.

I ran from the bed and tripped over my bag. When I got up, I limped over to the doorway and flicked the main lights on. My brother was standing in a suit dialing his cellphone.

"About time. Mom and Dad are waiting in the lobby."

I wiped my eyes and pulled my suit from its hanger. I got ready as fast I could, splashing water on my face and trying to make myself look less exhausted. The doorway was half open and I could see Andy scrambling around in the hallway. As I fixed my hair, I could hear the muffled voices of my parents coming up from the elevator and onto our floor. I stopped for a moment and tried to listen. They sounded excited and happy. It made me smile. When I got myself together, I found everybody by the elevator.

"There he is!"

My dad laughed. We all exchanged hugs and headed for Cipriani. When we arrived, I felt my eyes grow wider in my head. The building had transformed. People stood outside the main doorway between the Greek columns. I felt the adrenaline dump into my veins as we headed into the building. Between the crowds of shimmering designer dresses and black suits, I could see my family's faces glowing with excitement. Colored fluorescent lights washed over the crowd from the main stage; candles danced over white tablecloths and bounced off silverware and glass. My mother whispered to my father and pointed at my sculptures as we passed them. Every so often somebody's eyes would jump, and they'd lean over and whisper about a celebrity they caught a glimpse of.

The event had what they dubbed a "green carpet," or a pet-friendly red carpet. We passed by the flashing cameras and celebrities posing with attendees of the event. Many of the celebrities had their pets with them. It was funny seeing people dressed so nice walking their dogs.

At one point, I saw a head of curly hair pass in my peripheral. I did a double-take and saw a lanky man with sunglasses walking next to a woman. I grabbed my brother's shoulder.

"Is that Howard Stern?"

"It is. Look, his wife's walking their bulldog."

It was crazy to see Beth and Howard, never mind the famous bulldog Bianca Stern. I stared at Howard Stern's sunglasses disappearing into the crowd. I thought back to the early years of my career as an artist, building tables, and wall art to sell at trade shows. I'd hear his voice over the radio I kept in my shop. Everything felt absurd for a moment—like I'd fallen off a cliff into a strange dream world. I was in Manhattan with my art exhibition at a celebrity event. It hit me so hard at that moment that it felt like it never occurred to me where I was or what I was doing. I could remember how crushed I felt when a local gallery owner shooed me away. I could still hear the strain and impatience in his voice; like I was a child annoying him with something that didn't make sense. Some of them even threatened me. Now I was standing in the middle of an upscale event organized by one of the world's largest animal leagues. Waiters and waitresses passed by me carrying hors d'oeuvres and champagne. A dome ordained with painted murals sat above my head. Within the spectacle of it all, my sculptures stood to greet guests. All around the building they were woven between crowds of people. They became part of the environment; the ecosystem of the moment. That was one of my favorite things about the exhibition. It was a strange "fly on the wall," type of experience at times, watching the way artwork integrates into an environment and how people interact with it. I could see from my table people holding and inspecting the table ordinances we built. I was happy we built them. They were at the center of everyone's dinner and conversation.

We were seated at our table and eventually served food. Andy and I drank complimentary Champagne and I listened to the forks clang and conversation roar around me. My miniature dog sculpture sat proudly in front of me while we ate, lit up by golden candlelight. As we ate, nobody discussed anything that was a burden. There was no talk of broken bottling equipment or rotted barn panels. They were engulfed in the moment, both for themselves and me. I felt grateful to have them around me. If it were all for nothing, it was still worth being with them. Nonetheless, a little person in my head was still panicking. The night was moving quickly, and I hadn't had a single inquiry about the sculptures.

As the night moved into the award ceremony, the crowd hushed down and remained seated. We listened to the North Shore Animal League discuss the purpose of the event and remind us about the core of why we were all there. Afterward, celebrities took the stage and talked about their support for the organization. The 2009 DogCatemy awards began. Celebrities submitted videos of them with their pets. Some were funny, some were endearing. The crowd erupted into laughter and mused at adorable pets of all kinds.

There was voting in regards to whose videos would win awards. Alongside the awards for the videos, many people were winning awards for their contributions to the animal league and their overall impact on animals in need. I tried to pay attention to the award ceremony, but I couldn't. I could feel my hand shaking and was working up a sweat. My family talked about things around me and it sounded like echoes. I'd be winning an award tonight for my art. I knew it all along but hadn't felt nervous until that moment. Something switched inside me and I felt like a kid again, tucked in the back of a classroom praying a teacher wouldn't call on me to read or speak in front of the class.

"You alright?"

I broke out of the spiral and found Andy staring at me, his eyebrow arched and concern on his face. I yanked the collar of my shirt and centered the knot of my tie.

"What do you mean? Do I not look okay?"

He stared at me and didn't say anything.

"You look okay."

"Cheers to that."

I clacked his glass with mine. It was good Champagne; probably expensive. I didn't even drink Champagne and I could tell it was. I took a deep breath and poured another glass, taking a sip while I closed my eyes and tried to listen to the speaker. My mother grabbed my arm and pointed discreetly towards the woman speaking on stage.

"And here tonight we have the artist responsible for these beautiful pieces."

Time was moving fast, and I hadn't been listening. I clenched my fist so my hand would stop shaking. I felt dizzy.

"Dale Rogers!"

I stood up; my legs felt like jello, but once I got them moving, I felt the adrenaline send a lightning bolt into my brain. People were clapping as I traveled to the stage. I could hear my father's clap within all of them, distinctive in its sound like some people's are. As I got to the side of the stage, I climbed the steps and felt the heat of the bright lights mounted on a steel bar overhead. I zoned in on the plaque in the speaker's hand and the eyes of the crowd melted away. It felt almost like moving in slow motion; like drifting underwater. The only thing I could feel for a moment was the heat of the lights and my dress shoes thudding the stage as I walked forward. I shook her hand

and grabbed the plaque. When I touched it the noises and sights of the room returned like someone had turned up a television set.

I could hear her announcing the next reward as I walked back. People simmered to silence between announcements and I could hear my shoes now, thudding along the floor between tables of people. I returned to the table and my family quietly congratulated me. When I passed my mother, I went to hug her and saw a look on her face I hadn't seen in years. It was the look from when I was in high school and the teachers gave me an award for my art. I must've taken it for granted at that time because I didn't remember it feeling as important as it did now. I was too young then to admit it, but now that I was here, I saw that making her proud trumped everything else.

When the awards were over, we sat and had some more drinks, talking about old times and plans for the future. My parents were talking about going on vacation, which I thought they should do more often. My brother and I both laughed about our kids while my mother asked Andy a million questions about how his mother was doing. Eventually, my parents tapped out and headed for their hotel room. I was surprised they'd even made it as late as they did.

The event would be clearing out soon. We were told we'd have to pack the exhibition up the moment the crowd departed.

"This is gonna be rough."

My brother had come back to our table with drinks for the three of us. We cheered our drinks.

"Amen to that."

We all looked a little crazy at this point—like we were put together but barely hanging on. We were starting to become bolder and get louder. When all the cups were empty it was my turn to order, so I walked up to the bar.

I sat swiveling on the stool until the bartender appeared wiping a glass. He stood looking at me intently.

"Three vodka sodas."

He began making them with no comment in between. I felt bad. The staff seemed like they'd had as long a day as us.

While I waited for the drinks, I caught sight of a woman walking in my direction. I couldn't tell if she was walking towards me or not. The bartender put the drinks in front of me and I closed the tab, digging through my wallet for a credit card. I finally found it and handed it over. When I was putting it back in my wallet, I felt a tap on my shoulder.

"Congratulations on your award. Your work is great."

I hadn't heard the voice before. I spun around and it was the woman I saw walking towards me. She extended her hand.

"My name is Cathy Bissell. Nice to meet you."

19

"I'd like to inquire about purchasing one of the exhibition pieces."

I sat back down on the barstool and she sat down a few seats over.

"I have some friends that I think would love it—an organization that's similar to the North Shore Animal League."

"Great—that would be great."

Mrs. Bissel asked.

"Is somebody waiting for drinks?"

I looked down at the glasses on the bar table. I'd forgotten all about them.

"No, no—its—

"Go drop them off. I'll be here."

I apologized and ran the drinks to the table. When I dropped them off my brother was about to say something, but I had to cut him off.

"I'm busy—I'll be back in a few."

"With what?"

I didn't have time to answer. I was already speeding back. I'd yet to sell a piece at an exhibition before. There was something inexplicably better about it than trade shows. I hadn't even discussed the sale yet and I already knew it was better. It felt more genuine; maybe because although it was apparent they were for sale, it wasn't the primary purpose of the exhibition. Sometimes, trade shows felt like you were a vendor at a flea market more than an artist. They were chaotic and people could be curt and rude. I hoped this wouldn't be the case with Mrs. Bissell. It'd sting even more if it were during an exhibition.

To my relief, I returned to the bar and she was still there. I sat on the same stool as before and talked casually for a little bit, telling her my story. I told her how *The American Dog* came to be, about the one on Exit 48, and the New England Exhibition. I finally caught my breath and swung the conversation towards the potential sculpture purchase. I asked her about her organization.

"I'm the founder of the Bissell Pet Foundation. We work with many animal leagues around the United States. There's an animal league particularly close to us that I'd like to purchase a sculpture for."

"In New York?"

"In Michigan. The specific animal league is the Western Michigan Humane Society." I nodded and sighed. I tried to do a rough estimate in my head of how much it'd cost to get it out there. After a moment I explained to her I couldn't drive it out without losing money. A perplexed look ran across her face.

"*You're* the artist. I believe it's more up to what you want to charge than what I would want to pay."

I stared at her for a moment and didn't say anything. I was slightly suspicious.

"I would just end up having to charge—"

She started shaking her head and motioning her hand for me to stop talking.

"I understand how these things are."

She looked down and began to go through her purse.

EXIT 48

"I'm in charge of putting events like this together. There's a lot that goes into it that people don't think about. What I'm trying to say is—"

She pulled a business card from her wallet and handed it to me. I could see my brother and Andy in the background leaving our table and gearing up to move.

"I'm no stranger to the expenses and planning it takes to do something like this. I understand you have to make a living."

I thanked her and told her I'd call and figure out details once I was back in Massachusetts. She walked off and I immediately got to packing things up. The venue was making it very clear we had to pack up as fast as possible. My brother ran to get the truck and trailer from the parking lot we parked it in while Andy and I began dragging everything out into the street.

"Who was that?"

Andy peered his head around the front of one of the dogs while we carried it down the front steps of Cipriani. We let it down onto the sidewalk and I loosened the knot of my tie.

"A potential buyer. She wants me to drive one of the dogs out to Michigan. Her name is Cathy."

I pulled the business card from my breast pocket and handed it to him. He held it close to his face and read her name out loud.

"Cathy Bissell."

When he said her name out loud it all once felt like a lightbulb exploded in my head.

"Bissell—like on the signs around the venue?"

My jaw dropped. Their logo was all around me. They were a huge sponsor of the event. I was exhausted, but still the shockwave was running through me now. They must've been a pretty serious pet foundation. The possibilities of what that implied ran through my head, but I knew I had to focus on moving the dogs. Once Andy and I were close to getting all of them out on the sidewalk my brother returned with the trailer. The three of us began the long process of lifting the sculptures onto the trailer and securing them down. The cocktails and energy drinks had long worn off and we worked idly with our ties and suit jackets draped across the hood of the truck. The wind became wintry through the city and the gusts of coolness began to make my eyelids sink. By the time everything was packed, my brother leaned against the side of the trailer with his eyes closed, shifting now and again when the sound of a passing car woke him from his half-sleep.

"Want me to drive it back to the lot? I still have the parking pass."

"That's alright."

I took the ticket stub from my brother and shuffled over to the driver's door.

"I'll see you guys at the hotel. I haven't been on a walk in a while anyhow."

Andy yawned while he nodded and poked at my brother. My brother jumped up from his slouch and blinked his eyes. They started for the hotel while I drove down to the address on the ticket stub.

When I arrived at the lot, I dropped the truck and trailer off and began to make my way back to the hotel. As I walked, I could hear the echoes of the bars closing. People laughed and shouted at one another and hailed taxis. Now and then, I could hear the echo of high heels and group chatter. I could barely keep my eyes open, but I felt filled with new hope and appreciation. I knew I had to drive the sculpture out to Michigan. I knew myself well enough to know

EXIT 48

I wouldn't pass it up; even if I told myself tomorrow, I wouldn't do it. It felt good to be back on track a little bit from the money made off the table ordinances. It was enough to keep going; no more and no less. In a way, it was a burden, as all truly good things are to some extent. Cathy Bissel's inquiry was the only possible sale I'd landed the whole night. It was the only potential sale of the whole exhibition since the first date. Nonetheless, it was a new frontier and a glimmer of hope.

I made it back to Cipriani and stopped outside. Bowling Green was right across the street. I'd been too busy to stop all day and night. I let a car pass and jogged over to the park. I kept walking until it sat right in front of me; its weathered bronze giving off a dull sheen from the streetlights. The *Charging Bull* stood frozen and poised to leap forward. One day, it showed up unannounced and survived attempts to be put away somewhere; labeled as unwanted half-rate artwork by the same people who now pass it on their way to work and feel pride. I wondered what the artist expected to happen when he dropped it off in the dead of night. Did he expect they wouldn't try to put it away? Maybe he knew it all along. No matter why he dropped it off and how he felt then I'm sure he felt good now. I patted it on the snout and made my way off to the hotel. We'd be leaving early in the morning.

When I returned home to Haverhill, things settled back to normal. I called Cathy the following week and finalized the trip out to Michigan. I'd drive out in the spring to the Western Michigan Humane Society's headquarters and drop it off for them. Spring was a ways out, and I had to keep everything from breaking back down, so I had trade shows lined up ahead of time. Many of them were booked long before we went to New York because I knew that even if I ended up quitting all of it, I'd still have no way out besides selling art.

Andy and I made haste finishing up whatever last sculptures were laying around unfinished. I didn't have enough money to start building anything new, and since I only set up one sale at the Gala, I had no choice but to piece up the New York Exhibition and sell them at trade shows.

It was strange going back to working out of a booth in convention centers, old armories and public parks. At times it felt downright absurd and cruel. Bringing the exhibition to New York had aged into a strange memory that felt as if someone had brought me into a glimpse of my hopes and dreams and then shoved me out. Now I was back to lugging my art around the east coast and getting haggled.

One particular show, I sat at my booth trying to sort out some logistics for driving out to Michigan. The months had gone by and I'd be leaving soon. I was writing down the phone number of a hotel I'd found in Michigan when I felt someone in my peripheral. I looked up and there was a short, older man giving me a blank stare.

"Are you the one that makes these?"

I shuffled out of my seat and closed up my notepad.

"Yes sir. Out of my garage in Massachusetts."

He walked around touching all the sculptures on display. He kept gravitating towards one of my newer pieces. After barely selling at the New York Exhibition, the six-foot dogs did great at trade shows. It hurt to break the limited-edition collection up but it felt better to have a little bit of safety cash in my pocket. I had enough where I felt a little brave and used some of it to build a new design.

"This owl."

"That owl?"

I walked over to him. He was gazing in its eyes.

EXIT 48

"I felt like it spoke to me when I walked by."

I smiled. I wondered if it was going to become one of my more popular pieces. It was hard to tell if a piece would hit its mark or not. There was a science to it, no doubt. I'd spent years learning how to understand it, but there was still some magic to it that eluded me.

"Thank you. It's one of my—"

"My granddaughter. My granddaughter loves owls. She saw one in the front yard and never stops talking about it."

He wandered around and looked at some other sculptures. One by one he inspected each tiny aspect of them, but he kept coming back to the owl and staring at it. Finally, he called me over.

"How much?"

He had a sort of grimace on his face. I couldn't tell if it was from the light being in his eyes or if he was doing it on purpose.

"For this one? I'd have to do three grand on this one."

"Not worth it."

"What?"

"Not worth it."

He shook his head violently. I was stunned and felt disrespected. I'd priced it low since it was new, and I was testing the waters. Even if he didn't think it was worth it, he didn't have to air his opinion out. I felt a new kind of disdain for people down talking my work. I didn't want to back-pedal to dealing with it all the time.

"Well look at it from my perspective. I have to buy steel, supplies, pay bills and employees—never mind drive it out. If you really want it, I could—"

"I'll give you nine hundred."

"Nine hundred?"

He stared with the same grimace on his face. I must've been

slack-jawed because it was getting worse.

"Unfortunately, I'm going to have to pass that offer up."

I walked back to the center of my booth and let him walk away. I expected him to try to talk me down nine hundred, not give me it as an offer. For someone so moved by a piece of art, he bartered for it like it was an old moped. Unfortunately, he wasn't the only one. I sometimes wondered if some people loved owning art or just loved feeling like they got something for as cheap as possible.

It was strange to me that people's opinions of my work and its worth shifted with the environment it was in. If it was a Gala in New York, they spoke about it with high esteem. If it was in a booth at an art fair, they talked down upon it. It made me ponder strange things about art. Did anybody like something just because they liked it? If it wasn't just about liking the piece of art, then what was it actually about?

It was safe to say I was ready to drive out to Michigan. Any hardship it implied was better than sitting around and remaining stagnant. I loaded the dog up into my truck and stocked what I needed to get to Grand Rapids, Michigan. I drove west through Massachusetts towards the Berkshires and then up into upstate New York. I followed Route 20 through farmland and colonial villages until I passed Buffalo. Once I was up by The Great Lakes, I slept in a motel along Lake Erie. When I woke up, I got an early start and headed towards Cleveland. The land slowly flattened, and the wind bolstered as the New England sphere of influences subsided and the industrial decay of the rust belt began to emerge in scattered glimpses along the lake.

The only time I'd been to Michigan was on my bike expedition home from studying abroad. The only person I knew out there was my old friend Mike Regan. I figured I'd see what he was up to and maybe catch up since I didn't know if I'd be back in that corner of the country any time soon.

"Hello?"

"Mike? It's Dale. Hey, listen—I'm gonna be in Grand Rapids tonight. I know it's short notice but if you're around I figure we should grab a drink somewhere."

"You're in Michigan? I wish you would have let me know sooner. You caught me in the middle of a vacation with the family."

I looked at the clock on my phone. I probably wouldn't be in until late anyhow.

"Why the hell are you headed to Grand Rapids anyways?"

"I got a commission for my work. I'm dropping off a sculpture at The Western Michigan Humane Society."

I heard Mike mumbling at someone wherever he was. He put the phone back to his face.

"You're still kicking with the sculpture work? Not that I'm surprised—but congratulations buddy. They're a big deal out here."

I thanked him and laughed. Talking to him reminded me of older times. It was bumming me out that we couldn't catch up. There was a silence over the phone.

"I wish you didn't catch me on such a busy week. But listen—I went to this thing out here last fall. It's called ArtPrize. I haven't seen an Art event like it before. It's a competition and the winner wins a quarter of a million."

"Competition?"

"Yep. It's a lot to explain; look it up when you can. Maybe you can set something up."

I recited the name of the competition in my head over and over. *Art Prize. Art Prize. Art Prize.* As I recited it to myself, I saw Cleveland far in the distance.

"I'm gonna look into that. Thanks for tipping me off. But I'll let you go."

"Sounds good. Congrats again buddy. Take Care."

I said goodbye to Mike and repeated the name periodically as I drove. When I made it to Grand Rapids I checked into my motel and searched *ArtPrize* on my phone while the television chattered. I found their website and read their "about" page:

"ArtPrize is an open, independently organized international art competition which takes place for 19 days every fall in Grand Rapids, Michigan. $250,000 in prizes are awarded by smartphone-enabled public vote, including a $200,000 grand prize."

I kept reading. The competition took place all over the city. The streets themselves became a gallery for an immense amount of artwork. I'd never heard of an event like it. The grand prize was enormous; enough to do life-changing things with. I couldn't help but think about the doors it would open up: better equipment, no debt, maybe even a revamped exhibition. Public voting was crazy to me as well. The smartphone era was just beginning to bloom and things were changing in unexpected ways. The public's vote sounded much more organic and exciting than a panel of judges. I knew I had to find a way in.

In the morning, I brought the sculpture to the Western Michigan Humane Society. They loved it and we fell into conversation about the work their humane society does in the Midwest. I told them about myself and explained the origins of the sculpture they were receiving; about the exhibition in New York and how I met

Cathy. Eventually, when the conversation began to fizzle, I went for it.

"Have either of you by any chance heard of ArtPrize?"

One of the coordinator's eyes lit up.

"Of course. We were there for its debut last year in 2009."

"Have you thought about partnering with an artist?

I had thought about it through the night and on the drive to meet them. After doing some research I noticed many of the artists partner with brands and organizations. Ever since the New York exhibition, I wanted to keep doing work that benefited humane societies. It seemed like a positive choice all around.

"We've discussed it a good amount, actually. Are you going to propose we partner for the event?"

I shrugged and put my hands up.

"I'd love to come back out with more of my work—and it's a cause I'd love to support."

They both hesitated for a moment and flashed glances at each other. One of them tilted her head and smiled at me.

"I think that's a phenomenal idea, but there are other people who have a say in it as well. Could we get your information and we'll—"

"Of course!"

I dug through my pocket and gave her a piece of paper from my notepad with my name and email. She nodded and thanked me for driving out. I told them I was happy to do it and thanked them as much as I could. I also told them that I hoped to hear from them and then headed back to my motel. The following morning, I drove home. It was a long trip back to Massachusetts, but when I finally made it back, I arrived to find out they'd said yes. *The Big Dog Show* would be headed to Michigan to compete in the 2010 *ArtPrize*.

20

I once heard somebody call ArtPrize the "wild west" of art competitions. It was comparatively fresh and new from the old quota of art competitions, more akin to an election than an academy award. It required the average individual's participation to function rather than a panel of judges, and the competition brought artists and observers alike to the streets of Grand Rapids, Michigan in droves. For a short time every year, a midwestern city's serious and practical landscape turned into a hub for eccentricity.

It was autumn of 2010 when I loaded up the original *American Dog* exhibition and drove out to Grand Rapids to reunite with the West Michigan Humane Society. It was the competition's second year and there was overwhelming nervous energy in the air. I was amazed at the things I saw while setting my sculptures up. People hung things from buildings and bolted installations down in the middle of foot traffic. Artists worked on their pieces while being installed and argued amongst each other as equipment was moved. I didn't know how the event could get away with it; I was so used to months of planning and negotiation to get a single sculpture exhibited in a park. Either Michigan had very different laws than the East Coast or they were winging it. However, they were making it happen, there was electricity in the air.

I talked to some people who had bet their lives on winning—on hauling the quarter of a million back halfway across the country to where they lived. I'd think about them while I explored the city. Out in the streets would be hordes of eager crowds getting early glimpses of the art. Banking on winning was like banking on a scratch ticket; no matter how much of a dreamer I was, even I knew that. There was a building in Grand Rapids nicknamed the 'Big Old Building', or 'B.O.B' for short. It was the beating heart of the event, and only a few artists were lucky enough to get their work exhibited close to it. It became apparent before things even kicked off that I wasn't going to beat somebody with their work near the B.O.B, and neither were any other of the artists scattered about the city. I wasn't too bummed out, though. I couldn't even fathom that type of cash dropping in my bank account all at once, so it was pretty easy to leave it in the back of my head and focus on finding some new connections in the Midwest.

    I drove around the chaos looking for my assigned site to set up. I knew enough that it was a park and was relieved I wouldn't be somewhere too metropolitan. Plus, the color palette of the old Industrial City would swallow my sculptures in plain sight. After some more frantic searching, I found 6th Street Park. It sat along the Grand River and was filled with green grass and russet autumn foliage. It was a strip of vibrance separating the steel-blue of the city and the steel blue of the river. It would be a place where my sculptures would be complemented by the trees overhead and stand in contrast to colder hues in the distance. It was a short walk from downtown and I hoped I'd have a few crowds stroll my way and hang out.

    As I pulled the trailer in, a few volunteers from West Michigan Humane Society were already waiting. They'd been kind enough to send me some help for setup and loading out. My partnership with the West Michigan Humane Society was loose and easygoing, which worked just fine for me. Like everybody in attendance, we were winging it. Most other competitions prohibit any form of partnership between artists and organizations, but ArtPrize was new and taking its first steps. Artists partnered with restaurants, local schools, outlets, and nonprofits. Representatives of different brands and organizations suited up to spread the word about themselves, carrying promotional material. Everybody wanted to be part of the commotion. Years later, this freedom for anybody to stick their hand in the pot would cause some hiccups for ArtPrize; it had to find a means to become more self-contained eventually. I thought it was a shame. On one hand, it may have opened the floodgates for things to stray away from the art, but on the other, it offered opportunities for artists. It never bothered me to see an artist earning the money or publicity they deserved.

Regardless of how specific or nonspecific it was, there was an obvious benefit to the partnership between the West Michigan Humane Society and I. I'd agreed to donate a percentage of any sales that occur to them, and my work naturally resonated with people sympathetic to their cause. Partnering with an artist gave them a connection to the event and being from states away I benefited from their locality. They were also great about helping me with the many logistical issues of exhibiting at the event. I was flying solo this time and they'd been nice enough to lend a few volunteers to help me set up. They also let me store my trailers and equipment on their property.

There were other benefits on each end of the deal, but at the end of the day it was just for kicks. We were both there to spread the word about ourselves and have a little fun. On the morning of kick-off day, I double-checked the dogs. It was early, and the streets were just beginning to swarm. I made quick time moving everything to the

EXIT 48

Humane Society's headquarters and made it back to the park with a little time to kill. I could feel pain in my stomach. I always felt a little nervous before shows, no matter the context. Sometimes I felt like I was less nervous when everything was falling apart. When things went smoothly I had too much time to think. I realized I hadn't eaten yet. I'd smelt food on the way from the shelter and decided to go downtown to look for it.

I walked on foot and found a little pizza shop that sold by the slice. On my way back I took my time weaving between the swelling crowd of people forming. The broad, open streets of Grand Rapids filled in with people, leaving no room to see cutouts of open sky between buildings. People met up with one another and huddled in groups, trying to figure the voting system out on their phones as the event took off. Shop owners came out to mingle in the excitement. The city air smelt of exhaust, beer, and popcorn. I passed several artists with installations on sidewalks and the sides of buildings. I felt the excitement rush through me and hoped I'd be able to explore what others had done. There was something surreal about seeing so much artwork clinging to the city. I thought it was how it should always be. Like the people in the streets, the art-filled in the gaps of the city. Cities are famously a place where creatives flock to, but they're just as well a place where creativity struggles to persist. They have an exhaustive and burdening—even sedative, quality to them. It is so easy to fall under the current of nightlife and endless work; under the grumble of rush hour and the subway terminals. Sometimes when I am in the city and surrounded by so many people, I forget that any of us even are people. The art around the city breaks through the noise and reminds me we're all still here.

When I got back to my sculptures there were already people

wandering from downtown and making their way between the dogs. It made me smile to see them drop in and out of interest, sometimes looking together at the dogs and then becoming momentarily occupied with something else. It was one of my favorite aspects of installing the exhibition at parks. They became a part of people's surroundings and environment, rather than something they stood around that was isolated from them.

    I took a seat and spoke to whoever wanted to talk. Now and then I'd notice someone giving my work a vote. It felt great every time; especially since my sculptures weren't the first ones they saw. My favorite part of the event turned about to be wandering around when I had the chance. I met a lot of great artists and felt inspiration flicker inside of me. The more I spoke to artists the more I saw the beauty in ArtPrize. Many of the artists I spoke to were inexperienced and just taking the first steps into their potential careers. If they were to go all-in, then soon standing before them was a life of aimlessness, struggle, and ongoing financial and emotional instability. For all of my trudging around and sleepless nights, I knew that I was lucky in comparison to most. Most aspiring artists didn't make *anything*, and in regards to that my sales at trade shows were a blessing that kept me afloat. It felt great to see positivity and happiness in the faces' of so many artists. Although only one of them would win, this event gave them all a reason to keep the dream alive another day.

    A couple of days in, I arrived at the site early and found a car parked near my sculptures. I stepped out of my truck and tried to get a look at who was there. Back when I did the New England Exhibition, I'd arrived on site one day to find one of my sculptures knocked over and left lying in the dirt. I remember the sentiment was like a punch to the gut. When somebody tries to steal your art, there's a strange sliver of pride that makes it not so bad. When they uproot it from its metal base just to leave it tipped over on the ground there's not too much to be proud over. Ever since then, I'd been a bit on guard, and as I approached the car, I caught sight of a woman walking around the dogs. She didn't look like she was trying to sabotage the exhibition, but I was still confused about why someone was pacing around my sculptures at the break of day.

I got closer and rubbed my eyes. Of all people, it was Cathy Bissell. She caught sight of me and waved, smiling. I felt bad for assuming so quickly it'd be someone doing something negative.

"How's it going?"

"Good! I'm surprised to see you here so early."

I was surprised she even recognized me. She was jotting things down on a little notepad. She seemed involved and occupied with something and didn't look up for long from her writing. I put my hands in my coat pockets. The wind through the park turned frigid as it swept over the river. I hoped the sun would warm things back up later.

"I'm just making some notes—for the adoption event next weekend."

"Oh."

I crossed my arms and nodded. I caught a glimpse of her notepad and saw the compiled data, cleanly bulleted with indented sub-notes.

"I think right here—"

She pointed at the grass a few feet in front of us with her pen.

"Right here would be a good spot to set up the tables."

She motioned for me to follow. She was talking about the main event of ArtPrize for both of us. The Western Michigan Humane Society was hosting an adoption event. They'd be wheeling in a whole troop of dogs from their shelters looking for a new home. My sculptures would be the backdrop of the event, serving as the scenery to families hopefully meeting their new best friend. I knew Cathy and the Bissell Pet Foundation were sponsoring the event, but I didn't expect to see her up early in the morning checking out the site. At most I thought she'd just send a volunteer. She scanned the park while we walked, calculations, and concerns jumping about her head. We'd walked to a shady spot under one of the trees that were scattered around the park. Two of my sculptures neighbored us.

"I think this would be a great spot to set up an area for people to get to know the dogs available for adoption."

I looked at the ground and then up at the treetops, trying to think of something helpful to say. I had no idea what variables were being thought out, but I trusted she knew what she was talking about.

"I think so too."

She smiled and swooshed a checkmark on something she wrote down. I followed her back to our cars.

"So, how're you enjoying ArtPrize?"

"It's great. I've never seen so much great artwork at once."

She agreed and told me about the previous year; the different artists there, the highlights and ups and downs. She asked me if I caught anyone voting for my work and I told her how great it felt. It felt even better when they came up and spoke to me about it. She smiled and waited for me to stop ranting.

"You know, a few of my friends mentioned your work."

I pointed at myself and she laughed and nodded.

"Yes, yours. Keep up the good work. I'll see you at the adoption event."

We'd arrived at her car. She got in and drove off while I stood somewhat perplexed. In a way, I felt somewhat enlightened—or maybe inspired. It was humbling to see someone put work into something they're passionate about that they don't have to. The fact I was surprised to see her up early and surveying an event site was a testament to her character and work ethic. There are so few people in the world who put everything into what they care about—who stay on task and keep their goal clear in front of them. It reminded me of my own goals and made me think of what else I could be doing to move forward. I started to fret around my sculptures brushing any fallen leaves from their backs. I thought about the questions from the exchange that perplexed me much more. I wanted to know who her friends were and what they said about my art. It ran through my head like a freight train until I couldn't think anymore.

As the week went by, I forgot she'd ever mentioned it. I got myself to stop thinking about it by telling myself it must've been something good they said, and regardless of what that implied it had to be a good thing. Once the hustle and bustle of running an exhibition and navigating a citywide art festival took hold, the thought drifted into the back of my mind. The excitement of the crowd and contestants were culminating into a barreling force. Each day, more people filled the streets to vote and the first heavyweights were starting to emerge from the flurry of cellular votes. I was getting left in the dust, but it was no big deal to me. I was amazed at how many people I got to speak to. It was significantly more than some of the New England dates I put together. Nonetheless, toward the end of the first week the honeymoon stage of exhibiting in a distant place began to wear off. I began to remember that I was making nothing off of trucking out to this event. I was grateful the Western Michigan Humane Society had helped me out so much, as it softened the financial blow of the whole thing. Still, I was losing money—both in lost time at trade shows and straight from my bank account to make it out to the Midwest.

I was approaching the same old dead-end I always did. I had met amazing people during ArtPrize, but none that opened many doors for me to come back out west. For a moment, the entire event felt like the New England Exhibition; full of excitement and hope but surmounting to the realization I had no idea what I was doing or what I wanted. I despised the feeling of doubt in the back of my head. I still couldn't completely sell myself on the life I was living. It was exhilarating and full of emotions of triumph, but equally devastating and difficult. When the smoke cleared, I was always in the same place; run-down, broke, and hundreds of miles from my family. The feeling of reluctance felt like a burn that wouldn't heal, and with each negative experience it seared away any healing I'd developed over time. It all felt absurd. I had no clear direction forward or back.

On the day of the adoption event, Western Michigan Humane Society had their tables set up in the park by the time I had arrived. Soon enough a small army of energetic dogs appeared one way or the other. The bulk of them came in a truck, wheeled in and unloaded in their crates. Some stragglers came after in cars with volunteers. Before I knew it real dogs surrounded my sculptures of dogs. They were brought out on leashes and reeled with excitement at the new scenery and the growing curiosity of onlookers passing the park.

As we moved forward into the day, the humane society's volunteers worked diligently to talk to curious visitors. Now and then, I'd see a family walk over to the table and sign the papers promising a little dog a new life. It made me happy to see and helped sway me from the dark outlook I was continually developing about being an artist. When I saw a young couple or two parents with their younger children hold the dog they'd soon bring home, it reminded me I was contributing to something admirable. It made me feel proud; prouder than any amount of payment could make me.

I caught up with Cathy later on. She'd spent the day running back and forth, helping to educate people and introduce animals and potential owners. She worked throughout the day right beside the volunteers, and I only saw her for split moments at a time as she bustled from one place to the next.

When things settled for a bit, I was standing with her and all the volunteers. There were only a few people in the park now. One of the volunteers picked up a puppy and brought it to a little girl sitting in the grass under the canopy of trees. The puppy sat beside her while she talked to the volunteer.

"What do you think?"

Cathy had turned from talking to a member of the humane society.

"I think it's amazing. It feels good to be a part of something like this."

She smiled while she looked at the puppy playing with the little girl.

"Ever since I was little, I've loved animals. My whole life it's made me so upset that animals are mistreated or neglected or just left out in the cold. That is why I started The Bissell Pet Foundation."

I nodded and thought about the dogs I had as a kid. We always had dogs around the farm; both for companionship and work. It hurt to picture any of them being abused or starving out in the street.

. I'd realized I wasn't entirely sure what her foundation's role was in the grand scheme of things. I hadn't known her well enough or had enough time to get into specifics; I was just grateful to be involved. I asked her about what they did.

"Well—we act as a source of aid to humane societies. There are already so many struggling shelters across the country with animals in need. I wanted to do my part to improve the ones that we already have."

I nodded slowly. I was learning about a lot of the inner workings of humane societies and sponsors as I went.

"Essentially, we raise the money that the shelters need to function. We host fundraisers and events and then the money goes towards medical bills and microchipping."

She motioned her hand towards the park around us.

"*And* we sponsor adoption events—like what's happening today! Lots of the time we help families with the costs of adoptions too."

"Huh—that's great. It definitely makes more sense now."

We talked for a while until another wave of people rolled in. Cathy got caught up talking to people and explaining what she explained to me to them. I gathered a small audience and spread the word too while also talking about my sculptures. I suddenly felt like we were all part of the same movement, and it put fire in my step to interact with onlookers. I bustled around until the empty cages were tossed into the humane society's truck and the tables were folded up. The day was coming to a close and I felt worn out, but full of good feelings. It's hard not to feel great after being around puppies all day.

I was gathering my stuff to head back to my motel. I walked with Cathy to my truck with a bag of things.

"Cathy, thank you so much. Today was Amazing."

Cathy replied.

"You were a big part of making today great. The Big Dog Show was a big hit."

Everybody around us looked the same—in high spirits but drained of energy. The park had cleared out and now a few stragglers wandered about to themselves. Cathy unlocked the door to her car and looked at me.

"Hey—I've been talking to some friends in a humane society we work with. Remember I told you we hold fundraiser events?"

I nodded.

"Do you have any upcoming exhibitions planned?"

"No—to be honest, I'm not sure when I will next."

I had stopped with my bag in my hands. The cold wind was coming back over the river now that the sun had faded.

"So, you'd be available to come back? We'd love to have you as the featured exhibition of our event. It's here in Michigan—in Little Traverse Bay."

I stopped for a moment. I tried to think of the answer in my head, but my brain was at a standstill. I didn't want to commit in either direction.

"You have our number. Whatever you need, we can make it work. Give us a call."

She smiled and walked off to her car. I stood for a minute in the brisk air before walking back to my truck. I was half afraid of this happening—and all at once hoping more than anything. I'd been thrown another rope and if I didn't grab it, I had the ominous feeling I'd sink. If I did hold on, it'd pull me deeper out into the river.

I spent the rest of my time at ArtPrize thinking about it. The days flew by, one at a time. Eventually, the winner was announced, and the crowd disappeared until it was time for the artists to go home. As they all broke down their installations and exhibits I walked around the city. It looked like the end of the night at a house party in Haverhill—the discarded remnants of something that was once entirely in the present now a foggy memory that emanated a distant feeling of joy and happiness.

    The Humane Society helped me load everything up the following day and then I made my way home. I listened to audiobooks while I drove, letting the midwestern flats twist back into the mountain cities and oceanside I grew up in. I made it home a day and a half later. It was nighttime—far past my sons' bedtimes yet when I opened the door and shuffled in, they were awake. I was surprised at first, but not so much at the fact they were still awake. I was surprised at how old they had gotten. None of them were babies anymore, each of them now their own person beginning to develop out of the blank slate of infancy. I felt shocked at the realization and knew what it would take to make it back out to Michigan. I tucked them into bed and later laid up on the couch scribbling numbers on my notepad.

    I awoke in the same position, with my notepad still open on my chest. I sat up and yawned, feeling the soreness and ache of the uncomfortable conditions I'd slept in the past few days. I picked up my cell phone and called Cathy. I told her if I were going to come out, I had to bring my family with me. I had to make enough to do that. I told her how much it was—and she told me she couldn't wait for us to come out, and that she wouldn't have it any other way.

21

"Are we going to be at the Cabin tomorrow?"

"We'll be there the day after. Try to get some sleep, though. We have a long day ahead."

I patted Jude's head and yawned. I switched the light off and left the hotel room, heading out into the hotel parking lot. Outside was my new trailer, alongside the older one I had to reweld years ago. I'd gotten into the habit of checking on the dogs before bed. If they were stolen, it wasn't like I could go out with a local officer and recover them as I did with the original *American Dog* years ago. Still, there wasn't much reason to go out and check anymore; it was just an old habit. My old utility trailer was so rickety I used to worry someone would be able to drive away with it.

Coming out to Little Traverse Bay would be my first paid exhibition, and because of that, I was able to use the money I made at trade shows to secure a replacement. My parents towed it the whole way in their truck and it was a massive relief not having to worry about some type of dangerous mishap due to old and failing equipment. Plus, the new trailer was a bit larger and able to hold six dogs, rather than the four the old one could. It allowed me to move two dogs from the larger trailer and relieve some of the strain I was constantly putting on it.

When I woke up the next morning, we continued westward. We

left bright and early and were somewhere in the eastern side of Pennsylvania and traveling along Lake Erie; the same route I'd traveled a year ago to compete in ArtPrize.

"Are we going to have a campfire?"

"I bet we could. We'll have to see when we get there."

I smiled at my son, Tripp, through the rearview. They were all very excited about the spot we rented for the exhibition. It was a semi-rustic cabin sitting along a beach that stared out into Lake Superior. The photos online looked beautiful, and I had to admit I was just excited as all of them were. It was certainly going to beat a motel or the back seat of my truck.

"We still have to stay at another hotel on the way. We're too far out."

Tripp nodded. He looked a little disappointed he wouldn't get to see the cabin tonight, but soon we'd be staying there for five days. At the beginning of the exhibition, there would be an upscale cocktail party and fundraiser event. Everybody had their best clothes packed.

It'd be like the Northshore Animal League's Gala in Manhattan all over again. I thought about how it was starting to be funny to see my father dressed up so often. As far back as I can remember, he rarely wore anything besides his work clothes. I could only think back to him wearing a suit at the occasional funeral or wedding. Between the Gala and this event in Little Traverse Bay, he dressed up more than he had in a long time.

Both my parents trailed behind us. The kids hopped between driving with me and them the whole ride out. They were overjoyed at some points, their faces pressed to the window and looking out at the foreign scenery. Other times they fussed and fought one another and became difficult to manage. Either way, my attention was always on them, and I was beginning to feel a worry come over me. Before Cathy's offer, I could never bring them along, and the thought of missing out on their lives haunted me through each trip to trade shows or events. Now, as they laughed and argued in the backseat of my truck, I felt terrified that they were with me. I'd spent years taking America's highways to different strange places to sell art. At many points, I felt in danger in some way—be it a swerving eighteen-wheeler on the interstate or a shady character outside my car as I tried to catch sleep. It never meant much to me; I grew used to it and the only thing that worried me about my well-being was leaving my children behind. Now, they were right beside me and shared the risks I took.

It made the drive even more tedious. I tried to act in high spirits but clenched the steering wheel until my knuckles ached. I scanned the road constantly for erratic drivers and hovered over them at rest stops. I didn't want any of my kids to notice I was tense; I didn't want them to be nervous too. When one of them would make a loud noise or yell I'd jump in my seat and try to recover before any of them took enough notice to ask why. They didn't seem to notice during any of the trip. There was too much to take in and talk about to worry about their nervous dad at the wheel.

We drove throughout the day until we arrived in Harbor Springs, Michigan. Tucked away at the top of the country, the city sat like an art installation itself. Every building's paint was immaculate; every lawn and shrub tamed to a degree that almost felt uncanny. It reminded me of the wealthy ocean towns along the east coast, but it possessed a more reserved and stowed away feeling. My children weren't very impressed until we arrived at our home for the duration of our time in Michigan, sitting quaint and quiet on the water. They woke each other up and jumped from the truck when we arrived, running around the yard and sandy beach.

"They have a fire pit! And a canoe!"

I smiled and turned from them to help my parents get their things. I grabbed my mother's duffel bags and brought them inside. The cabin was stripped down but cozy. It had basic amenities but was rustic enough to feel campy. It was warm inside and smelt of cedar, the pores of the bare walls breathing into the rooms and making the air summery and weighted. It reminded me of camping with my parents as a kid. I looked at my sons, who had just barreled inside and were inspecting the rooms. My mother was laughing at them. I thought that's how my brother and I must've looked years ago.

Once I got everything situated at the cabin my father and I left my mother with the kids and drove out to the event space. As we drove, I had to keep my jaw from hanging open. The entire surrounding area was gorgeous. I'd never heard about it, but I saw now that this was a haven for important people tucked away in the quiet Midwest. The homes reminded me of the homes that sat along the most coveted beachfront in Massachusetts—each of them unique and maintained to the level of impeccability, sitting upon massive lawns that abutted the waterfront.

"I certainly wouldn't mind retiring here"

My father laughed from under his John Deere cap. We both looked a little out of place. I'd gotten used to it, and I could tell he was beyond caring about anything like that. No matter what type of suit we dressed ourselves up in we couldn't hide; we were both from a Farm in the Merrimack Valley. A long time ago, I would've resented that fact, but I learned not to mind one bit as the years passed. I sometimes wondered if people might even get a kick out of it.

EXIT 48

The event space was certainly intimidating. The Humane Society's fundraiser was being held at The Boathouse of Harbor Springs a private yacht club, painted grey with sprawling greenery surrounding its beaches. Sailboats and Yachts floated out in the distance, undoubtedly each worth more than half my neighborhood back home. My father seemed intrigued by the boats more than anything else and stared out at them and pointed while we began to set up.

"Don't see boats like that every day."

We lifted a baseplate onto the roller. I went slower than usual. I always worried about my own body getting hurt from the constant setups, never mind my father getting hurt. After we got the basics done, I went to gather some intel before we began moving things. I was happy to be acquainted with Cathy because she helped us navigate the upscale culture surrounding Little Traverse Bay. She was on-site when we arrived, and we caught up and had reintroductions. She gave us a tour of the yacht club and a detailed lowdown of how the fundraiser event would go. I took notes in my head about where to place the dogs, names I should remember, and names I should look out for.

The exhibition's main event would be the cocktail party at the yacht club. It had some heavyweight sponsors behind it and the humane society was anticipating a significant turnout. My father and I wheeled a dog inside the main floor of the yacht club. Inside, my eyes were immediately drawn to a showcase of amphibious vehicles on one side of the room. They looked old but in stunning condition. I was going to ask my father if he knew anything about the cars they had showcased when I noticed him looking at a banner on the wall.

"Well, would you look at that—"

My father had his face inches away from the banner, laughing to himself. It was a promotional photo of me posing with one of the dogs advertising The Humane Society's fundraiser. It felt good to see myself in advertisements. It made me feel professional—legitimate. My father pointed behind me and I swung around and caught sight of a large banner with the same promotional printed across it.

"These folks aren't messing around."

"No, they are not."

I felt a little fire in my heels and started moving quickly to get everything set up. In the days forward, it felt a lot like any other exhibition. I hung out around the Yacht Club lawn and chatted with people, be it bystanders or people who worked there. My kids and parents came with me, and they explored the various things to do in the area. At one point we discovered the Bay Street Drinking Fountain.

"What are they doing?"

My mother had a look of horror on her face. Pedestrians walked up and filled their water bottles from the fountain, indulging in big gulps of water while they lounged around. I unscrewed the cap of a bottle of water my son Jude was drinking. I dunked it under one of the fountain's streams.

"It's spring water—safe to drink. Cathy told me about it."

I handed the bottle back to Jude and he took a sip. He smiled and gave my mother a thumbs up. She still didn't seem to trust it. I have to admit I'd never heard of something like it either, but this place was strange in many ways in terms of what we were used to.

It almost began to feel like I was on vacation. It wasn't until the middle of the exhibition that I felt the fire under my heels again. On the night of the fundraiser, I chased my sons around trying to get them into their formal attire. My father paced around fixing his tie and my mother tried to help me wrangle them.

When we finally made it to the yacht club all of us were taken aback. Round tables filled the room, each with white linen tablecloths and reserved seating. A violinist drifted between groups of chatting socialites, the music from his strings echoing out into the cavernous ceilings of the building. People in suits and designer dresses lounged by the waterside and amongst my sculptures, sipping champagne and humoring each other's stories. We sat at our table and took it all in. I wanted to introduce myself to people but felt in the presence of a different world. Some of the jewelry around people's necks belonged in a museum. The concept of it being a casual cocktail party boggled my mind.

I found Cathy and tried to meet people by hovering around her. I eventually broke the ice with some people and began paving a way into socializing. It felt absurd to talk to someone for a half-hour just to discover a little bit afterward that they were the heir to a brand of candy I used to buy at the corner shop as a kid—or maybe a head executive to a gas station I filled my tank at the day prior; to brush elbows with people that controlled the nation's finances and economy, as well as their fashion sense and favorite sport all alike.

Dinner was catered while different members of the humane society spoke and outlined their mission. It always felt nice to hear what the end product was for the money generated by these events I found myself frequenting more and more. Any feeling of overindulgence or boastfulness was culled back by the bigger picture; it was all in good spirit and benefiting something great.

I spent the rest of the night trying my best to network at moments, and at others trying to stand still and see what was happening in front of me. Now and then I'd catch my sons engrossed in an imaginary game they were playing—totally oblivious to what was happening in front of them and unconcerned with who they tiptoed around. It put a smile on my face.

Eventually, the party simmered down, and happy couples hailed their drivers, disappearing into the night. My mother had long brought the kids home and my father was off socializing with whoever still wandered around. For the most part, it was event staff and members of the humane society, tiredly picking up their feet and gearing up for the final haul of labor to end the night.

I walked out to the waterline. Cathy was there speaking to an older couple and saying goodbye to them. When she wasn't occupied, she walked over beside me.

"Thank you. Tonight was a great success."

I looked out from the shore at the clouds above the lake. The water had turned subdued and gray.

"Actually, I was just about to say the same thing. I don't know where I'd be if you hadn't lent me a hand with the exhibition."

She waved her hand.

"I wouldn't have offered if I didn't know your art was good. Everybody else seemed to think so too tonight. In fact—"

She raised her eyebrows and lowered her voice.

"We raised roughly eighty thousand tonight for the Little Traverse Bay Humane Society—and you were a part of it. That's something to feel good about."

I smiled and looked back out at the water. I did feel good about it. The Humane Society's fundraiser made me remember there was something more driving me forward than financial security. When I was a kid sitting in art classes I never even thought about this side of being an artist. I never would have dreamt I could help

EXIT 48

do something like that with my art. I was able to exhibit my art and make a difference at the same time, and I was so lost in the trance of it all that I almost didn't notice when Cathy spoke up.

"Before you go—"

She clicked a pen and began to scribble something on the back of a business card.

"I wanted to put you in contact with a friend of mine. She may be able to offer you some opportunities out of my reach."

She handed me the card and I looked down at it. There was an email address with the name "Sara" inscribed above it.

"Who's Sara?"

"Just a patron of the arts."

She smiled keenly before waving goodbye. I put the business card in my pocket and made my way to the truck. My father was there waiting with his hands in his coat pockets. I'd seen him standing like that so many times before in my life, outside our barn or the bottling plant. It felt so strange to see him so far from home, still in his old Carhart and looking at me like nothing had ever changed. We both got in the truck and drove back to the cabin. I was physically exhausted from the day's work but felt like a fire was burning inside me. I couldn't wait to get back and be with my family. I peered over quickly at my father. He was staring with tired eyes at the passing landscape.

"Cathy says they raised eighty grand for the Little Traverse Bay Animal League."

He turned to me as if I'd broken him from a trance.

"That sure is a lot of spare change. How much did you say they paid you for coming out?"

"They paid me what I asked. I just wanted to be able to bring everyone out and not lose money."

My father squinted and fixed his hat. He re-postured himself as if he were waking up.

"Well, how much did you ask for?"

"About twenty grand."

"That's not bad."

I sighed and tapped my hand on the steering wheel.

"Well—I gave them a ten-thousand-dollar sculpture credit too."

He huffed and puffed in disapproval. I could tell from the beginning of the conversation where it was headed. I already knew what he had to say, and I knew he was right.

"Don't you think it was about time you started asking for more?"

"Well, I—"

"Think about it. Do you think I'd of sold bottles of milk all those years if it only paid for the bottles?"

I nodded, trying to show I was understanding what he was getting at.

"We all see by now it's possible—but you've gotta let it work. Five more grand to them is much less than it is to you. You need to stop selling yourself short."

He rolled the window down and put his arm out. The breeze came into the truck like the current of a river.

"It's great this can sustain itself, but I think it's about time you think about making it into something more than that. People will pay—I know it."

I smiled and rolled my window down too. The air felt good on my face, and the sound of the wind filled the cab.

We returned to the Cabin after the sun had set. There was

EXIT 48

a small light glimmering down by the water. We walked down and found my mother and the kids huddled around a firepit, the embers reflecting their orange hue onto their faces.

"We decided to make smores."

My mother smiled in the dancing light while my sons picked at melted chocolate and marshmallow on their hands and clothes. My youngest, Jude, held up a box of graham crackers smiling. My father walked up to him and patted his head.

"I'm awfully tired. Do you think you could make me one?"

He smiled and fished a marshmallow out of the bag. He hadn't quite gotten the hang of cooking marshmallows yet. When he presented the s'more to my father the marshmallow was blackened and burnt to a crisp. He ate it anyway and I laughed next to him.

"We were talking about taking the canoes out tomorrow before we go."

"That sounds like a great idea to me."

I grabbed a marshmallow from the bag and started roasting it over the fire. We all sat into the night while my mother told farm stories to the kids and my father and I joked around. When it came to be everybody's bedtime I went inside and sat on the couch in the living room of the cabin. I could hear the sink running and there was an orange light pouring out from the bathroom door on the far side of the room. Parker was brushing his teeth before bed.

"Hey. You wanted to go on the canoe?"

I saw his shadow move until he emerged from the doorway. He nodded.

"Why don't we take it for a test run?"

He smiled and ran back into the bathroom to finish brushing his teeth. I grabbed our hoodies from the duffel bags and we met outside, dragging the canoe across the sand and letting it drift afloat into the water. He jumped in first and then I pushed it out, jumping over the side and crawling up to the bench seat while it drifted out past the shallows. Everything was silent, aside from the thrush of water from the oars and the birds rustling in the trees. I taught him how to row and steer the boat with the oar. The wind was soft but cold from blowing across the vast span of water. We eventually let the canoe float on its own and I could see the cabin looking over the dark silhouette of the waterline.

"What do you think? Have you had fun so far?"

"Yeah."

I could see him smiling with his head down through the dark. It made me remember our time spent on my bicycle during the New England Exhibition. I thought back to running around the different shops in Portsmouth and Newburyport with him and his brothers. All of them all of the sudden looked so much older to me. It happened so fast; within as little as a year. I wondered if I'd be thinking the same thing a couple of years further down the road.

"What are you laughing about?"

Parker was looking at me and beginning to laugh too. I hadn't noticed I was laughing out loud.

"I was just thinking about that prank shop in Portsmouth. I wanna go back."

"Me too."

We both sat quietly for a while and listened to the boat drift. The stars had become clearer than I'd seen them my whole time in Michigan.

"Hey, Dad?"

"What's up?"

He didn't say anything for a moment. I could sense a tenseness in his voice all of the sudden.

"Is this how you being an artist is going to be from now on?"

A gust of wind blew and rustled the tree line far behind us. I looked down at the dark outline of my feet and tried to think of the words to say.

"I'm working on it. I want it to be this way."

He nodded, looking out at the water in a slouch. I leaned in and nudged his shoulder.

"I'll make sure things are more like this. I promise."

He smiled at me and I handed him an oar. We rowed back to the shoreline. I thought about what he said over and over. It wouldn't leave my head. I thought about it for the rest of our time in Little Traverse Bay, trying to take in each precious moment with my three sons and my parents. If I could find a way for it to always be like this, I knew I'd be alright, and everything would be okay.

At the end of our stay, my parents and the kids ended up flying back. I took my father's truck back and booked a flight a few days later to grab the rest of the exhibition. The night my brother dropped me off at Logan Airport, it was pouring across Boston. The weather was even worse in the Midwest. While I sat at the airport, I emailed Sara Carruthers. I didn't know much about her, but Cathy seemed to hold her in high regard, and I trusted her judgment. I was still staring at the email when my flight was announced, trying to dig for anything unprofessional or imperfect in my writing. I finally closed my eyes and pressed 'send,' as I passed through the terminal.

It was a rocky flight, but I made it to Michigan as the sun was coming up. I took my truck from the airport to get the sculptures, then drove into the afternoon until I arrived at my friend Mike Regan's house. He looked and acted just as I'd remembered all those years ago; maybe just a little weathered by the years. When I saw him outside his door, I realized that I hadn't seen any of the friends I'd made in college since I started chasing my dream. I rarely spoke to Gene since he stopped going to trade shows and pursued his bigger plans. It was a poignant reminder that just like them, I was racking up the years. I tried to think in my head whether I'd made good time through the decade. I still couldn't tell if I was on the wing of something great or scrambling around in the dark.

While we were inside his house, he heated leftovers from dinner earlier that night and we sat in the living room.

"Paving your way, eh?"

I laughed over the bowl of pasta in my hands. He said it with the same cadence he used to tell jokes in college, but when I looked up from my food there was a seriousness in his face.

"You could call it that."

"Yeah, yeah. I knew you weren't gonna get a job in marketing."

I laughed and he picked up the remote to the television and flicked on a rerun of a football game.

"What's the deal with you spending so much time out in Michigan anyhow? Tired of Massachusetts?"

"Well—"

I swallowed my last bite of pasta and placed the bowl on an accent table by the couch.

" Remember you told me about ArtPrize?"

"Sure."

"Well I mentioned it to the folks at the Western Michigan Humane Society when I delivered their sculpture and they agreed to enter it collaboratively. After that I received an offer to exhibit in

EXIT 48

Little Traverse Bay from the Bissell Pet Foundation and now here I am, hanging out with you like old times."

A sarcastic smile cracked across his face.

"People should start listening to me more often."

We both laughed. Eventually, he went off to bed and I rested my head back on the couch cushion, watching a ceiling fan slow to a halt. I suddenly remembered I'd sent Sara an email yesterday and turned over to find my phone. I opened my email to see Sara Carruthers had replied, saying she'd love to help me set up an exhibition; somewhere in Ohio most likely. I smiled to myself and couldn't help but laugh. Mike was all jokes, but I hope he knew I was grateful. It was so strange that taking somebody's inkling of advice could send your life in a new direction. I began to miss all of my old friends, and I felt grateful for them all at once. I don't know where I'd be without their help.

In the morning, I tossed my backpack into my truck and double-checked the trailer. Mike came out of his house yawning.

"Coffee?"

I shook my head.

"No thanks, I'm running late. But hey—"

He sipped his mug and arched an eyebrow. I walked up to him and hugged him.

"Thanks for going out of your way. You're a good friend."

"Oh, come on now."

I jumped into my truck and waved as I hauled the dogs out from in front of his street. When I got back to Massachusetts, I got back into the groove of trade shows. I needed to stockpile some funds because I had another exhibition already booked, and I had no idea what would come from my correspondence with Sara Carruthers.

We talked back and forth as I continued my typical trade shows and made ends meet. The anticipation I felt grew as details began to roll in. We were going to be partnering with a humane society and there were a few high roller exhibition sites on the table. I felt filled with gratitude to be corresponding with a promoter so involved.

The day I received the confirmation, I was ecstatic. Sara Carruthers had landed me an exhibition in the prestigious Pyramid Hills Sculpture Park. I was well aware of Pyramid Hills by now. Artists spoke about it at Trade Shows, and in some ways served as a rite of passage into greater things. I said yes immediately and months later I was setting up there in the weeks approaching June of 2012.

We arrived at Pyramid Hills with the full exhibition in tow. The park was beautiful, as beautiful as I'd read about it written years ago in magazines like *The Atlantic*. It was a bit North of Cincinnati, bordering Indiana. Inside the park was like a paradise. It consisted of acres of rolling fields and ancient Ohio tree lines. It felt sacred in a way, with permanent installations of many different sculptors of different styles tucked away along the winding trails and forested paths. I felt like I was walking down a path I was supposed to. I had no idea how to find my way around, but it revealed itself more by the minute.

My work would be the featured exhibition of the summer. I set two dogs up right out front of the cobblestone entrance facing each other with the central walkway in between. Inside, I positioned the dogs in a cluster about the size of two football fields. With all of the available exhibition space, I was tempted to put them everywhere, but by now I'd well learned the visual beauty of *The Big Dog Show* existed in the cohesiveness that dogs provided each other when they were grouped.

The Big Dog Show would be partnering with the Animal Friends Humane Society. I met them as I was setting up and was excited to see they were very enthusiastic about the exhibition. At some point, an Ohio News Station showed up to interview me. I felt uncomfortable on camera, but it was exhilarating and surreal. Even being at a place as well regarded as Pyramid Hills, the press and public reaction always felt dreamlike.

I spent another day finishing preparations. Sara and the Animal Friends Humane Society arrived, and we planned for the main event; a cocktail party for many generous sponsors participating in a fundraiser for the humane society.

The cocktail party was held under a canopy in the sculpture park with live music. Above the heads of all the attendees, the beams of the canopy were lit with blue fluorescents. I'd brought a few of the dogs under the canopy just for the event, and guests chatted and drank among one another as I drifted about, taking in the moment and hoping I wouldn't forget it. I looked over to Sara interacting with attendees. I didn't know much about her but just seeing the event she coordinated I knew she never had to give me the time of day. All around me were people who had more than I had to offer, be it wealth or power or connections, and she spoke to me with the utmost respect. It instilled great respect in me for her, and it bolstered my confidence as an artist. People were viewing me through the lens of my work and there was nothing better than that.

When the event ended, I thanked Sara and expressed my appreciation. The dogs stayed there until August 1st. From there I was asked by another organization to exhibit in Ohio and accepted. After that, I landed a couple of exhibitions in Florida. The dogs didn't have time to come home to Haverhill in between. It was easier to leave everything on sight and move from one place across the country to the next. I drove with my parents south through the United States.

My father and I towed the sculptures and equipment through the Midwest and American South down into Orlando, Florida. We arrived and set up the exhibition at the Mennello Museum of American Art. The relatively young museum was based around a collection of art by Earl Cunningham and was named after the family that donated the pieces. I exhibited my work in the family's sculpture garden attached to the museum. I positioned the dogs around a locally well-loved tree called "The Mayor." It was an oak tree covered in moss that was over 350 years old.

The owner of the museum was kind and accommodating. It was great to see a private museum making an effort to pay contemporary artists and help out the community around them. From the Menello Museum will, I took the expedition further South to Bonita Springs, Florida. The land shifted into tropics with salty air coming in on warm gusts from the gulf. The tree lines melted into swaying palms and I could see my mother in the rearview taking photos from the passenger seat of my father's truck.

Bonita Springs was different from the past few exhibition spots and in many ways reminded me of the exhibition in Beverly, Massachusetts. My sculptures would be exhibited in celebration of a brand-new dog park. The town and local government had gathered around in a park nearby on the fresh open lawns adorned by palm trees. I could feel the contentment in the air as the city gained a new place to enjoy. I felt like I became a member of the town, celebrating something new and good to look forward to. My sculptures blended into the happiness, their heads peeking up from behind droves of running children and elderly couples discovering a new place to stroll in the afternoon.

I could tell my parents could feel the joy too, and in many ways, it felt just as good to merge with an entire city's happiness as it did to be a premier artist at a black tie fundraiser.

When Bonita Springs was a wrap, I drove my parents to the airport in Florida. I didn't want to keep them jumping from state to state any longer, and I knew I'd figure something out for where the dogs would go next. I carried their bags in and we sat in the terminal. Sunkissed vacationers sat in rows around us, coming and going from the Sandy beaches and gulf waters. I looked at my mother in her big sunhat and sunglasses. My father sat next to her fanning himself with a magazine and fatigued by the heat. They were both getting older. I noticed it as they traveled with me the past year or so. My father walked more each day with the step of my grandfather. Sometimes for a moment, I'd watch him walk up to look at a sculpture or historical landmark and I'd feel like I was a teenager going to the Agawam with my grandfather. Even the way he drank coffee in the morning began to carry a certain weight.

My mother gave me the same assuring smile she had since I was a boy. I paused for a minute and didn't know how to get my words out. She sat waiting patiently, just as she had through my years of struggling with reading and writing.

"I just—wanted to say thank you. I know I've dragged you guys around the past couple of years and I wouldn't have been able to do it without you."

My mother stared at me with her head tilted. Even from behind her sunglasses and hat I could see her face soften. My father looked down at the tiles on the airport floor and chuckled to himself.

"That's a weird way to put it. I was just about to tell you thanks."

He smirked and leaned forward in his seat.

"I've spent most of my life delivering bottles of milk and tending a farm. Same with your mother. We've seen more in the past year than we've seen in a long time."

My mother nodded in agreement and smiled at me. I couldn't keep from smiling too and swelled with pride. A voice crackled over the intercom announcing it was time to board the flight to Logan Airport. I hugged both of them tight and sent them on their way.

With each place I exhibited, I embedded myself a little more into the region's artistic community. I learned which trade shows were hot and which weren't, I befriended gallery owners and artists and organizers. Thanks to Cathy and Sara my name spread through the ranks of humane societies across the United States and I remained in communication with many of them. For the first time in my life, I was beginning to occasionally turn opportunities down. It felt wrong to me each time; I was so used to reaching for anything to grab onto to stay afloat. I had enough of a footing to take logical steps and even though I was busier than I'd ever been in my whole life, my mind felt clear-headed.

Someone had tipped me off to an event in Houston, Texas. The event was called the Bayou City Arts festival. After doing some research and finding photos I decided I wanted to go. I was excited to hit Texas and had rarely passed through before. I was also excited to give a little light to my other designs in different parts of the country. The Big Dog Show was becoming a bigger project each day and I wanted my other pieces to follow suit. A part of me was beginning to miss the grind of selling individual pieces, although being able to get paid for an exhibition had been a dream come true.

Andy and I loaded up a wide range of my favorite pieces into

EXIT 48

the trailer and headed for Texas. With each opportunity that presented itself, he became an integral piece of the puzzle. We'd become a true team in the past year and managed a system like a well-oiled machine. He'd surpassed the learning stages of metal-work and I could put confidence in him to manage the building side of things as I toured America.

When we arrived, both of us were captivated by the culture in Houston. It was clear as day that something exciting was happening. The city had become an amalgamation of the brightest attributes of each region comprising the United States. It possessed the warmth and hospitality of the south, the ingenuity and grit of the west, and the creativity and progressive thinking of the east. It felt like a big social experiment, and I was filled with excitement to see the festival's setup in person. It was in the middle of Houston's urban heart and the city had shut down the streets just for the event. White tents filled with art lined each inner-city road and food trucks and entertainment were budding from the different corners of the buildings and bar fronts.

We took in the life of the city while we set up our tent. We jumped from restaurant to restaurant, gallery to gallery while live music echoed out from the open doors of barrooms. The smoke of grilling meats and vegetables floated between tents and mingled with the beating Texas sun. In many ways, it reminded me of ArtPrize. It felt as if we were there to sell art, but just as equally to celebrate art itself.

We hung out for the duration of the festival letting the weather tan us. We handed out promotional material like madmen and people seemed interested in our optimism and personality just as much as our art. We made great friends and secured some healthy sales along the way. In the middle of the madness, I was approached by a woman with a professional air to herself, but with the same bright disposition I'd been feeling from people all week.

"I heard about your work through the grapevine. Now that I'm seeing it in person, I definitely think they're beautiful sculptures."

Andy and I both thanked her and introduced ourselves.

"Nice to meet both of you."

The three of us talked amongst each other about Houston. We explained our admiration for the city and the people we'd met so far. She told us what was good to eat and where, and things we should do before we left. I told her about the past year exhibiting in different parts of the country and the hectic climb it's been since. She asked what my favorite spot had been, and I couldn't give her an answer. They were all so unique and full of ups and downs. I told her that all I knew was Texas had Michigan beat in terms of weather. She laughed and poised herself.

"While I was looking at your work, I was wondering to myself if you often exhibit in Texas."

Andy began to go off checking on the sculptures and making sure our table looked prim. This was my first time down here, but the idea sounded right on track.

"Not often— but depending on the situation we certainly wouldn't be opposed."

"Great. I've been toying with the idea of requesting an exhibition—and perhaps purchasing something for my homeowner's association."

When she said, "homeowners association," my heart dropped into my stomach. I saw Andy visibly wince out of the corner of my eye. We'd made sales to members of homeowner's associations multiple times and almost all of them were nightmares. People would ask to buy a piece and it would get denied by the rest of the association. Then we'd be stuck in a lousy business situation where we'd already have coordinated a delivery for them. In between, it often involved months of confusing emails.

"That sounds like something right up our alley. Here—"

I signaled Andy while he was over at our table to grab a pamphlet. He handed it off to me and I handed it to her.

"Take this and contact us through phone or email. I'd love to talk about it more."

She took the pamphlet and looked excited. We talked some more and eventually, she handed me her card.

"I'll be in touch."

She went on her way and we waved. I looked over at Andy.

"It'd be awesome to come back. To sell something would be great too. I just don't want to end up having to keep it."

He nodded in agreement and we both took a seat, feeling the heat cut through the white vinyl of the tent canopy. I looked down at her business card and squinted.

"Dang."

Andy jumped in his seat and looked at me.

"What's wrong?"

I laughed and cursed under my breath at the same time.

"She's not part of a homeowners association, she *works* for one."

"What's that mean?"

I pointed to her title and put the card up to his face.

"It means she's a representative for a company that builds entire housing projects."

He shrugged slowly and unsure.

"Well, hopefully she calls."

I sent her a follow-up email while we were still in Houston. I didn't know what would come of it and what her proposal was, but I was interested. The rest of our time was well spent, and I was a little bummed to have to leave. The city had an exciting aura to it—it seemed like it was discovering itself and I wanted to be a part of the conversation. We loaded up the sculptures and counted our blessings, though. On the drive home, we braved the Midwest again. It was becoming strenuous driving through flat farmland constantly. I was beginning to think most of what I ever saw was stalks of corn.

As I drove closer to home and nearing the Appalachians, I stopped at a gas station in Tennessee. I bought a coffee and took big gulps, feeling it leave streaks of burns in the back of my throat and tongue. Andy walked up to me, sipping his coffee.

"One of the guys in there says there's a trail down the road. It leads up to an abandoned fire tower."

"I don't know if we should leave the sculptures in an empty lot."

He shrugged as if to show he didn't mind either way. I could tell he wanted to check it out, though, and the more I thought about it the more I did too. I sighed.

"Alright fine, let's do it."

We drove down the road and found the dusty lot the man was talking about. I wasn't sure who owned it, but it was filled with broken-down vehicles and debris. We cut into the rocky forest via a grown in trail and began the ascent up. The land began to steepen as we moved further up the small mountain. The sun began to flicker away, I began to think of turning back, the gravel became loose and traction less under my feet. I saw the outline of the tower peeking over the hill. We pushed forward through the brush until we arrived at the tower swaying in the wind.

The sun was still out; just barely hovering over the tree line. From the top of the tower, we saw the entire forest and surrounding towns drenched in a glimmering tangerine hue. I could see my trailer full of sculptures, a speck in comparison to the massive expanse of earth, waiting patiently at the bottom.

I wanted to get a photo before it turned completely dark. I pulled my phone out, but before I could switch to the camera setting, I noticed an email notification on my lock screen. It was the representative of the housing developments in Texas. She replied to me saying they wanted my work to exhibit on their property. My eyes scanned the screen frantically and caught a cash offer.

'One hundred thousand.' Andy was leaning on the fire tower's railing next to me, his face now turned my way.

"What? What's wrong?"

I looked up at him from my phone and blinked twice. I had to look back at the email to make sure I wasn't hallucinating.

"Nothing. Nothing at all."

I turned my gaze back to the overwhelming outward pouring of light across the land. Now that I could see it, it was incredible to think I ever considered turning back.

22

My life had changed. Looking back, it was hard to tell when. Many of the years chasing the Big Dog Show's tail was like ascending a cliff, stone by stone. I was too scared to look down and kept my eye on whatever I could to pull myself another foot higher. Landing Texas deal had sent a shockwave through my life that hailed a new era of my career as an artist.

The exhibition in Texas for the Johnson Development Group was a large-scale exhibition featuring the Big Dog Show visiting their properties. When all was said and done, we even worked out a deal to build a custom piece for their organization.

After years of counting pennies, the check I received for the exhibition's time in Texas was the lifeboat I'd been waiting for as I floated through the dark. It wasn't necessarily the hundred grand that changed my life. A hundred thousand is a heap of money in any regard, but in terms of running an exhibition, much of that money disappears before it hits a bank account. That being said, it was the first time I had enough money to initiate significant change for myself, and from there it snowballed. I returned home and renovated the shop, adding an addition to my home and reserving the old garage workspace for storage. I caught myself getting sentimental as the new edition was built and we dragged equipment out of the old workshop. It was like saying goodbye to and old friend. A flood of memories rushing in and the tears swelling in my eyes until the memories faded away.

The ceilings and garage doors were high in the new shop; high enough so that we wouldn't have to finish pieces in the driveway and rub elbows. It was designed with sculpture-making in mind and even had an office in the back. Any tool on its last leg got dumped and replaced with newer, safer, and more efficient ones. With the expanded space and finances came an expansion of our team. I hired two more welders, Evan and Dave, as well as an office assistant, Samantha.

After the conversation with my father in Michigan, I began upping my prices on my work. It wasn't all over newfound confidence, though. Expenses for coming out to exhibit or sell work were rapidly climbing. The bigger the *Big Dog Show* got, the more it needed to be fed. The transition to more appropriate prices was smooth and sales didn't go down. The years of traveling to trade shows, as well as exhibiting *The Big Dog Show,* had finally paid off and I'd become well recognized through a large portion of the country. The recognition brought a new budding market for me of custom builds for individuals and organizations alike. We built custom pieces for a multitude of private individuals, municipalities, and academic institutions.

I returned to ArtPrize twice after my initial entry there. The first year, we launched a special exhibit for the event called *Metal Monkey Mania* and built a hundred metal monkeys and hung them from the Blue Bridge in Grand Rapids, Michigan. I'd remembered how inspired I was my first year at ArtPrize witnessing the interaction between the artwork and the city and had designed the metal monkeys to depend on said interaction. One of their arms reached above their heads, and it was specially designed to be able to grip and hang from a multitude of different platforms found throughout everyday life.

The third time attending ArtPrize, we launched my exhibit *Flight,* which consisted of nine floating stainless-steel birds. They were suspended from steel frames of varying heights and had twelve-foot wingspans. I created the exhibit in commemoration of a concept that had ruled over much of my life; the struggle to balance fear and freedom. I'd been terrified for so many years as an artist but I'd finally come to see it as symptomatic of any freedom; freedom to go where a person wants, to be what a person wants to be. Any hesitation or hiccup I ever succumbed to was rooted in fear, and the moments I was most proud of were in the pursuit of some kind of freedom. *Flight* went on to win "best use of urban space," at ArtPrize and later exhibited across the country from the campus of Southern Illinois University to the parks of Florida, to back home in Massachusetts.

Meanwhile, *The Big Dog Show* continued to grow, and we got more and more requests to exhibit. I was able to begin shipping my purchased sculptures which allowed me to dedicate more time to touring with my exhibitions. I brought my dogs to different locations around Massachusetts, Connecticut, New Jersey, Texas, Florida, and the various spots around the Midwest. On my way back from every exhibition, I'd see my *American Dog* sculpture by Exit 48 and I'd know I was home. It never got less strange to think back to dragging the original off the highway and making the sporadic decision to replace it with a larger one. I'd often wonder what happened to the first; I'd sold it off years ago, eager to make anything I could. I hoped the first Exit 48 *American Dog* meant something special to its owner, where or whoever they were.

As I began to feel truly comfortable for the first time in my life, I started to be able to focus more on my social life. I started going on dates more often and putting effort into finding a relationship worthwhile. It was all to no avail until one night after a botched date in Ipswich, I walked into the Choate Bridge Pub. To my surprise, I recognized the bartender. It was Mary, the woman I talked to at the Bradford Common during the very first Big Dog Show. I went up and talked to her and we were both surprised we recognized each other. I asked if I could see her again, and within a couple of years I'd call her my fiancé.

In Haverhill, I began to see an old side of the world emerge again. I'd sometimes go for a bike ride through the city and watch things I hadn't in decades. I'd rest my elbows on the railing of the bridge between Bradford and the center of Haverhill and watch a train pass covered in russet brown and red. I'd watch the leaves tumble between streetlights and see the school buses marching through downtown in the late afternoon. Sometimes I'd see a group of teenagers hanging out in the Market Basket parking lot or crossing the street in Lafayette Square and I'd think of my old friends. It made me sad to think of them. So many had been swallowed up by the dark side of life, many weren't even alive.

I walked through downtown one day taking in how the city had changed. Haverhill had risen and was becoming a social hub of sorts. Rows of new bars had emerged from seemingly out of nowhere and still old local staples like *The Tap* thrived and became the gathering place for new generations. Hair salons and local Barbershops like *Knots* passed hands from master to apprentice and restaurants renovated and expanded. There was a new coffee shop called *Battlegrounds* that all of the guys in my crew stopped at during their lunch breaks and I wanted to try it for myself.

I stepped inside. There was a line of people swerving out from the front counter. I tried to squint and look at the menu. I was too far away to read anything, and my eyes began to travel around the room. On the couch in the corner was an older woman I recognized from long ago.

"Ms. Paradis?"

She looked up, smiling calmly. She waved to me as if I'd just graduated yesterday. I walked over and sat down.

"I see that business degree worked out in an interesting way."

I laughed and nodded. I felt embarrassed and proud at the same time. We drank coffee and caught up. I tried to tell her anything I could, but there was so much that had happened I didn't know where to begin. She waited patiently as I scrambled to tie my ideas together just as she did when I was in her class. Finally, when I quieted down, she smiled, sighing and shaking her head.

"I always knew you were meant to pursue art. Art was pursuing *you*."

I sat quietly, staring at the floor and smiling.

"Thank you for looking out for me."

She laughed.

"Thank you for being what you wanted to be."

After I left the coffee shop, I felt lost in the past for the rest of the day. I began to think about my old cubicle she let me keep outside her class; how that small act of kindness allowed me to not only discover my art but in the grand scheme discover myself as a person. I'd finally brought my work and myself outside the walls I'd built away from the world, but if somebody didn't let me hide inside them, I would have never known they were even there.

It took me a minute to remember where I even found that old cubicle. It was with my old friend Tommy—skipping class somewhere in the A-Wing at Haverhill High School. I laughed thinking about our antics, but then I began to feel a bit somber. He was a great artist when we were kids, and I wondered if he still worked on art. I hoped he was doing alright.

The more time I had to myself in the city, the more I felt like I owed it something. Certain cities carry a looming weight to them, and Haverhill is undoubtedly one of them. Still, it was a weight everybody in the city felt together; from the parents of the people I knew to their children.

I began to give back here and there to the city. More specifically, I wanted to offer something to the place where I first truly felt the spark that drove me to pursue art; Haverhill High School. We installed multiple sculptures on the high school campus in the coming years. One of them was a memorial honoring the terror attack victims during the Boston Marathon, which had wounded New England's heart a short time ago. Another was two steel pillars installed in the school's fountain in remembrance of the attack on the world trade centers. Finally, we installed a good old *American Dog* in the school's central garden area. The garden had to be accessed from the school's hallways, so in the spirit of my old antics, I made sure to weld a ten foot American Dog on sight that couldn't ever be brought back out a doorway. The sculpture's finishing touch was a plaque dedicated to the teacher that saved me when I was a student in need. It was the least I could do for Susan Paradis; I don't know where I'd be if she never helped me find my way out of the dark.

After the high school sculpture, we did other things to try to remain engaged and spread positivity throughout the city. We often bought our lunches from local restaurants and cafes and I gave some of them *American Dog* keychains, miniature tabletop *American Dog's,* and copies of an exhibition photo book to stock in their shops and grab a percentage from. I even tried my hand at teaching and taught a class at Brooks Academy a private high in North Andover. The class focused on sculpture concept design and metal fabrication.

Through it all, there was something that still irked me in the back of my mind. I was digging through old movies with Tripp and Jude one day when I found a copy of the documentary that was filmed on *The Gates*. All these years later, *The Gates* still amazed me, and as I remembered back to beginning as an artist one of my immediate dreams was to exhibit something as immense and awe-inspiring as *The Gates* exhibition. I still had yet to do that, and I began to feel the burn of frustration as I remembered the runaround and denial I received from Boston when I proposed the hundred dog exhibition I'd dreamt up. In reality, everything was set in motion from that denial. I'd only decided upon the smaller touring exhibition because I was denied a larger one of a grander scale.

After that realization, I was quick to contact the city of Boston to pitch my original idea once again. I figured that I'd certainly put the time in and had much more of a name to prove myself now. After all, *The Gates* took twenty years to coordinate and I'd figured I was already pushing half that amount of time since I last asked. I'd exhibited in major cities all around The United States since then, and somebody down in Boston must've at least heard my name. To my dismay, that was exactly the problem. They answered my email swiftly and said *The Big Dog Show* had circled around too much to be an interest to them. I couldn't help but throw my hands in the air and laugh.

A short time later, I received an email from an organization in Charlestown; an outskirt neighborhood in Boston. It wouldn't be the same as putting a hundred dogs in the common, but I was in.

EXIT 48

The Big Dog Show came to the Charlestown Navy Shipyard in the summer of 2018 by the skin of its teeth, after a quarrel over email and a representative telling us it was going to be a "hard no." Nonetheless, they changed their mind, and it was enough for the time being to not march into the statehouse.

As things leveled out in my life, they began to feel much more domestic. Some stresses came with each corner of success or movement forward. I spent more and more time hashing out emails in the office, crunching numbers, and coordinating the artistry that was in some ways, becoming a business. Everything had to be planned months and months, if not years, ahead. The only way to sustain things as more money appeared was to simultaneously spread it thin, and things were still in many ways a slippery slope. I was by no means worrying about buying food, but I continually worried about accidentally taking the wrong step and hurting my life and the life of the people that were now linked to my art. Andy had a child now and had just found out his wife was going to have another baby. He had grown up through the years and now had a mortgage on a home. My children were approaching their teenage years; many of the things they wanted and the things they wanted to do were more expensive than those when they were younger— never mind that college would be right around the corner if they decided to do so.

I began to feel a bit bogged down and decided I'd call someone I hadn't talked to in a very long time. I held the phone to my ear and listened to it ring, a bit nervous at what I was doing. Finally, I heard the ringing pause.

"Hello?"

"Gene?"

I felt a bit of a knot in my throat. I was annoyed at myself I felt so estranged from an old friend.

"Woah—how the hell are you buddy?"

"Good—good. Just calling to complain about how my life's going good."

He laughed through the speaker. We began talking and I felt dumb for thinking it'd ever be awkward or strange to catch up. We both complained to each other and listened to each other talk about their lives in the past years. It felt no different to crack jokes and brood the same way we did years ago, though now it was over very different things. It felt as if we were completely different people and the same as when we were nineteen all at once.

It was great to listen to Gene's stories. He'd gone and built a life for himself. He frequented circles of important people and it seemed like whatever the master plan was he once concocted, it was working out. I was happy to be able to report mine was on its feet too.

"So, you're happy where you are?"

I scratched the back of my head and kicked my feet on my coffee table.

"Well—yes. I don't want to stop here though. I still feel like I'm in the middle of a climb, you know? I just don't know what to do next."

"Hmm—"

The line was quiet for a moment. I could hear Gene walking about while I waited for him to answer.

"Sorry; people coming over later for dinner. I'm trying to clean the kitchen up a little. What I was going to say was you need to jump into the corporate world."

I laughed at first. I thought he was making a joke about getting a day job.

"No, no. Think about the exhibition you did in Texas. That was brand sponsorship, right there. If you can make a marketing deal with big real estate developers, why not Starbucks or Walmart? Why not Petco? You build metal dogs for god's sake."

I laughed and told him I understood what he was getting at. I'd spent most of my time doing private commissions, making private sales, and exhibiting for non-profits. Otherwise, I was organizing exhibitions with a local municipality. I'd rarely dabbled in the private "for-profit" sector of potential clients. I'd found my way as an artist through nonprofits and public exhibitions. It wasn't as common to hear about artists landing deals with brands; most art would be hard to base a marketing campaign around. However, I'd begun to view things from a different angle in the past few months. My sculptures were by nature designed to be marketable. I'd begun my art career building things I thought people would buy to furnish their homes with, then later graduating to pure sculpture work. The transition wasn't seamless, though. At first, I was selling my sculptures to the same audience that bought my wine racks, and I knew if I were to sustain myself, I had to sell my work to people from many walks of life. My reliance on my art to put food on the table wove marketability into its inherent nature. I attributed where I was not only to my artistic passion but to the know-how and business tactics I'd picked up from trying to survive.

After I said goodbye to Gene, I got to thinking about how I could get my foot in the door. I spent the next few weeks paying attention to different company's marketing styles and techniques. When I went to the grocery store or a gas station, I looked at each product and asked myself if there was a pitch I could offer them.

I didn't want to approach a brand empty-handed. I knew that I'd only have one shot if any. Still, I was impatient. I knew that it'd take weeks to open up any sort of dialogue with a company, and before all of that, I still needed to find one and come up with an idea.

One night I ordered takeout from a bar in Haverhill called "The Barking Dog." I stood leaning against the varnish bar top while they ran my credit card and bagged the Styrofoam boxes of food. I scanned the bottles along the wall. Most of them were the typical, age-old liquors I'd remembered being in bars ever since I could first go, but in between the bunch was a bottle of *Tito's Vodka*. I knew the company, but I didn't know where it came from. Seemingly out of nowhere, they'd become popular in the last few years. It was affordable and American made, and I was beginning to see it at almost every social gathering I attended.

The bottle had a cardboard cone on the top I didn't recognize. It was red, white, and blue and from my line of sight I could make out the silhouette of a dog on it.

"Excuse me, what does the cardboard tab on top of that bottle of Tito's say?"

The bartender looked up from the register confused, but she investigated for me. She walked over to the bottle and read it aloud.

"It says 'Vodka for dog people: supporting pet prosperity and rescue.'"

She smiled and handed me the bags of food. I thanked her and walked back to my truck in a rush. When I got home, I did some digging around online. I found out that Tito's had a large hand in supporting animal rights events and was involved with several non-profits. The next day I walked over to Andy at the shop.

"Do you drink Tito's?"

He shrugged.

EXIT 48

"Sure. Tastes better than most of the stuff out there. I know they're right down in Texas."

The gears were turning in my head. I walked over to my office and pulled up their email on the computer. I sat stalemated looking at the white screen. I thought about my first attempts at working with public municipalities. I was just dipping my feet into public installations and was rejected over and over for years. I didn't have that type of time and patience and I knew that jumping into a new market like this would most likely be a repeat of back then.

I chewed on the cap of my pen trying to think of something that could get their attention. I tried to recount some of my favorite sculptures and how they ended up where they were.

"To hell with it."

I stood up and walked over to Andy. There was one particular sculpture that stuck out in my mind. It was the *Charging Bull* on wall street. The artist must've known he'd never make it through the crowd; that he'd get shot down as soon as he put his foot through the door. He skipped the mess and dropped it off right where he wanted. He knew they wanted his art before they did.

"What are we looking at for sculptures right now?"

I walked out into the yard and looked at the newer pieces built to hit the trade shows in the coming weeks. Andy trailed behind me and I rested my hand on a new dog.

"By the end of the week, we're shipping this to the Tito's headquarters."

"We haven't even—"

"We're gonna skip all of that. I'm scheduling a pickup now."

I'd be losing money doing it, and I didn't know how they'd respond, but it was burned into my brain and I was determined. We mailed the dog out on the back of a freight truck a few days later. Once it was bound for Texas, I felt fidgety. The anticipation was surmounting from the moment it left the parking lot. The guys at the shop frequently asked whether they answered, and word got around. The nature of the transaction was confusing to them, and I had to admit I didn't know what I was doing myself. It felt a lot like gambling more than anything. The impatience irked me for weeks until one day I picked up my phone and found a rep for Tito's on the other end. I walked outside into my driveway.

"Hi, this is Dale Rogers."

"Hi, Mr. Rogers. We recently received a metal sculpture with a brochure directing us to this number."

I could hear papers rustling and a keyboard clicking over the line.

"Do we owe you money? I can't seem to find any record of anything."

"No—I just figured I'd send it over."

There was silence from the other end; a long, painful drawl of empty static.

"Well thank you, Mr. Rogers. Have a nice day."

The representative hung up and I stood there unsure what to do with myself. When I walked inside all of the guys were standing up from their workbenches.

"What happened?"

Andy had his welding hood pulled up and was wiping his face. I looked over at my two other workers, Evan and Dave. They were both listening intently. I shrugged slowly and put my hands up.

"They said thanks."

"Thanks? Did they say anything else?"

"Not really."

I put my head down and walked into the office. Their feet started to shuffle behind me as they got back to work. The only thing that nulled my sense of disappointment was that I knew they were a good company that routinely gave back. If nothing came of it, I could at least tell myself they deserved it as a gift. The whole thing began to slip from my mind until we received a follow-up email from them a few days later. It was something about the *GoPro* Mountain Games in Colorado. They said we may have some type of luck contacting them, and that they'd put a good word in for us. I shrugged it off and told my new office worker, Andrew, to inquire about it.

There was no answer back initially, and in the coming months I fell into a routine. It was an elevated routine from before, but it was no less straining. I was back on the trade show circuit, rushing from state to state. We ran the Big Dog Show locally here and there, but it was nothing more and nothing less than before.

I had more money, but I was wondering if I jumped the gun on celebrating. It seemed like I spent the same amount of time at trade shows, in some field or armory I'd never heard of talking to strangers for short bursts of time. After whatever trade show I was at, I'd limp back to a cheap hotel and stay the night alone, away from everyone I knew and loved. I'd call and text my kids as much as I could. They'd grown into their teen years. Parker was halfway through high school and talking about becoming a barber. We were working on finding him an apprenticeship. Tripp and Jude were both accepted to Central Catholic Highschool; they'd be thinking about the rest of their lives before I knew it. I felt older than ever before. There was so much to be grateful for, but so much to reach towards. I didn't know what to do with myself.

I sat up in a motel one night in Pennsylvania, watching an old western flick. I was exhausted from talking to people all day and moving sculptures. There's something about the constant hum of conversation and waves of people that scatter my brain. I wanted to sleep more than anything, but my mind was stricken with worry. There was so much planning to sift through—emails from customers and trade shows and city organizers. Some plans needed to be made for permanent installations in schools and town squares, for orders of raw material and tools. On top of that came the obligations for my kids, from parent-teacher conferences to baseball games to giving rides to their friends.

I scrolled through my email, feeling the wave of anxiety build. I clicked a random unopened message about a trade show when suddenly my phone vibrated.

'Good news. Call ASAP.'

That's all the text from Gene read. I sat up on the hotel bed and called him.

"Hope you missed seeing my face. I think you've got an obligation out here in Arizona."

"What are you talking about?"

"Alright, settle in. This is gonna take a minute to explain."

He told me about the crowds he'd been running in lately—the events and dinner parties and meetings he kept up with. He told me he couldn't stop thinking about the breakthrough I found in non-profits; how I'd been used as the centerpiece of events to raise money for massive animal rights foundations.

"Turns out a lot of the people I know—and people they know, are either involved or gearing up to be involved in sponsoring some type of event. Listen—"

EXIT 48

I pressed the phone to my ear. He paused and made sure he had my attention.

"We're going to plan a fundraiser bigger than anything you've exhibited at yet. I'm talking city-wide, with plenty of compensation for your end of things. I've got sponsors and a foundation already on board. Once you say yes, we just need to pass everything by the municipalities in Phoenix, but they'll say yes."

"Did you say Phoenix?"

I heard him scoff.

"Yes—where else would we? I don't think you're hearing me. We're not going to throw an event this big in some desert plot."

I took a deep breath and stood up.

"Okay, okay, I trust your judgment. Let's do it."

"Awesome. Stay glued to your phone or computer for the next few days. I'm eventually going to put you in contact with the foundation. Talk to you soon."

He hung up the phone and I stood there, the television still playing. In the coming weeks, we got the details, and Gene was right. It was going to be the most significant exhibition I ever did. It had massive sponsorships behind it, and they were still coming in. The local government was getting involved and the planning became more elaborate each day.

The commission would be more than I'd ever received. When I shared the news, the shop was alive with excitement. There'd be enough funds for me to bring all of my employees, my family, and Andy's wife and children. I was immediately interrogated with questions.

"I don't know. We'll figure it out later."

I waved them off, smiling ear to ear. A new ledge to climb up had materialized from the help of, of all people, my old friend Gene. I couldn't wait to catch up in person.

I headed over to the family farm to spread the good news to my parents. My mother was out somewhere but I found my father in the living room. He'd been sick for some time and I hadn't seen him doing his typical things.

"Hey there, how ya been?"

He smiled and motioned me to sit down. I carried two bottles of spring water and handed one to him.

"I just finished securing an exhibition in downtown Phoenix. It's going to be the biggest one we've ever done—music, a parade; like a festival or fair. They're giving me enough to bring everybody out."

He smiled and nodded slowly, taking his time. He put his hand a little way above the armrest of the chair.

"I remember when you were this tall—getting dragged by a Heifer at the Topsfield Fair. Too stubborn for your own good."

We both laughed. I could remember being dragged in front of all those people like it was yesterday.

"The Heifer—she was stubborn too. Probably the least practical of the group you could've picked—but you two were locked into a stalemate by each other."

He leaned back into the cushion of the seat.

"I suppose it was a bit of foreshadowing. You were too stubborn to keep yourself from getting dragged all over the place for no practical reason. But—"

He winked.

"Unlike that mean little cow, you've managed to take hold of life by the horns and prove the doubters wrong."

I looked down at the floor smiling. I couldn't think of words to say. He coughed and then started to laugh to himself.

"Reminds me of the exhibition you had in Chicago. Trying to carry everything in a single trailer like a crazy person."

I shook my head and sighed. "You were so worked up about letting down Amy Amder. Then when we got there, rows and rows of banners with your sculpture on them on every streetlight downtown. Wasn't that something to see? They did a great job."

I could feel the flashback of stress and worry hit me. Amy had helped me tremendously that day. I was intimidated by working with such an esteemed promoter and she ended up being one of the most understanding people I'd ever met. My father was right and had helped me make things work like he always had. I looked over at him. His eyebrows were still raised like he was looking at the banners they made for the exhibition when we went to Chicago.

"Thanks for everything, Dad. I know you've gone out on a limb for me."

He stared straight ahead, taking shallow breaths and sinking into the seat a little bit more.

"That's funny—I was going to thank you. Traveling to your exhibitions, your mother and I have seen more of the country than we ever had before.

He turned his head to me.

"It's made this growing old thing a little more fun."

He laughed and put on the television. We watched whatever was on for a bit until my mother came home. I spoke to her for a bit and then hugged them both, saying goodbye. A few months later, my father passed away. As my whole family gathered for the funeral, I couldn't stop thinking about watching him work when I was little making his daily routes and talking to regulars. I felt a strange wave of absurdity and awe pass through me as I realized I was doing the same thing as him.

One morning a few months after the funeral, I stood outside my house and looked at the twenty dogs I'd taken across America time and time again. Ten years before where I stood, I loaded them for the first time and exhibited down the street in the Bradford Common. Back then, I could barely manage to move them a half-mile. I could still taste the black smoke in my mouth from cutting the trailer beam by the road as my father watched. It never got much easier.

The air was beginning to get warmer around New England and their metal bodies were drenched in early morning dew. They were the central culmination of everything I had ever worked towards. The revolutions of my life followed them as they traveled state to state. I once thought I was leading them out to meet the world, but I saw now that I was the one who was following them. Somewhere along the way, they outgrew my bounds, just like my children were now as they grew into adulthood—and just as I once outgrew the orbit of my parents and the farm I grew up on.

I stepped forward and touched one of the dogs. I could feel grooves and scratches along the rusted metal. My eyes scanned the small dents on each dog from the years of exhibitions. Through their tiny wounds, each of them had grown from a carbon copy into something unique. I could remember almost all of their wounds like they were my own.

Some of the memories made me laugh, some sent a quick spike of rage through me. Many of them made me choke up. Any memory of the Big Dog Show now filled me with a quiet somberness, as the months after my father's passing hung over my head like a gloomy fog. I tried my best to think forward and be excited for Arizona, but the dogs stared back at me now like reflections of the past; shadows along a smoke cloud dissipating.

I was still outside when my crew arrived at the shop. I met Andy and Dave as they traveled across the front lawn.

"I realized the other day it's the ten-year mark."

"Since the first show?"

I nodded and blew into my palms. I held the door for them as steam rushed into the shop. Evan and Andrew were arriving a few yards behind. I sat at the table looking around at the sculptures we were working on. The shop was hectic and undone. We had a continuous flow of orders coming in and had to produce pieces for trade shows on top. When everybody settled in, I knocked my knuckles on the table and they looked my way.

"So—Arizona. What do you guys think of building a new set?"

"A new *Big Dog Show*?"

Evan put his welding hood on the workbench. He and Dave hadn't been there for the original build, and I think I shocked them. I shocked myself a little when I said it. Andy leaned against a wall in thought, counting the weeks on his fingers.

"We've got work stacked up until the week we leave—and Evan's still getting the hang of things."

"I know. I just—"

I tried to think of the words to explain myself.

"It's been ten years. Things have changed a lot, and I think we should build an exhibition that has a piece of all of us in it."

They were quiet for a moment. Dave crossed his arms and looked at the ground. Andy nodded at me.

"Alright. Let's do it."

"Yeah?"

I looked around at Dave and Evan and they were already nodding and letting their welding hoods fall over their faces.

For the rest of the months leading up to Arizona, we worked around the clock. There was too much to do to cover in a typical workday and I helped move things around the shop and in the office at the same time. Andrew did the same, taking breaks from editing videos and photos and coming out to help load a piece onto the truck or carry a shipment inside. The constant sound of sparks crashing into steel echoed often into late hours of the night. The air became hot like fire as summer came over New England. We were cutting things tight, and the closer we got to Arizona the more run-down everybody looked. My crew showed up extra early and left extra late; coffee cups and energy drinks lay strewn across the shop floor.

Somewhere between the chaos, I got word that Gene's father had passed away shortly before mine. It filled me with sadness to hear and dug into a wound of mine that had yet to stop bleeding. As a final push, we designed and built a sculpture to commemorate Gene's father. It was finished with little time to lose, and after a couple of days of recuperating we were chasing the dream of Arizona and whatever came next.

23

The rain came down hard; harder than I'd ever seen in my whole life. I could barely see in front of me as the wind barreled in from the farm fields of Oklahoma. Andy and I leaned forward looking for the red glare of brake lights. Evan, Andrew, and Dave were somewhere up ahead driving my truck and one of the trailers. We drove in my father's old truck with the second trailer in tow. I gripped the steering wheel hard and could feel the frame of the trailer fluttering. The dogs rattled inside and sent a roar through the back window. I prayed the tires didn't catch a pool of water and skip.

We'd been driving for a couple of days, staying in motels across the states. It was the beginning of Autumn and the leaves in New England were falling as we left. We took highways across the country and watched the foliage turn to wilted yellow as the waves of preserved southern heat hit us. The storm had come from seemingly nowhere as we traversed the lower Midwest towards Arizona.

"Pull off at the next exit! Can you hear me?"

Andy was shouting into the phone. I felt my head pound from straining my eyes, searching for an exit sign while the windshield wipers shivered and flopped against the glass. I just barely caught the exit and felt the trailer give behind me. Andy gripped the door handle and looked behind us. Up ahead, I could see a sign for a gas station. I followed the arrows and pulled into an old shell positioned in the middle of a flat open field. There were cars parked under the gas station canopy seeking shelter and we joined.

We all got out of the trucks and leaned against the trailers. Evan and Dave ran the pumps and filled up our tanks.

"Any update on the engineering plans?"

Andrew looked at me with a pained face and shook his head. I'd been sick with worry the whole drive. The night before leaving, one of Phoenix's city planners called me notifying me I needed to send her engineering plans for the sculptures and their installation. I told her there was no possible way for us to make it happen on a night's notice and she wouldn't budge.

"There's just no way we can get them."

I couldn't think of a feasible way to get them within our time frame. I kept trying to push it away from the forefront of my mind, but I knew things could go very bad if we didn't get them. Andrew looked frantically through emails on his phone. I held my hands on my head and looked out towards the storm. The rain moved sideways, hammering the grass down and blurring everything into a gray haze. Every couple of minutes a vein of lightning danced across the sky and sent a flurry of thunder flying towards the gas station. It felt as if the thunder was coming up from the ground.

"Just keep trying to find something"

He nodded and we sat around the trailer for what seemed like forever. There was no way I could make it through the storm with the dogs in tow. There wasn't anybody else out on the road and I knew we should take the hint from the locals.

We bought sandwiches and stood around the bed of my father's truck talking. While we ate, I noticed a small child staring at the dogs. His parents followed after him and I waved to them. They walked over to get a closer look at them.

"What's all this for?"

"An art exhibition in Arizona."

I smiled at the couple and they nodded slowly. Their kid seemed to understand more; he was walking around the trailer and very curious about them. I heard voices behind me and turned around to see another family walking towards the couple. Soon there was a crowd of people who had wandered out from their stagnant cars to see what the commotion was. We answered questions and introduced ourselves to people while everybody's children made friends and ran around the trailers. It felt like I was at a cookout full of people I'd never met. Many people didn't understand the point of the dogs, but it made them all the more curious and they hailed over other friends and family members. We had some pins and stickers and gave them out with brochures. They were braving the rain just to see what we were all about and I felt humbled.

When the sky cleared, we waved to the congregation of people and kept moving. The sun was beginning to peek through the gray and cast light upon endless stalks of corn that now soaked the pooling water across the land. We drove on through the top of Texas and settled for the night in the middle of New Mexico somewhere. We woke up early and hit the road as quickly as possible, making a pit stop for convenience store coffees.

"Good news."

I wiped my eyes and nodded at Andrew. He was reading something intently from the studio's email account.

"GoPro finally got back to us. Nothing set in stone, but they answered at least."

"Awesome. Let's reel em' in."

We drove and sipped our coffees while the farm fields disappeared into dust. The desert heat swelled, and it felt strange to feel hot air come in through the truck windows in the middle of October. We made good time and Andy had mentioned he wanted to see Devil's Bridge in Sedona, Arizona. It was only a couple of hours from Phoenix and I figured it wouldn't hurt to hit it along the way.

The further we drove north after crossing into Arizona, the more alien the land became. The soil took on a rich orange hue, and the golden light of the ending afternoon made the atmosphere a dreamy pinkish red. The land became full of hills and then later full of jagged mountains and cliffs. The road through the strangely shaped landscape became increasingly unkempt and narrow until we got ourselves locked into a perilous winding roadway through cliffs.

"I didn't expect it to be this bad."

I glared at Andy through the window. He was driving the other truck now and I pulled ahead while he followed. Evan looked out from the passenger seat at the sun lowering in the sky. The turns were becoming too tight for the trailers. I hit the gas and pulled the trailer up a steep incline. It was a sharp curve around a rock structure to our side, and as I came upon the narrow pathway, I caught a glimpse of the drop over the edge, sloped with jagged rock and trees. It made my stomach drop, and as the truck struggled to bear the weight of the sculptures, I felt the tires lose traction for a moment and slide. I closed my eyes and pounded the brake as the truck drifted backward. I caught a grip on the ground again and stopped, Evan and I both sighing and throwing our heads forward.

When we finally made it out and back towards Phoenix smoke began to pool from the hood of my father's old truck. The truck was older than mine and had spent the last few years traveling as my father followed me to different events around the country. It lived a long life of work and towing things it was never meant to tow. I feared I may have finally pushed it to its edge trying to haul the sculptures up a cliff. Nonetheless, it got me safely to Phoenix by the end of the night. We dropped the trailers off at the Phoenix Humane Society and I parted ways with my crew for the night. I'd be staying at Gene's.

When I arrived, I walked up to the front door, rang the bell, and then fell and leaned against the doorway. I'd barely got up from my seat in my truck most of the day but felt exhausted. There were numbers, problems, and concerns pelting my brain like a downpouring storm. I heard muffled footsteps and then the latch of the door turn.

"You look like you had an easy trip." I rolled my eyes and hugged Gene.

He peered around me at my truck in his driveway. Small streams of smoke still seeped from below the hood.

"That doesn't look good."

I shook my head.

"Least of my problems."

He laughed and we headed inside. He referred me to a good mechanic to call and I scheduled a time in the morning to bring my truck in after we brought the trailers to the site. After that, I spent most of the night catching up with his family and settling in. He introduced me to his wife, Whitney, along with their three children, Carter, Stella and Cecelia. As I spoke to all of them, I felt proud of my old friend and the life he'd created for himself.

Towards the end of dinner, we discussed the logistics of setting up and the later festivities.

"The city seems to be making a big deal about it. They're excited."

"Yeah?"

Gene swallowed a forkful of food and nodded.

"Sure thing. They're calling it 'Howl-o-ween' or something like that. There are flyers all over town. We can hunt one down. And get this—"

He dropped his fork and it clanged around his plate. He pointed his finger.

"I got Mike Regan and Jamie Munson flying out to come see the exhibition."

"Oh god."

I laughed and ate a forkful of food. We hadn't all been in one place since we were in college. I couldn't believe Gene somehow managed to wrangle everybody into one place.

"Hopefully it goes better than when we'd go out in ."

He cackled and picked up his empty plate.

"I'd hope we'd at least grown up a little bit since then."

I shrugged and followed behind. After dinner, I felt the inevitable wave of fatigue hit me like a ton of bricks. I told him I had to take a breather and knock out early and he understood.

The next morning, I met my crew at the Phoenix Humane Society and drove the trailers to Margaret T. Hance Park in Phoenix. We jumped out and began getting ready to set the dogs up. Dave began undoing the ratchet straps around the dogs and turned to me.

"Did we ever work out that issue with sending the plans?"

I sighed and lifted my hands.

"We set up now—we ask for forgiveness later"

I began to turn away to go help with the trailer when I nearly collided with a person behind me.

"Forgiveness for what?"

A woman was smiling at me. I could tell immediately she was

one of Arizona's city planners.

"Hello, I'm Dale Rogers."

I extended my hand and smiled shyly. She introduced herself and confirmed my suspicion of her title.

"Were you notified you needed to send engineering plans before the event?"

"There was no time to—"

I paused and rubbed the back of my neck. My crew had stopped and was looking at me and I could feel a sense of panic rising in myself. The city official sighed.

"I can't let you set up until we have the right documentation. It's the city's call, not mine."

I nodded and looked down at the ground. I was convinced there had to be a way out; I couldn't have made it this far to be struck down because I didn't have a few pieces of paper.

"I'm going to call the Phoenix Humane Society. I'm sure they'll be better at handling this than me."

I frantically dialed their number as she stood in front of me. As the phone rang, I wondered what exactly would happen if I set the dogs up anyways. Whatever it was, I didn't want to find out.

Thankfully, the Phoenix Humane Society picked up and came to the rescue. They somehow managed to contact an engineer and arrive with her in barely any time. I stood a distance away as the engineer and humane society representative spoke to the city planner. I kept my hands in my pockets to try to hide that they were shaking. I prayed over and over in my head as the engineer walked up to me to break the news.

"Okay, you're good to go for now."

I sighed and threw my head back. She told me that she gave

the city planner her verbal certification and that she'd have the plans in her office by noontime. I thanked her repeatedly and then ran to the Phoenix Humane Society and representative and thanked her equally. They both waved it off humbly, but I was truly at the end of my rope before they arrived. I'd never come so close to losing everything while I was at the heels of everything I ever wanted.

We spent the rest of the day rushing to make up time. When it was finished, I looked out over the congregation of *American Dog* sculptures, just as I had so many times through the years. Through the haze of panic and frenzy, I almost ignored the sense of completeness rising in me. I looked over at my crew. They were joking amongst each other and hanging out by one of the trucks. I had to admit we all did a damn good job.

The following day was the main event of the exhibition. Andy's wife, Jill, arrived with their children and my fiancé, Mary and my three sons. We picked them up at the airport in between making final touches to the exhibition. I stopped for a moment when I saw them all at the park. As Andy double-checked the sculptures with his toddler son pulling at his arm, I felt like I was looking at a younger version of myself. I thought of the small moments I spent with my sons during different exhibitions; how no matter how fleeting they were, they were some of the most precious moments of my life. A part of me feared that Andy would end up following in my footsteps, constantly trying to build a stable life on top of shifting sands. To be able to give him, Dave, Evan, and Andrew a lifestyle in which they can travel the beautiful corners of the country and be comfortable doing it was the vision I'd always reached towards. Now, it was happening in front of me and we were becoming something like a family. I looked at all my three sons and beautiful fiancé. I was amazed I'd ended up as lucky as I did and knew in a different world I wouldn't be able to offer them the same things.

Soon following our arrival came a flood of staff and organizers, manning their positions and waiting still. Before my eyes, the park then filled with more people than I've ever seen at one of my exhibitions. They arrived from all walks of life and of all different ages, dressed in costumes to celebrate Halloween. Many of them brought their dogs with them for the festivities, who were equally well dressed in creative costumes. A pet parade commenced, with the citizens from all over Phoenix walking their dogs together. I stood baffled watching the massive troop of happy pets marching with their owners around the park. Radio stations set up tents in the park to talk about the exhibition and fundraiser. All around me, people enjoyed their afternoon and walked among my sculptures. News sations arrived to cover the event and I jumped from camera to camera talking about my sculptures and talking about humane societies.

A high school marching band clung to the parade and performed as they passed. We joined in the festivities and celebration, and later on we got word that Phoenix Mayor Kate Gallego had declared October 27th, 2019 as Howl-o-ween dog day. I was full of pride.

I caught up with Gene later in the day. The event was coming to a close and things were becoming less chaotic for everyone involved in organizing.

"Mike and Jaime are waiting for us downtown. We made reservations."

We brought our partners and children to Gene's favorite restaurant in Phoenix. Mike and Jaime were waiting when we arrived. We spent the night catching up on everything we'd all missed in each other's lives. Each of us had followed paths that lead far from each other but had arrived at a crossing point in Phoenix. The four of us went out and did different things together for the rest of the week. I stood guard at the exhibition site during the daytime and talked to anyone interested in my work. I let Andy take the truck to see the Grand Canyon with his wife and children.

Eventually, I said my goodbyes to Mike and Jaimie. I hugged them and told them I was grateful they came out; that it meant the world to catch up with them. Gene dropped them off at the airport. The following day was the last before I'd be catching a plane home myself. We presented the sculpture we made in his father's memorial, and which would be installed at his house. The sculpture itself was a *Grateful Dead* quote. It was a line emblematic of our friendship:

'What a long, strange trip it's been'.

Etched into a plaque on the bottom front of the sculpture read a favorite quote of his father's:

'In the long run, the true value will assert itself.'

We both stood staring at the sculpture in silence. The other guys were getting antsy and beginning to shuffle about, but I couldn't stop staring at the sculpture. There was something so absurd about it; about the moment in general. I looked over at Gene. For a moment he looked sentimental and somber; slightly out of character for his usual quick wit. It turned into an outburst of laughter and he looked at me.

"Sometimes I can't even process all of it. It's like life makes complete sense and nonsense at the same—"

"Hey! Hey!"

Everybody turned around and stared at Andrew. He held his phone up pointing wildly.

EXIT 48

"We got into the GoPro Games. They want *The Big Dog Show* to exhibit."

Everyone was facing me now as I looked at each of their faces. Gene shrugged.

"Just what I was getting at."

He laughed and began to clap.

"Clear your calendars for June."

A cheer erupted amongst the guys and I felt the absurdity and joy of the moment all at once.

Later on, Gene and I headed back to his house. Returning to a friend later in life is strange in the way you learn things that they seemingly never bothered to speak about in their youth. After a hike with Mary, and my children through Camelback Mountain in downtown Phoenix, we all sat in Gene's living room talking about our childhoods. It was great to hear some new stories about Gene's past. More importantly, it was wonderful to hear stories from my children about how they remember growing up chasing the Big Dog Show around the country. My kids were no longer little children, they were all young adults. I could see now, how they truly understood what I was trying to achieve. It was the greatest validation I had received in my life.

My time in Arizona was coming to an end and we were all exhausted. Mary and my children went up to bed as Gene and I stayed up talking.

"It's weird. There's this thing we used to do that I've been thinking about a lot lately."

He said nothing and nodded, fixing his glasses and waiting for me to speak.

"So, we had this bull on the farm, right? We used to hop the fence and get real close. When he noticed he'd get all pissed and start chasing us and we'd run for our lives back towards the fence."

He arched one eyebrow and looked at me funny. I closed my eyes and tried to remember the bull's face.

"And you know—I know I wasn't thinking about the bull when I ran. If I did, I know I would've frozen up mid-sprint. I remember just trying to think about the fence. Just hyper-focusing on it—you know?"

He nodded slowly, smiling.

"What's that face for?"

"I just think it's crazy what you farm kids called fun."

We both laughed. The look on his face reminded me of another memory that made me start laughing agian.

"Hey, how about that Belgium girl in India? Remember her?"

"Is that a serious question?"

He closed his eyes and looked up to the ceiling.

"I remember her like it was yesterday."

Even after all the years had gone by, I still could hardly believe he spent that much to impress a girl. I thought it was even more absurd that his expenditure is what ultimately introduced me to the trade show circuit. I leaned back in my seat.

"Well—was she worth it?"

"What do you think?"

He waved me off, shaking his head as if I'd answered a question wrong. He stopped for a moment and gathered himself.

"I didn't think about it then, why would I now? It was never about actually obtaining anything. You see—you and I don't have a whole lot in common—but there's one thing that we do."

EXIT 48

I leaned in and asked him what it was. He pushed his glasses back up the bridge of his nose.

"It's that we both run towards, and not away from. Money—subjective worth, it's all retrospective. Those things imply you're running from something: fear, instability, pain."

I nodded. I felt like what he was saying was something I always knew, and never knew how to bring to the forefront of my mind.

"Now passion, knowledge, adrenaline—greatness even; those are things you can keep running towards forever. You have always been running towards your dream. A dream that is uniquely yours."

He stood up, yawning, and heading towards the kitchen.

"But how do you know *I'm* that way?"

He turned around in the lit doorway and pointed at me.

"Because you made it to the fence"

I watched the light flick off in the kitchen.

Life takes as quickly as it gives. I think back to the path I took to get where I am, and it is less a timeline and more a tangled web of faces, color, and sound. One of the most striking things I've learned in my time here is the lack of control any of us have. It's contradictory in a way, as the most valuable thing I ever learned to do was take self-initiative and live on my terms. It's how I learned to distinguish myself—as well as how I coped and found positivity in the negative aspects of the hand life dealt me. The happiest people I've met are the ones who think and do for themselves, and the least were those who remained passive. It's the ones who run towards the fence line and not away from the charging bull; the ones who make hay when the sun shines.

Yet, to assume one has full control over the trajectory of their life only leads to heartache. For all the effort I put in—all the critical decisions I made—some things happened out of pure happenstance that were vital in bringing me to the height of my career. Oftentimes, it was the random kindness of others. Sometimes it was as trivial as petting an old farm dog. It's easy to go crazy tracing the lines and realizing in another world, it could all of never happened.

After Arizona, the world seemed up for the taking. We began expanding our social media, pumping out content and new designs, and talking about bigger and more ambitious concepts. I never lost the dream of Boston; my own *Gates* level exhibition commandeering the Boston Common and outwards. I was sketching up the rest of my life, but time and time again it seems life responds to order with chaos.

I never did make it to the GoPro games. My life, and the greatest momentum of my career as an artist, came to a dull halt when the United States experienced its most widespread and unsettling pandemic in over a century. I remember watching the newsreels about the Covid-19 virus and knowing immediately that my life, and the life of everyone around me, was about to change forever.

Within weeks, the machine I'd created had nothing to power it. All trade shows and exhibitions were canceled. The GoPro Games were shut down, prices of raw material climbed, and companies we worked alongside recoiled as they began to settle into a defensive position.

I had to cut my crew down to Andy and Andrew and bring any of the once budding projects we initially had to a temporary halt. All of my hopes of providing an alternative lifestyle for my family and the families of my employees began to disintegrate.

EXIT 48

I didn't know what to do, and for a while, things looked increasingly bleak. There was no fallback for Dale Rogers Studio. I racked my brain for a solution until one day, Andrew notified me about a commission—and then shortly after about another, and another. Out of nowhere, I suddenly had more commissions at once than ever before. Almost all of them were locals from the New England Area; many of whom I met on the first few exhibitions *The Big Dog Show* ever did. They were people who were once met with kindness when kindness was all I had to offer. I could've never known any of them would buy a sculpture so many years later.

I spend the most time at home now; more time than I've spent home in a decade. It's back to the old way of things around the studio, as each morning I fire up the welder and I work on building the pieces with Andy. There's been much to think about, sitting from day to day and moving in no particular direction. It's hard to say where to go from here, but through the growing chaos of the outside world and the growing complexity in maintaining the heartbeat of *Dale Rogers Studio*, there's only one thing that makes perfect sense. I learned long ago that it makes sense because it doesn't. On old Exit-48 in Haverhill, Massachusetts, there is a sixteen foot metal dog standing guard. I once thought it was a young pup braving the road that leads towards the unknown. I see now it's an old hound, proud to return to the place that raised it. Chasing that dog singlehandedly led me on the greatest adventure of my life, and as a new adventure begins, I think it's time I build a bigger one!